Mobil
Travel Guide®

NATIONAL
PARKS

ACKNOWLEDGMENTS

30449 3990

We gratefully acknowledge the help of our representatives for their efficient and perceptive inspections of the lodging and dining establishments listed, the establishments' proprietors for their cooperation in showing their facilities and providing information about them, and the many users of previous editions who have taken the time to share their experiences. Mobil Travel Guide is also grateful to all the talented writers who contributed entries to this book.

2

ISBN: 9-780841-60742-2   Manufactured in Canada.
10 9 8 7 6 5 4 3 2 1

TABLE OF CONTENTS

3

CELEBRATING 50 YEARS

Because time is precious and the travel industry is ever-changing, having accurate, reliable travel information at your fingertips is essential. Mobil Travel Guide has provided invaluable insight to travelers for 50 years, and we are committed to continuing this service into the future.

The Mobil Corporation (known as Exxon Mobil Corporation since a 1999 merger) began producing the Mobil Travel Guide books in 1958 following the introduction of the U.S.-interstate highway system in 1956. The first edition covered only five Southwestern states. Since then, our books have become the premier travel guides in North America, covering all 50 states and Canada.

Since its founding, Mobil Travel Guide has served as an advocate for travelers seeking knowledge about hotels, restaurants and places to visit. Based on an objective process, we make recommendations to our customers that we believe will enhance the quality and value of their travel experiences. Our trusted Mobil One- to Five-Star rating system is the oldest and most respected lodging and restaurant inspection and rating program in North America. Most hoteliers, restaurateurs and industry observers favorably regard the rigor of our inspection program and understand the prestige and benefits that come with receiving a Mobil Star rating.

The Mobil Travel Guide process of rating each establishment includes:

★ Unannouced facility inspections
★ Incognito service evaluations
★ A review of unsolicited comments from the general public

For each property, more than 500 attributes, including cleanliness, physical facilities and employee attitude and courtesy, are measured and evaluated to produce a mathematically derived score, which is then blended with other elements to form an overall score. These scores form the basis that we use to assign our Mobil One- to Five-Star ratings.

This process focuses on guest expectations, guest experience and consistency of service, not just physical facilities and amenities. It's fundamentally a rating system that rewards those properties that continually strive for and achieve excellence each year. The very best properties are consistently raising the bar for those that wish to compete with them.

Only facilities that meet Mobil Travel Guide's standards earn the privilege of being listed in the guide. Deteriorating, poorly managed establishments are deleted. A Mobil Travel Guide listing constitutes a positive quality recommendation. Every listing is an accolade, a recognition of achievement.

We hope that your travels are outstanding and that our books help you get the most out of every trip you take. If any aspect of your accommodation, dining, spa or sightseeing experience motivates you to comment, please contact us at Mobil Travel Guide, 200 W. Madison St., Suite 3950, Chicago, IL 60606, or send an e-mail to info@mobiltravelguide.com. Happy travels.

5

MOBIL RATED HOTELS

Whether you're looking for the ultimate in luxury or the best bang for your travel buck, we have a hotel recommendation for you. To help you pinpoint properties that meet your needs, Mobil Travel Guide classifies each lodging by type according to the following characteristics.

★★★★★The Mobil Five-Star hotel provides consistently superlative service in an exceptionally distinctive luxury environment. Attention to detail is evident throughout the hotel, resort or inn, from bed linens to staff uniforms.

★★★★The Mobil Four-Star hotel provides a luxury experience with expanded amenities in a distinctive environment. Services may include automatic turndown service, 24-hour room service and valet parking.

★★★The Mobil Three-Star hotel is well appointed, with a full-service restaurant and expanded amenities, such as a fitness center, golf course, tennis courts, 24-hour room service and optional turndown service.

★★The Mobil Two-Star hotel is considered a clean, comfortable and reliable establishment that has expanded amenities, such as a full-service restaurant.

★The Mobil One-Star lodging is a limited-service hotel, motel or inn that is considered a clean, comfortable and reliable establishment.

Recommended A Mobil-recommended property is a reliable, standout property new to our guides at press time. Look for a Mobil star-rating for these properties in the future.

For every property, we also provide pricing information. The pricing categories break down as follows:

$ = Up to $150
$$ = $151-$250
$$$ = $251-$350
$$$$ = $351 and up

All prices quoted are accurate at the time of publication, however prices cannot be guaranteed.

RESTAURANTS

All Mobil Star-rated dining establishments listed in this book have a full kitchen and most offer table service.

★★★★★The Mobil Five-Star restaurant offers one of few flawless dining experiences in the country. These establishments consistently provide their guests with exceptional food, superlative service, elegant décor and exquisite presentations of each detail surrounding a meal.

★★★★The Mobil Four-Star restaurant provides professional service, distinctive presentations and wonderful food.

★★★The Mobil Three-Star restaurant has good food, warm and skillful service and enjoyable décor.

★★The Mobil Two-Star restaurant serves fresh food in a clean setting with efficient service. Value is considered in this category, as is family friendliness.

★The Mobil One-Star restaurant provides a distinctive experience through culinary specialty, local flair or individual atmosphere.

In each section, we indicate whether the restaurant has a bar, whether a children's menu is offered and whether valet parking is available. If reservations are recommended, we note that fact in the listing. Because menu prices can fluctuate, we list a pricing category rather than specific prices. The pricing categories are defined as follows, per diner, and assume that you order an appetizer or dessert, an entrée and one drink:

$ = $15 and under
$$ = $16-$35
$$$ = $36-$85
$$$$ = $86 and up

PARK IT

Hike part of the Appalachian Trail in Shenandoah. See the incandescent rock formations as the sun strikes from different angles in Bryce Canyon. Visit crocodiles and alligators in the Everglades—the only place in the U.S. where these two reptiles reside together. Or peer down into that big crevice in the middle of the desert known as the Grand Canyon. America's national parks are those special places that have been set aside to preserve land from development and offer a refuge for wildlife. They are the untouched parts of the country that remind us of what makes America beautiful—and they simply must be explored.

See how the thick mixture of all the brush and trees in the Smoky Mountains creates a haze from the water and hydrocarbons thrown off by their leaves, resulting in a "smoky" appearance. Or marvel at how wind and water have carved curiously sculptured formations in the badlands.

Hike, bike, observe the wildlife, meet the rangers—get away from it all and take a moment to enjoy the great outdoors and gawk at mother nature.

The first national park, Yellowstone, was established in 1872 (some say it's still the grand dame). By 1916, the National Park Service was put in place to manage the new additions to the system, and today there are 58 parks in total. Together, the parks cover millions and millions of acres of untamed wilderness preserved for everyone to enjoy. Denali National Park in Alaska alone covers 6 million acres—an area roughly the size of Massachusetts.

In this guide, we've put together the 15 hands-down must-see national parks and provided essential information on what to see and do once you get there. We've also gathered the best places to stay, whether it's a campsite outdoors or a lodge, a rustic cabin, a quaint bed and breakfast or a luxury suite with a plasma TV. We've also got great places to eat along the way (no beans out of a can necessary here). Pack a backpack or your fancy leather luggage— these national parks are for everyone. Happy trails.

ACADIA
NATIONAL PARK

THE MAJESTIC ROCKY COASTLINE AND THICK WOODLANDS FILLED WITH wildlife make Acadia National Park a favorite spot to visit in Maine. The 47,633-acre park takes up almost half of Mount Desert Island, a 14-by-12-mile lobster claw–shaped island made predominantly of rugged granite. The park also comprises smaller areas on Isle au Haut, Little Cranberry Island, Baker Island, Little Moose Island and part of the mainland at Schoodic Point. Created by the force of glaciers more than 20,000 years ago, the coastal Acadia area has countless valleys, lakes and mountains that were forever changed by the great fire of 1947, which burned for over four weeks and scorched more than 17,000 acres. As a result, instead of only fir, pine and spruce, the forests in the area now include younger, more varied tree species. Although small compared to other national parks, Acadia still hosts more than 2 million visitors annually, and it's the only national park in the northeastern United States. Situated 160 miles north of the state's capital, Augusta, Acadia can be reached by plane through Bangor, Maine (50 miles), the closest airport that serves national airlines.

Native Americans were the first inhabitants of the Acadia area, and lived here for more than 6,000 years before Europeans began arriving in search of natural resources. French explorer Samuel de Champlain officially founded Mount Desert Island in 1604. Shortly thereafter, French Jesuit missionaries settled here until they were driven off by an armed vessel from Virginia—the first act of overt warfare between France and England for control of North America. Until 1713, the island was a part of French Acadia, and not until after the Revolutionary War was it officially settled. It soon became a popular summer destination for wealthy vacationers who bought land and built mansions or "summer cottages." In 1916, President Woodrow Wilson proclaimed 6,000 acres of land as Sieur de Monts National Monument. It was changed to Lafayette National Park in 1919, and finally, in 1929, it was enlarged and renamed Acadia National Park.

The expansion of the park is largely thanks to land donated by private citizens who loved the area and wanted to preserve its natural beauty. One of the best-known contributors to the park was John D. Rockefeller, Jr., who built the popular carriage road system to avoid motorized vehicles. He later donated 11,000 acres of land—roughly one-quarter of the park's current acreage. Because of private gifts like these, the park grew piecemeal throughout the 20th century, so much so that Congress could only establish its official boundaries in 1986.

Mount Desert Island, Maine, 207-288-3338; www.nps.gov/acad

WHAT TO SEE

The best way to see the Mount Desert Island part of Acadia is via two circular trips—the 27-mile **Park Road Loop** goes around the popular eastern part of the park, while Route 102 travels through the "quiet side" on the western half. Just before entering Mount Desert Island, you'll find the **Thompson Island Information Center** (Route 3; open May to mid-September), located on the Mount Desert Narrows.

As in many northeast seacoast areas, the towns surrounding Acadia and the park services essentially shut down during winter months. Acadia is best visited between mid-April and mid-October. During warmer months, you'll find a plethora of charming seaside hotels and century-old historic homes-turned-inns and bed and breakfasts.

Eastern Mount Desert Island (Park Road Loop)

Travel east along Route 3 and make a stop at **Hulls Cove Visitor Center** (Route 3; April 15-June 8 a.m.-4:30 p.m., July-August 8 a.m.-6 p.m., September 8 a.m.-5 p.m., October 8 a.m.-4:30 p.m.). Watch the 15-minute introductory video and get your park bearings using the center's 3-D map. During the off-season, visitors can get information from the **Park Headquarters** (Route 233, three miles west of Bar Harbor, 207-288-3338; November 1-April 14, daily 8 a.m.-4:30 p.m., April 15-October, Monday-Friday 8 a.m.-4:30 p.m.). From the visitor center, follow Route 3 and bear right (southwest) onto the Park Loop Road to Cadillac Mountain Road. Ascending to 1,530 feet, **Cadillac Mountain** is the eastern seaboard's highest point. From here, the mountain offers sweeping views of forests, lakes and the endless ocean beyond the Frenchman, Blue Hill and Penobscot bays. After descending back to the bottom, take a right to backtrack and pass by Route 3, where Park Loop Road becomes one-way.

The Park Road loop leads first along the eastern coast of Mount Desert Island before coming back up through the center of the island past Jordan Pond and Eagle Lake. On the eastern side of Mount Desert Island, you'll first head into the Sieur de Monts Spring Area, considered the heart of Acadia Park. Check out the **Sieur de Monts Nature Center** (June-October) before heading to the paths that cut through the **Wild Gardens of Acadia** at the foot of Dorr Mountain. Established by the park and Bar Harbor Garden Club in 1961, the small site is a microcosm of the island's vegetation and attracts an abundance of birds, which flit by the brook and through the host of native trees, shrubs, wildflowers and ferns. In the same area, from May to November, learn about thousands of years of Maine's Native American heritage at the **Abbe Museum** (Sieur de Monts, 207-288-3519; www.abbemuseum. org; another location is open year-round at 26 Mount Desert St., downtown Bar Harbor). Heading south again on the Park Loop Road, pass the Entrance Station and the Sand Beach swimming area to **Thunder Hole** along the island's steep granite cliffs. If you time it right (at about three-quarters tide with the tide coming in), you can hear the sea rush in to produce an explosion of air forced from a cavern (hence the name). Continuing on to the western portion of the Park Loop Road, make time for a stop at **Jordan Pond**. On the southern edge of this glacier-carved pond, enjoy tea and a snack—Jordan Pond Restaurant is famous for its popovers—on the lawns of the Jordan Pond House (mid-May to October), the park's only dining facility.

Western Mount Desert Island (Route 102/Western Loop)

To access the western part of the islands from the Park Loop Road, head down Route 233 and then go west to Route 198 toward Summerville. From Route 198, drive south on Route 102 toward Southwest Harbor. Passing **Somes Sound** to the east and **Echo Lake** to the west, eventually Route 102 hits the short 102A detour. Head down this road to Bass Harbor Head, the end of the road and

southernmost point on the island, to see Mount Desert Island's only lighthouse: **Bass Harbor Head Lighthouse**. Built in the 19th century, it is currently the Coast Guard unit commander's private residence. Here you'll find several short trails to walk for great ocean views and nature sightings. Returning back up 102A, take a left onto 102 toward Tremont. Past Seal Cove Pond, make a stop at **Pretty Marsh**, where the name says it all. Perfect for a picnic lunch, the rocky Pretty Marsh Harbor faces Bartlett Island and Western Bay, and the area is covered in evergreens and a thick carpet of moss.

Schoodic Peninsula and the Islands

If you have some extra time, consider a side trip to the Schoodic Peninsula, the only part of the park located on the mainland. Located off Route 186, drive six miles down the one-way road to reach **Schoodic Point** at the peninsula's southern tip. This part of Acadia has granite outcroppings and pounding surf that add to the beauty of the bay and island views, and is usually not crowded.

Some parts of the park, including **Isle au Haut**, **Little Cranberry Island**, **Baker Island** and **Little Moose Island**, are harder to reach than the other portions of the park. These islands are served by mailboat or tour ferries, weather permitting, from Northeast and Southwest Harbors (check for schedules at the Visitor Cen-

★
★
★
★

ter). To explore Little Cranberry Island's maritime past, check out the exhibits of ship models, toys and photographs at the **Islesford Historical Museum** (mid-June to September).

WHAT TO DO

HIKING

There are 125 miles of trails in Acadia, not including the 45 miles of crushed-stone carriage road, which has 17 granite bridges and is ideal for easy scenic walks through the park. For complete information on hiking in the park, check out www.nps.gov/acad/planyourvisit/hiking.htm.

———— **EASY** ————

Cadillac Summit
0.4-mile loop
Trailhead: Cadillac Summit parking lot
This short stroll provides panoramic views of Frenchman Bay.

Wonderland Trail
1.4 miles round-trip
Trailhead: Route 102A, one mile south of Seawall Campground.
For a relaxing hike, this jaunt passes through an evergreen forest to reach the rocky shoreline.

———— **MODERATE** ————

Beech Mountain Loop
1.1-mile loop
Trailhead: Follow signs from Somesville to Beech Mountain.
The Beech Mountain loop has a watchtower on top and vistas of Long Pond and Echo Lake.

Cadillac Mountain North Ridge Trail
4.4 miles round-trip
Trailhead: North Ridge Trail parking area on the Park Loop Road.
This open ascent trail looks onto Frenchman Bay.

———— **STRENOUS** ————

Perpendicular Trail (Mansell Mountain)
2 miles round-trip
Trailhead: South end of Long Pond (near Southwest Harbor).
This trek up Mansell Mountain has rocky stairs and requires climbers to use iron rungs.

Cadillac Mountain South Ridge Trail
7.4 miles round-trip
Trailhead: Route 3,100 feet south of Blackwoods campground entrance.
The mountainous South Ridge Trail runs through forest before gradually transitioning to an open granite ascent.

BUS TOURS

Bus tours are a great way to sit back, relax and get a good overview of the park. National Park Tours (Testa's Restaurant, 53 Main St., Bar Harbor; 207-288-0300; www.acadiatours.com; mid-May to October) offers a 2.5-hour narrated trip around Bar Harbor and through the park (adults $25, children 12 and under $10). Besides giving information on the local history, park and other subjects, the tour makes short stops

ACADIA

at points of interest, including the top of Cadillac Mountain, Thunder Hole and the Jordan Pond House. Another good option, Oli's Trolley, takes riders around the park on a trolley-style bus (207-288-9899, 866-987-6553; www.acadiaislandtours.com; One Harbor Place, 1 West St., Bar Harbor). One-hour trips run July to October (adults $15, children under 12 $10); 2.5-hour trips run May to October (adults $29, children under 12 $15).

CARRIAGE TOURS

Horse-led rides in uncovered carriages are available through Carriages in the Park at Wildwood Stables (Park Loop Road near Stanley Brook Road, June-October, 207-276-3622; www.acadia.net/wildwood). Tours vary from a one-hour trip around a coastal mountain with thick forest and views of the ocean, Schoodic Peninsula and the Cranberry Isles (adults $16) to a two-hour, early evening sunset ride to the summit of Day Mountain (adults $22). The Jordan Pond House tour includes a stop for tea and popovers.

SWIMMING

To escape the summer heat, head to one of Acadia's two beaches which are patrolled by lifeguards and are ideal for a quick dip or a lazy afternoon swim. For saltwater ocean swimming, the **Sand Beach** is located just off the Park Loop Road. Keep in mind that the water temperature is usually 55 degrees or colder. For freshwater swimming and warmer waters, **Echo Lake** is located on the island's west side. Both beaches are open Memorial Day through Labor Day.

BOATING

As the park is virtually surrounded by water, there are many options for exploring the area by boat. The Bar Harbor Whale Watch Company (1 West St., Bar Harbor, 207-288-2386, 888-942-5374; www.barharborwhales.com) offers a variety of cruises from May to October that depart from the Bluenose Ferry Terminal aboard catamarans *Friendship V* or *Bay King III* to view whales, seal, puffin, osprey and more. Alternatively, from mid-June to mid-September, you can cruise to the Cranberry Islands and see native wildlife while learning about the island's history with the Cranberry Cove Boating Company (Southwest Harbor, 207-244-5882; www.cranberryisles.com/ferry_cranberry_cove.html; six departures daily from Upper Town Dock). For a ranger-led boat excursion, from late spring to early fall, the park offers four cruises: the Islesford Historical Cruise (207-276-5352) for a history lesson on life on the Maine coast, the Baker Island Cruise (207-288-2386) that heads to a remote island, Dive-In Theater Boat Cruise (207-288-3483) to see and even handle local sea life, and the Frenchman Bay Cruise (207-288-4585) that sets sail aboard a 151-foot schooner.

★
★
★
★

To explore the area on your own from May to October, rent a canoe from Acadia Bike & Canoe (48 Cottage St., Bar Harbor, 207-288-9605, for tours 800-526-8615; www.acadiabike.com).

Animals both big and small thrive in this island climate. Though rarely seen, **moose** and **black bear** roam Acadia year-round. Much more likely sightings in the park include the **white-tailed deer** that feasts on grass and tree buds, and the **red fox** that hunts the area's numerous small rodents and hare that populate the fields and marshes. A variety of aquatic mammals call Acadia home as well including:

Beaver: Beavers love the freshwater ponds, brooks and streams scattered throughout the park, but they were once in danger of disappearing from the area altogether. In the 1900s, hunters overhunted these broad-tailed dam builders for their sought-after fur. In 1920, park superintendent George Dorr released two pairs of the animal into the newly formed national park, and thanks to his conservation efforts, these pairs thrived and contributed to the rebirth of the area's beaver population.

Seal: The harbor seal is another Acadia favorite and the namesake for the Mount Desert town of Seal Harbor. These playful creatures measure 4 to 6 feet in length and have grayish-brown fur. Seals can often be seen sunning themselves on offshore rocky ledges during low tide, while during high tide, they head out to look for dinner: North Atlantic fish like herring and mackerel.

Whale: Finback, humpback and minke whales call the Gulf of Maine home. The more common finback can be anywhere from 30 to 70 feet in length. The humpback whale, measuring between 30 and 60 feet, is the liveliest of these whales—often breaching and visible moving about the cold Atlantic Ocean waters. At less than 20 feet long, the minke is the area's smallest whale.

BIRDS

Acadia National Park is a birdwatcher's fantasy. More than 300 species of land, sea and shore birds either nest or pass through the park due to its pivotal location between Canada's colder arctic region and the more temperate southern United States and tropical zones. **Sea ducks**, brightly colored **warblers**, **puffins** and **buffleheads** are just a few of the species in the area. In the 1960s, another park resident, the **peregrine falcon**, was on the brink of extinction. In fact, until reintroduction efforts began in earnest in the 1980s, no peregrine falcons had inhabited the park since the last pair had been spotted in 1956. But like the **bald eagle** soaring overhead, these swift raptors have again become self-sustaining park residents, mainly nesting along steep cliffs like those overlooking

14

ACADIA

Jordan Pond. Almost 100 chicks have been born in the park. For the best chance to see these falcons, try the Peregrine Watch at the Champlain Mountain breeding cliffs (Precipice Trail parking area; mid-May to mid-August). Before winter, many other raptors—sharp-shinned hawks, American kestrels, osprey, northern harriers and merlins—travel from Canada and Maine to warmer southern climates. To spot one in late summer or fall, check out Acadia's Hawk Watch on Cadillac Mountain.

WHERE TO STAY

CAMPING

Only limited camping is available in Acadia National Park. On Mount Desert Island, the 306-site Blackwoods Campground is open year-round (Route 3, five miles south of Bar Harbor; reservations recommended May 1-October 31, 877-444-6777; www.recreation. gov), while the Seawall campground's 214 sites are available late May to September 30 (Route 102A, four miles south of Southwest Harbor; first-come, first served). Both campgrounds are located in the woods within a short walk from the ocean. On the Isle au Haut, the primitive Duck Harbor campground only has five sites and is open May 15 to October 15. Reservations are required; call 207-288-3338 or use the form at www.nps.gov/acad/planyourvisit/upload/iahreserve.pdf.

HOTELS

Bar Harbor
Balance Rock Inn
21 Albert Meadow, Bar Harbor, 207-288-2610, 800-753-0494; www.balancerockinn.com
Named for a rock precariously balanced on the shore, this quiet property is set on secluded land on the ocean. Built as a "summer cottage" in 1903, the inn has preserved its early 1900s feel with manicured lawns, flower gardens, veranda and afternoon tea, complete with sweets made by the dessert chef. At night in the main house, cozy up to your own fire on your deck or enjoy the secret garden in what was once the carriage house.
23 rooms. Closed late October-early May. Wireless Internet access. Complimentary full breakfast. Bar. Pool. Pets accepted. **$$**

Bar Harbor Grand Hotel
269 Main St., Bar Harbor, 207-288-5226, 888-766-2529; www.barharborgrand.com
This newer hotel was built to replicate the 1875 Roddick House and is an ideal location for those wanting to stay in downtown near shops and eateries. Rooms are clean and spacious and a free shuttle is nearby that takes guests to several points in Acadia Park.
70 rooms and suites. Closed December-April. High-speed Internet. Complimentary continental breakfast. Fitness center. Pool. **$$**

15

ACADIA

★
★
★
☆
☆

★★★Bar Harbor Hotel/ Bluenose Inn

90 Eden St., Bar Harbor, 207-288-3348, 800-445-4077; www.bluenoseinn.com

From its hilltop location on Mount Desert Island, this hotel offers scenic views of Frenchman Bay from many of its guest rooms. The well-appointed accommodations feature four-poster beds and balconies and include mini refrigerators, CD and DVD players and bathrobes. After exploring the park, guests can enjoy gourmet dining in the restaurant, and then the next day, walk down to the dock and catch the *Cat Ferry* for a day trip to Yarmouth, Nova Scotia. Enjoy gourmet dining in the Rose Garden Restaurant.

97 rooms and suites. Closed early November-late April. High-speed Internet access. Restaurant, bar. Fitness center. Pool. $$

★★Bar Harbor Inn

Newport Drive, Bar Harbor, 207-288-3351, 800-248-3351; www.barharborinn.com

The Adirondack chairs on the grassy lawn of Bar Harbor Inn, set on eight nicely groomed acres, overlook Frenchman Bay and are the perfect place to take a book or just watch the boats sail by Bar and Sheep Islands. Service is friendly, and three guest buildings feature rooms with patios overlooking the ocean or manicured grounds. Take a meal in the hotel's Reading Room Restaurant or Terrace Grill—both with water views—or enjoy a spa treatment in the inn's

brand-new spa facility.

153 rooms. Wireless Internet access. Complimentary continental breakfast. Restaurant, bar. Fitness center. Pool. Beach. Spa. $$

★★Bar Harbor Regency

123 Eden St., Bar Harbor, 207-288-9723, 800-234-6835; www.barharborregency.com

Fronting the water, this large gray stone property offers oceanfront or garden view rooms and is approximately one mile from downtown Bar Harbor and near Acadia National Park. Guest accommodations are spacious, and rooms include refrigerators. A putting green, marina and walking trail are offered onsite, and a coin laundry is available to guests who are traveling light.

278 rooms and suites. Closed November-April. Two restaurants, two bars. Fitness center. Tennis. Pool. $$

★★★The Bayview

111 Eden St., Bar Harbor, 207-288-5861, 800-356-3585; www.thebayviewbarharbor.com

This eight-acre inn is within five minutes of the town's center but still offers a private setting next to the water down a long, wooded drive. The propety includes condos for guests on longer stays. Rooms are spacious and feature French doors that lead to wide, private decks overlooking the water and are furnished with four-poster beds, inlaid wood tables and armoires.

26 rooms. Closed November to

16

ACADIA

mid-May. Complimentary full breakfast. Fitness center. Tennis. Pool. $$

★★Harborside Hotel, Spa & Marina
55 West St., Bar Harbor, 207-288-5033, 800-328-5033; www.theharborsidehotel.com

This downtown Bar Harbor hotel on Frenchman Bay is minutes from Acadia National Park and offers luxury guest rooms, studios and penthouse suites; each has a balcony and nearly all have incredible views. Spend an afternoon relaxing at the hotel spa or lounging at the outdoor pool while taking in a panoramic harbor vista. Spend the evening at the Italian wine bar.

187 rooms and suites. Complimentary continental breakfast. Two restaurants, two bars. Fitness center. Pool. Spa. $$

Southwest Harbor

Kingsleigh Inn
373 Main St., Southwest Harbor, 207-244-5302; www.kingsleighinn.com

Built in 1904, this Queen Anne Victorian is perfect for those looking for a relaxing place to stay. Some of the tastefully decorated guest rooms have private decks, and the downstairs wraparound porch even has a hammock for long lazy afternoon naps.

7 rooms, 1 suite. Closed November-late April. Children over 12 only. Complimentary full breakfast. $$

Northeast Harbor

★★★Asticou Inn
15 Peabody Drive, Northeast Harbor, 207-276-3344, 800-258-3373; www.asticou.com

Rooms at this sprawling Victorian inn have been restored to their original turn-of-the-century beauty and are decorated with Oriental rugs and traditional furniture. The grounds include beautifully landscaped gardens with Northeast Harbor views as well as clay tennis courts and an outdoor heated pool.

28 rooms, 14 suites, 6 bungalows. Wireless Internet access. Complimentary continental breakfast. Closed mid-October to mid-May. Restaurant, bar. Tennis. Pool. $$$

— ALSO RECOMMENDED —
Maison Suisse Inn & Peregrine Lodge
Kimball Lane and Main St., Northeast Harbor, 207-276-5223, 800-624-7668; www.maisonsuisse.com

Maison Suisse is a restored, shingle-style summer cottage set amid a rustic garden that was once a speakeasy during Prohibition. Rooms are outfitted in antiques and unique furnishings. Peregrine Lodge, with a kitchen that can seat 14, is often rented by groups.

11 rooms, 5 suites. Closed November-April. Wireless Internet access. Complimentary full breakfast. Pets accepted. $$

17

ACADIA

★

★

★

★

WHERE TO EAT

Bar Harbor

★★Maggie's
**6 Summer St., Bar Harbor,
207-288-9007;
www.maggiesbarharbor.com**

For years, Maggie's has been a Bar Harbor favorite. This small, intimate restaurant is located on a short side street in downtown Bar Harbor. The chef/owner, who once owned a local fish market, uses only regional farm produce and meats and fresh local seafood to support her seasonally changing menu. Everything is made from scratch, with all breads and desserts oven-baked onsite. The simple country décor and candlelit ambience make this a cozy spot for a delicous meal.

International menu. Dinner. Closed Sunday; late October to mid-June. Bar. Casual attire. Reservations recommended. Outdoor seating. $$

★★★Reading Room
**Newport Drive, Bar Harbor,
207-288-3351, 800-248-3351;
www.barharborinn.com**

Located on the oceanfront, this restaurant offers a panoramic view of the harbor and nearby docks through large windows. This is the place to come for seafood; you'll find everything from lobster pie to local diver sea scallops on the menu.

American, seafood menu. Breakfast, lunch, dinner, Sunday brunch. Closed December-March. Bar. Children's menu. Casual attire. Reservations recommended. Valet parking. $$$

★Route 66
**21 Cottage St., Bar Harbor,
207-288-3708;
www.bhroute66.com**

Route 66 is part roadhouse, part soda fountain and part country store. The interior features faux marble Formica booths, a 1954 juke box, model train, and tin and neon signs everywhere. Some of the windows are stained glass from an old church, and an old Mobil gas pump sits next to the door. Traditional New England dishes are offered along with a good selection of diner food such as burgers and sandwiches.

American menu. Lunch, dinner. Closed mid-October to mid-May. Bar. Children's menu. Casual attire. Reservations recommended. Outdoor seating. $$

Southwest Harbor

★Beal's Lobster Pier
182 Clark Point Road, Southwest Harbor, 207-244-3202, 800-245-7178; www.bealslobster.com

The lobster at this self-service eatery is boiled to order, and the other local seafood offerings are just as fresh. Enjoy the steamed clams, fresh fish, chowders and sandwiches at this casual restaurant located next to a working wharf with picnic tables.

Seafood menu. Lunch, dinner; Labor Day-spring closes 5 p.m. Casual attire. Outdoor seating. $$

18

ACADIA

Northeast Harbor
★Docksider
14 Sea St., Northeast Harbor,
207-276-3965
Inside this white seafood shack, locals love the homey, relaxed atmosphere. Dig into the fresh- est lobster, New England clam chowder and other classic seafood dishes local to Bar Harbor. An outdoor deck is open for dining alfresco.

Seafood menu. Lunch, dinner. Closed Columbus Day to mid- May. Children's menu. Casual attire. Outdoor seating. **$$**

19

ACADIA

★

★

★

★

BADLANDS NATIONAL PARK

THIS MOONSCAPE OF STEEP CANYONS, SPIRES, PINNACLES AND FLAT-topped tables sits amid a sea of the largest protected prairie in the United States. The Badlands National Park occupies 244,000 acres in South Dakota's southwest corner, and its stark and simple beauty is the result of the geologic processes of deposition and erosion.

An inland sea, an age of flooding and eventually a river and the wind formed three distinct layers of soft sediment deposits, which cemented together into a flat floodplain over the course of 68 million to 77 million years. But not until 500,000 years ago did water begin to carve through the cemented sediment (its one-inch annual erosion rate makes it one of the world's fastest-eroding landscapes) to form the sculpted forms we see today. Oxide deposits have painted the land its various red and brown hues, and amazing fossils have emerged from the wearing away of Badland's rock. The exceptional fossil collection sets the Badlands apart. In fact, the fossilized bones of the saber-toothed cat, the rhinoceros-like brontothere and other prehistoric animals make this area one of the world's best Oligocene epoch fossil beds.

Long after prehistoric animals disappeared, the Paleo Indians settled the Badlands area around 11,000 years ago. The Arikara, whose descendants live mostly in modern-day North Dakota, followed these little-studied Indians. The middle of the 19th century brought the Great Sioux Nation, a seven-band tribe that forced other Indians out of the area. It's from this group of Sioux that the area, called *mako sica* ("bad lands"), gets its name. Eventually homesteaders arrived from the East Coast and Europe in the early 1900s to try to farm the semiarid land. In 1939, President Franklin D. Roosevelt designated 122,000 acres as a National Monument, and 37 years later, 122,000 acres that had served as an aerial bombing range during World War II were added. The two areas, now known as the north unit and south unit, were redesignated the Badlands National Park in 1978. Located 88 miles east of Rapid City and other attractions, including the Black Hills and Mt. Rushmore, the Badlands can be seen as a stand-alone trip or as a day trip among other South Dakota highlights.

Badlands Loop Road, Interior, South Dakota, 605-433-5361; www.nps.gov/badl

WHAT TO SEE

The park is divided into two main units: North (east) and South (west). While the North Unit is marked by a long, winding park road, the South Unit has its own visitor center but is essentially without streets. You'll want to check the weather forecast before venturing into either section of the park, as weather conditions in the Badlands can be extreme and change quickly. In particular, be cautious of slick and icy conditions in winter months and rapid lightening storms during the hot summers.

NORTH UNIT

One of the easiest ways to see the North Unit is by car on the **Badlands Loop Road** (roughly one hour's drive). Begin at the **Northeast Entrance** (Route 240) where the **Big Badlands Overlook** has great views of the **Wall**—a 60-mile multicolored ridge of sedimentary rock. A close look at the Wall allows a glimpse of up to six different sedimentary layers of the Badlands. The darkest and bottom layer, the black Pierre Shale, is the 69–75 million year old hardened mud from what was once a sea floor. Above that, observe the softer Yellow Mounds (a fossil bed) and grayish Chadron Formation, once home to prehistoric rhinoceros-like mammals. The upper layers include a light brown Brule Formation that hosted herd mammals, a layer of volcanic Rockford Ash, and finally the upper—and most rugged—Sharps layer, which serves as the Badlands' spectacular peaks today. Big Badlands Overlook is just the first of a whole host of overlooks that are ideal for viewing the geology and natural beauty of the park.

There are several short trails to explore (see "What to Do: Hiking") before reaching the **Ben Reifel Visitor Center at Cedar Pass** (Badlands Loop Road, Highway 240, nine miles south of I-90, exit 131). The center has exhibits and an audiovisual program, and it's open all year (an entrance fee of $15 per vehicle or $7 per person applies; good for seven days in the park). Permanent exhibits feature geology, paleontology, wildlife and resource management, and evening programs and activities conducted by ranger-naturalists are offered during the summer.

Follow the Loop Road for more hiking trails and a series of overlooks, including the **Yellow Mounds** and **Pinnacles Overlooks**. You may choose a spot to view the following day's sunrise or sunset—visitors rave about the stellar vistas and photo opportunities during sunrise in the Badlands.

Just five miles beyond the Pinnacles park entrance and south of Wall (the town) lies a short detour and side trip opportunity down Sage Creek Rim Road. Venture down the unpaved road, and you'll find **Robert's Prairie Dog Town** (along with some other native wildlife) and some breathtaking views of the landscape.

BADLANDS

SOUTH UNIT

A stop at the **White River Visitor Center** (Pine Ridge Reservation of Highway 27, 605-455-2878; open summer), 60 miles southwest of the Ben Reifels Visitor Center, is the perfect way to learn about Native American culture from the Oglala Sioux who staff the center. They can also provide recommendations and directions for your exploration of the park's south unit. These 122,000 acres remain undeveloped and have few roads and trails, but there are many beautiful areas worth trekking to for experienced backcountry hikers and those willing to risk driving the rutted tracks. (See park maps before heading out into the South Unit, as you may encounter private property lines.)

Begin exploring with a drive up to the **Sheep Mountain Table**. To get there, follow Pennington County Road 589 four miles south of the town of Scenic. Signs indicate Sheep Mountain Table Road, one of the few roads in the South Unit. A drive to the top of the steep cliffs offers a stunning view of the Badland's rock spirals and pinnacles.

Stronghold Table is an extremely sacred place for the Sioux, whose ancestors chose this grassland site in December 1890 to dance the last "Ghost Dance"—a ritual in which the dancers fell into trances and "died" while imagining the paradise (a land filled with wild game and no white men) that awaited them.

WHAT TO DO

HIKING

There are several designated hiking trails near the Ben Reifels Visitor Center in the north unit that offer a great range of shorter and longer walks. For more details on area hiking, check the *Badlands Visitors Guide* at www.nps.gov/badl and www.stateparks.com/badlands.html.

──────────── **EASY** ────────────

Door Trail
0.75 miles round-trip
Trailhead: Northern end of the Door and Window parking area two miles northeast of Ben Reifel visitor center.
This trail will take you to the heart of the eroded badlands by passing through "The Door"—a break in the Badlands Wall.

Fossil Exhibit Trail
0.25-mile loop
Trailhead: Five miles northwest of the Visitor Center.
On the Fossil Exhibit Trail, park naturalists give presentations on the fossilized specimens of extinct animals on display.

Window Trail
0.25 miles round-trip
Trailhead: Center of the Door and Window parking area.
This trail provides a great view of an intricately eroded canyon through a "window" in the Wall.

MODERATE

Castle Trail

10 miles round-trip
Trailhead: Door and Window parking area. Or Fossil Exhibit Trailhead.

The Castle Trail, stretching between the Fossil Exhibit Trail and the Door/Window parking area, is the park's longest trail. Because it's not heavily used, it offers a great chance of spotting wildlife or exploring alone.

Cliff Shelf Nature Trail

0.5-mile loop
Trailhead: Half mile north of the Visitor Center.

For a 200-foot climb to view the valley, try this loop-shaped trail, which offers a spectacular view as it meanders through a juniper forest along the Badlands Wall. Ponds attract wildlife, including bighorn sheep.

Notch Trail

1.5 miles round-trip
Trailhead: South end of the Door and Window parking area.

For a bird's-eye view, put on a pair of hiking boots and hit the Notch Trail. The trail passes through a canyon, up a ladder and along a ledge for views of the White River Valley and Pine Ridge Reservation below. This trail is treacherous when wet and is not for those with a fear of heights.

HORSEBACK RIDING

There's no better way to explore the Badlands' varied terrain than by horseback. Riding is allowed throughout the park, but most people stick to the 64,000-acre Badlands Wilderness Area. Several companies organize trail rides, including the **Badlands Ranch and Resort** (HCR 53 Box 3, Highway 44 south of White River, Interior, 605-433-5599, 877-433-5599; www.badlandsranchandresort.com). This ranch offers a 1.5-hour ride with professional wranglers through the varying Badlands terrain. Horses are gentle, so riders of all ages and skill levels are accepted.

WILDLIFE

The best part of the park to see wildlife is in the Sage Creek unit of the Badlands Wilderness. Some mammal species are abundant and easy to spot in the Badlands, while rattlesnakes and porcupines are less common.

Bison: Roaming the Sage Creek wilderness area, a herd of about 600 bison live within the confines of the park. These large plant grazers had all but disappeared from the region in the mid-1800s but, like the bighorn sheep, were reintroduced to the Badlands in 1963. Today, park rangers carefully control the herd numbers to keep capacity manageable and prevent bison from wandering outside park boundaries.

Black-footed ferret: The black-

BADLANDS

★
★
★
☆

footed ferret has gotten a new lease on life in the Badlands. Native to the park, these ferrets were believed to be extinct in the 1970s. But in 1981, a small colony was discovered in Wyoming, and with the help of the U.S. Fish and Wildlife Service, were bred and reintroduced. Still, they remain one of North America's most endangered mammals, so you'll be lucky to spot one.

Coyotes: Coyotes are the most common carnivorous creatures in the Badlands. These doglike animals are often found near the prairie dog towns. They prey on smaller or weaker animals like the swift fox.

Prairie dogs: Popping in and out of their underground tunnels, the prairie dog is a visitor favorite. One of the best places to watch them play is at the Robert's Prairie Dog Town west on the Sage Creek Road. The animated underground rodents share their tunnels with the black-footed ferret and burrowing owl.

WHERE TO STAY

CAMPING

Campers can stay up to 14 days in the Badlands' two campgrounds, Cedar Pass and Sage Creek. Cedar Pass is located by the Ben Reifel Visitor Center and has 96 first-come, first-served sites for $10 per night (reservations are accepted between Memorial Day and Labor Day). The campground is open year-round and has water, flush toilets and picnic tables (but no showers or electrical hookups). The Sage Creek campground is in a more remote part of the park and can only be reached on unpaved roads (beware of bad weather). Sites at Sage Creek, available all year for up to 14 days, are in an open field. There's no water and only pit toilets, but staying here is free. For adventurers, backcountry camping is allowed (without a permit) a half mile from the road and out of sight. Campers are urged to register at the Ben Reifel Visitor Center or the Pinnacles Ranger Station.

HOTELS

Rapid City

Abend Haus Cottages & Audrie's Bed & Breakfast
23029 Thunderhead Falls Road, Rapid City, 605-342-7788; www.audriesbb.com

This bed and breakfast's pine log lodges and cottages sit on seven forested acres in the Black Hills, about an hour east of the Badlands. Both the cottages and the bed and breakfast itself have great mountain views, and Rapid Creek runs through the property (fishing poles are provided). Crickets and the gurgling brook are the only noise you'll hear from your private patio or hot tub at night, given the no kids or pets policy. 8 cottages, 2 suites. No children allowed; couples only. Complimentary full breakfast. $

★
★
★
★
☆

★★★Alex Johnson

523 Sixth St., Rapid City,
605-342-1210, 800-888-2539;
www.alexjohnson.com

Two mounted bison heads keep watch over the large lobby in the Alex Johnson. Named for the vice president of the Chicago and Northwestern Railroad who built this hotel in the 1920s as a "showplace of the west," this downtown hotel displays original Native American artwork and old-fashioned photos of the many celebrities—including presidents—who have stayed here. Everything has been restored to resemble how the hotel looked when it was constructed, right down to solid maple furniture in the guest rooms.

141 rooms, 2 suites. Wireless Internet access. Restaurant, bar. Airport transportation available. Business center. Pets accepted. Casino. $

★Best Western Town 'N Country

2505 Mount Rushmore Road (South Highway 16), Rapid City, 605-343-5383, 800-780-7234; www.bestwestern.com

Spacious and quiet rooms are the norm at this centrally located Rapid City hotel. Staff will help arrange a number of sightseeing tours. Plus, there's a daily soup and crackers reception and fresh-baked cookies every day.

96 rooms, 3 suites. High-speed Internet access. Complimentary continental breakfast. Restaurant, bar. Pool. Airport transportation available. Business center. Pets accepted. $

Wall

★Days Inn

212 10th Ave., Wall,
605-279-2000, 800-329-7466;
www.daysinn.com

Just seven miles from the entrance to the Badlands National Park, the Days Inn is a good option for travelers who want basic accommodations but don't want a long drive to park destinations.

32 rooms. High-speed Internet access. Complimentary continental breakfast. Fitness center. $

WHERE TO EAT

Rapid City

★Firehouse Brewing Co.

610 Main St., Rapid City,
605-348-1915;
www.firehousebrewing.com

Giant vats visible behind the bar brew ales right onsite at this brewpub. Housed in Rapid City's historic first firehouse, the unique setting is the perfect place to sip beer and enjoy the Midwest-meets-English pub grub menu, including a local favorite—the buffalo burger.

American menu. Lunch, dinner. Bar. Children's menu. Casual attire. Outdoor seating. $$

★Flying T Chuckwagon Supper & Show

8971 S. Highway 16, Rapid City,
605-342-1905, 888-256-1905;
www.flyingt.com

Buffalo, beef, homemade biscuits with honey and other western-style meals are served on tin plates at this lively restaurant. After din-

BADLANDS

ner, served at 6:30 p.m., the Flying T Wranglers entertain audiences with old-time favorites ranging from cowboy ballads to country western and bluegrass music.

American menu. Dinner. Closed mid-September to mid-May. Children's menu. Reservations recommended. $

Wall

★Wall Drug Store
510 Main St., Wall, 605-279-2175; www.walldrug.com

Ted and Dorothy Hustead bought the Wall Drug pharmacy in 1931 during the Great Depression. Business was lukewarm for five years, until Ted put up signs around town advertising free ice water. It worked—and business boomed. Now in the hands of a third Hustead generation, Wall Drug is a sprawling tourist outpost that attracts nearly 20,000 visitors on hot summer days, pouring some 5,000 glasses of ice cold water in the process. Today the Hustead's empire includes not just a drugstore but a 500-seat restaurant, where hungry campers come for classic hot beef sandwiches, buffalo burgers and homemade donuts. The coolest part: Coffee still costs just 5 cents!

Winter, daily 6:30 a.m.-6 p.m.; summer, daily 6:30 a.m.-10 p.m. American menu. Breakfast, lunch, dinner. Children's menu. $

Interior

— **ALSO RECOMMENDED** —
Cedar Pass Lodge Restaurant
20681 South Dakota Highway 240, Interior, 605-433-5460; www.cedarpasslodge.com

This restaurant right inside the park serves up burgers, sandwiches and steaks but if you're looking to sample a local favorite, bypass those standards and order the Sioux Indian Tacos, made with seasoned buffalo.

American menu. Breakfast, lunch, dinner. Mid-May to early October. Casual attire. $

BRYCE CANYON NATIONAL PARK

BRYCE CANYON IS A 56-SQUARE-MILE AREA OF COLORFUL AND FANTASTIC cliffs created by millions of years of erosion. Towering rocks worn to odd, sculptured shapes, called hoodoos, stand grouped in striking sequences, inspiring the Paiute Native Americans who once lived in the region to call this "the place where red rocks stand like men in a bowl-shaped canyon." Although termed a canyon, Bryce is actually a series of "breaks" in 12 large natural amphitheaters—some plunging as deep as 1,000 feet into the multicolored limestone. The rock formations appear to change color as the sunlight strikes from different angles and can seem incandescent in the late afternoon. The famous Pink Cliffs were carved from the Claron Formation, and shades of red, orange, white, gray, purple, brown and soft yellow appear in the strata. Plateaus covered with evergreens and valleys filled with sagebrush also stretch into the distance.

The natural beauty here has been appreciated for centuries; people have existed in the region for more than 10,000 years. However, because of harsh winter conditions, Bryce Canyon often served only as a place to pass through. Paleo Indians used the area as a hunting ground toward the end of the Ice Age, while Pueblo people, and later the Fremont and Anasazi tribes, used the region's grassy meadows and forests to find food. The Paiute Indians moved into Bryce Canyon in 1200, but, like those before them, used the area mainly for seasonal food gathering and never established permanent settlements. A host of pioneers later passed by the area in the 1800s before a group of families finally settled in tiny towns. Included among them were Ebenezer Bryce and his family, who in 1875 moved to Clifton and later to New Clifton. To gain better access to the timber surrounding the park, Bryce made a road through the pink cliffs that ended at the amphitheater, which soon became known among locals as "Bryce's Canyon." Although the Bryce family eventually left for Arizona in 1880, the name for the canyon endures. In March 1919, the Utah Joint Memorial asked Congress to set aside the area as a national monument. In 1924, Bryce's Canyon was designated a national park, and it soon became a popular destination with the advent of the Union Pacific Railroad's train service. Today nearly 1.5 million people visit the park each year.

Route 63, Bryce Canyon, Utah, 435-834-5322; www.nps.gov/brca

BRYCE CANYON

WHAT TO SEE

The long, narrow, north-south park showcases all four Utah seasons; a solid blanket of snow through much of the winter causes the park to look very different from its summer tones of red rock. But no matter when you plan to visit, you'll want to get oriented first at the **Bryce Canyon Lodge** (Bryce Canyon National Park, 435-834-8700; www.bryce-canyonlodge.com; open daily 8 a.m.-8 p.m., reduced winter hours). This national landmark, built in the 1920s, is the last of the lodges that architect Gilbert Stanley Underwood designed. Besides information on hiking, lodging, dining and guided programs, the 22-minute video *Shadows of Time* gives a good park overview.

Traversing the park is relatively easy, thanks to the free Bryce Canyon Shuttle which takes visitors to the park's most popular viewpoints, trails and facilities (late May-early September). If you choose to drive yourself, head to the main park road, which runs 18 miles along the eastern edge of the **Paunsaugunt Plateau** with natural amphitheaters spread out below. A series of overlook points provide spectacular views of Bryce terrain, and some also serve as trailheads for the many hiking trails you'll find here. The canyons make for exceptional hikes, while walks along the canyon rims also provide excellent views of the park. Stop at **Fairyland**, **Sunrise**, **Sunset** or **Inspiration**

Points to see the stunning **Bryce Amphitheater** from several different angles. Or, for the must-see panoramic view of the namesake amphitheater, go four miles south of the Visitor Center to **Bryce Point** and take in the full vista from this popular photo-op locale. One of the higher rim overlooks in the park, Bryce Point peers down onto the canyons, buttes and surreal hoodoos, typically bathed in warm shades of yellow and orange beneath the sun. For an even wider array of color and light, arrive at one of the overlooks at sunrise or make a return sunset trip to watch the changing light dance through the canyon and ignite the rugged landscape. Heading back toward the visitor center, make a detour to **Paria View**, which looks onto the Pariah River watershed, slot canyons and a castle-shaped hoodoo below.

If you have more than a day, you'll want to continue on past the major overlooks of the northern part of the park to explore the terrain further south. Heading toward the southern part of the park, turn left on the park road to reach the 8,000-foot **Swamp Canyon Overlook**. To the south, the **Mud and Noon Canyon Buttes** rise above this forested canyon, named for its relative wetness due to the spring and two creeks that feed it. Further along, **Farview Point Overlook** is aptly named—on a clear day, views can extend more than 100 miles and include sights like the **Aquarius Plateau** (pink cliffs) to the north,

★
★
★
★
★

Kaiparowits Plateau (grey cliffs) and **Molly's Nipple** (white cliffs). Incredibly, sometimes the **Kaibab Plateau** on the distant Grand Canyon's North Rim is visible on a clear day. In another contrast of color characteristic of Bryce, notice the beginning of a transition between Ponderosa pine and spruce-fir forests as the native vegetation changes and, at the next overlook, the iron-oxide rich red rock **Natural Bridge**, which spans two cliffs with a lush green ponderosa pine serving as a backdrop. With a view of the 10,000-foot-plus Navajo Mountain on the horizon further down the road at the **Agua Canyon Overlook**, two large hoodoos dominate the foreground—"the Hunter" to the left and "the Rabbit" to the right. The next major stop, toward the southernmost tip of the park, is the **Ponderosa Canyon**, which looks down on huge Ponderosa pine trees that can grow to be more than 150 tall and five feet in diameter. At the end of the park road, the 9,115-foot **Rainbow Point**, the highest point in the park, is surrounded by thick fir trees. It's the perfect place to end the tour with its sweeping view over the entire park.

If you choose to visit during winter, the views are equally impressive, although roads are often closed, depending on the weather. The upside is that there's plenty of snowshoeing and cross-country skiing.

WHAT TO DO

HIKING

Bryce Canyon is laden with hiking trails from short loops and stretches of overpass to long, strenuous, overnight treks. Keep in mind that the park is arid so you'll want to carry plenty of water (one quart/liter per 2–3 hours per person). Also, park elevations reach more than 9,000 feet, where even mild exertion may leave you feeling light-headed.

EASY

Mossy Cave
1.8 miles round-trip
Trailhead: Mossy Cave, Highway 12, north of Bryce Canyon Park entrance.
This easy trail follows a stream through Water Canyon. A left fork in the path leads to Mossy Cave, a grotto that was formed by an underground spring. In warmer weather, the overhang is covered with moss, while in colder weather, icicles hang from its ceiling.

Queens Garden
1.8 miles round-trip
Trailhead: Sunrise Point
Starting from Sunrise Point, Queens Garden Trail is the easiest way to get from the rim into the canyon below. Passing natural bridges, the trail travels through large collections of hoodoos that jut up like stalks from a garden. Look hard enough and spot what looks like Queen Victoria hold-

★
★
★
☆

ing court over the strange formations.

Rim Trail from Sunrise to Sunset Points

1.8 miles round-trip
Trailhead: Bryce Canyon Lodge
If you have little time to spend in the park, don't miss the unforgettable Rim Trail that runs along the top of the Bryce Amphitheater from Sunrise Point to Sunset Point. This level, paved trail offers an incredible bird's-eye view over the hoodoo-covered canyon and distant hills.

——————— **MODERATE** ———————

Hat Shop

4 miles round-trip
Trailhead: Bryce Point
The steep down-and-back Hat Shop trail begins at Bryce Point and descends 1,436 feet. Check out the balanced-rock hoodoos perched at the Under-the-Rim Trail.

Navajo Trail

1.3 miles round-trip
Trailhead: Sunset Point
The Navajo Trail leads from Sunset Point down several switchbacks 550 feet to the canyon's bottom, then climbs back by a different route that takes you over a recent rock slide. You'll pass Two Bridges, Thor's Hammer and Wall Street, a narrow, towering gorge. This hike can be extended by adding Queens Garden Trail.

Swamp Canyon

4.3 miles round-trip
Trailhead: Swamp Canyon
This trail is great for exploring a less-traversed portion of the park. From the Swamp Canyon Overlook, take either of the two trails that head down 800 feet into the spruce-filled canyon that's flanked by fins (long, narrow outcroppings) and hoodoos.

——————— **STRENUOUS** ———————

Peek-a-Boo Loop

5.5-mile loop
Trailhead: Bryce Point
Winding amongst the hoodoos, the steep path cuts from Bryce Point down through the Bryce Amphitheater to the canyon floor. Look for the famous Wall of Windows cut into a pale sandstone fin. This hike encompasses a net 900-foot elevation change and 1,555 feet of climbing.

Riggs Spring Loop

8.5-mile loop
Trailhead: Yovimpa Point
Starting at Yovimpa Point, the eastern portion of the Riggs Spring Loop has beautiful vistas as it passes along red cliff breaks and groves of quaking aspen. On the steeper western portion of the loop, a 2,248-foot climb, the trail passes through thicker forests of spruce, fir and bristlecone.

HORSE AND MULE RIDES

For a fun and relaxing way to see Bryce Canyon, consider a horse or mule ride from Canyon Trail

Rides (Bryce Canyon Lodge, 435-679-8665; www.canyonrides. com). The two-hour ride, leaving at 9 a.m. and 2 p.m., begins at Sunrise Point and descends into Bryce Amphitheater and down to the canyon floor. Along the way, local cowboys give history and geology lessons and point out areas of interest. For a more complete journey, the half-day trip leaves at 8 a.m. and 1 p.m. and lasts for about 3.5 hours into Bryce Amphitheater and along the Peek-a-Boo loop. Guides show and talk about canyon sites like The Chessman, Silent City and Wall of Windows. There are minimum age requirements and age restrictions, so call ahead. The cost is $40 to $65.

WILDLIFE

Bryce Canyon hosts 59 species of mammals within its borders, including the ubiquitous golden-mantled ground squirrel, rock squirrel and uinta chipmunk. Other creatures include:

Utah prairie dog: The Utah prairie dog is found only in southwestern Utah. It can often be seen running around the meadows in the northern part of the park. These threatened species have white-tipped tails and characteristic black "eyebrows" that distinguish them from the other five types of prairie dogs. Unlike the Great Plains species, the Utah prairie dog hibernates during the winter and emerges in March, just in time to greet park guests arriving with the warmer weather.

Mountain lion: The mountain lion ranges between 75 and 175 pounds and generally reaches eight feet from nose to tail and 30 inches at the shoulder. These cats are an extremely rare sight but can sometimes be seen at night along park roads.

Great Basin rattlesnake: Of the 11 species of reptiles here, the Great Basin rattlesnake is the only venomous snake in Bryce Canyon. Luckily for hikers, these brown and gray snakes are rarely spotted within the park. However, they are occasionally seen on especially hot days around the Fairyland Loop, Riggs Springs Loop and Under-the-Rim Trail.

Tiger salamander: The only type of salamander in Bryce Canyon, tiger salamanders are sometimes spotted in Swamp Canyon or backcountry springs. Although they are located throughout the park, you'll really have to look for the short-horned lizards. These flat-bodied reptiles are especially adept at hiding from predators by blending into whatever background they're against.

BIRDS

In Bryce Canyon, 175 species of birds have been reported, including the **California condor**, **peregrine falcon** and the dark brown and white **ospreys**. The ospreys have wingspans of five feet and nest in the park but feed primarily on a diet of fish from the nearby Tropic Reservoir. The much smaller **violet-green swal-**

low can be recognized by its white belly and metallic green back with purple accents. They can be seen everywhere along the Rim Trail but especially like to flock around Sunset Point.

WHERE TO STAY

CAMPING

Bryce Canyon National Park has two campgrounds in a Ponderosa pine forest near the Bryce Canyon Lodge Visitor Center. The North Campground (opposite the visitor center) is open year-round. Reservations may be made for most sites two to 240 days in advance for a stay mid-May to September (877-444-6777; www.recreation. gov). The Sunset Campground (one and a half miles south of the visitor center) is closed in the winter, and its 101 sites are first-come, first-served only. Sunset is closer to the popular hiking trails that start at Sunset Point. Both campgrounds have 14-day limits, restrooms and drinking water available, and cost $15 per night. During the summer, the nearby general store has laundry and shower facilities. Backcountry campers need a permit to stay overnight (available at the visitor center) in one of the eight campsites on the Under-the-Rim Trail or the four sites on the Riggs Spring Loop Trail.

HOTELS

★★Best Western Ruby's Inn
1000 S. Highway 63, Bryce Canyon, 435-834-5341, 866-866-6616;
www.rubysinn.com
Tourists have been lodging in this historic hotel since 1916. That's because this inn offers the closest accommodations to Bryce Canyon and is a great base for park exploration. Rooms are spacious, and a general store nearby is packed with souvenirs, food, drinks and other conveniences.
368 rooms, 2 suites. Wireless Internet access. Restaurant. Pool. Pets accepted. $

── ALSO RECOMMENDED ──
Bryce Canyon Lodge
Utah 63, Bryce Canyon National Park, 435-834-5361, 800-297-2757;
www.brycecanyonlodge.com
This rustic lodge has 40 cabins as well as guest rooms with private porches and balconies. Shops, dining and onsite hiking trails are within close proximity of the lodge, but the best part of this property is its location right inside the boundaries of Bryce Canyon National Park.
71 rooms, 3 suites, 40 cabins. Closed November-March. Restaurant. $

★

★

★

★

★

Bryce View Lodge
991 S. Highway 63, Bryce,
435-843-5180, 888-279-2304;
www.bryceviewlodge.com

Stay just a half mile from the park at this lodge on a high plateau overlooking Bryce Canyon. Rooms have been newly finished, and packages that include deals on horseback riding and other activities are available.

160 rooms. Closed November-March. Pool. $

WHERE TO EAT

★Foster's Steak House
1150 Highway 12, Bryce, 435-834-5227; www.fostersmotel.com

This restaurant, located less than two miles from the park entrance, has a friendly staff and is a great place to feast on steaks, prime rib and seafood after a day on the trails. The portions are large and fresh pastries and breads are baked daily. Or stop in for a picnic lunch before heading out.

American menu. Breakfast, lunch, dinner. Children's menu. Casual attire. $$

— ALSO RECOMMENDED —

Bryce Canyon Dining Room
2 miles south of the park entrance, Bryce Canyon National Park, 435-834-8760; www.brycecanyonlodge.com

The only restaurant inside the park's boundaries, this rustic dining room is located in the Bryce Canyon Lodge. Fill your belly with hoodoo buffalo wings, quesadillas and pasta while enjoying the Ponderosa pine forest views. The lodge, though a white tablecloth kind of place, maintains a casual atmosphere, which along with its prime location makes it quite popular—you'll want to make a dining reservation well in advance.

American menu. Breakfast, lunch, dinner. Closed November-March. Children's menu. Casual attire. Reservations recommended for dinner. $

Bryce Canyon Pines Restaurant
Milepost 10, Highway 12, Bryce, 800-892-7923; www.brycecanyonmotel.com

From the huge cowboy steak and fresh rainbow trout and homemade mashed potatoes, the comfort food at Bryce Canyon Pines, just minutes from the park, goes perfectly with its relaxed atmosphere. Save room for dessert: The restaurant is famous for its banana blueberry and banana strawberry pies.

American menu. Breakfast, lunch, dinner. Bar. Casual attire. $

★
★
★
★

DENALI NATIONAL PARK & PRESERVE

TUCKED AWAY IN INTERIOR ALASKA 240 MILES FROM THE STATE CAPITAL, Denali National Park and Preserve is one of those places that, despite its breathtaking beauty, many Americans may never see. But they should. Considered one of America's last great wilderness frontiers, the park did not become accessible by paved road until 1972. Even today, it has only a single 92-mile-long gravel road through it—a nominal distance, considering Denali covers a jaw-dropping 6 million acres (an area roughly the size of Massachusetts). Those who make the trek to Denali, one of the United States' northernmost national parks, come to experience unparalleled hiking, wildlife and the unforgettable varied landscapes that range from open tundra to snow-capped mountains. If you visit during the summer, you'll catch more than 20 hours of daylight, while fall brings brilliant foliage and spectacular northern lights.

Cutting through the park, the 400-mile-long Alaska Range is hard to miss. The giant chain, which includes the highest point in North America, the nearly four-mile-high Mount McKinley, is a result of the Pacific Plate colliding and slipping beneath the North American Plate. Volcanoes have had their hand in shaping the land, and the Ice Age brought grinding glaciers that plowed out the now-emerald valleys that run through the region. In fact, the park still contains more than 20 glaciers; the Kahiltna glacier serves as a base camp for climbers of McKinley and other surrounding peaks.

The first human presence in the Denali area can be traced back more than 12,000 years ago, when ancient hunters roamed the land for elk and bison. In later years, the Athabaskan people settled the region. By the early 1900s, a short-lived gold rush to the Kantishna Hills brought an influx of prospectors, who soon depleted the area's gold deposits. Charles Sheldon, who came to Denali in 1906 to hunt Dall sheep, fell in love with the area and stayed for two years. He then spent the next nine years lobbying to preserve the area. Recognizing Denali's awesome beauty, President Woodrow Wilson signed the Mount McKinley National Park into existence in 1917. In 1980, Congress expanded the park and changed its name to Denali (meaning "The Great One" in the Athabaskan language). Today, the area sees more than 1 million tourists, mountaineers and outdoor adventurers each year.

Alaska Route 3 (George Parks Highway), approximately 240 miles north of Anchorage, Alaska, 907-683-2294; www.nps.gov/dena

WHAT TO SEE

The first place to begin any Denali experience is at the **Visitor Center** (located near the park entrance; open May 15-September 18, daily 8 a.m.-6 p.m.) to learn about the various park services. During the winter months (mid-September to mid-May), the nearby **Murie Science and Learning Center** acts as the Visitor Center (daily 9 a.m.-4 p.m.). An entrance fee of $10 per person or $20 per vehicle, good for seven days' admission, is collected upon arrival.

The next stop is the **Wilderness Access Center** (Mile 0.6, Park Road, 907-683-9274; May 15-September 18, daily 5 a.m.-8 p.m.). Buy tickets for the daily shuttle buses that leave from here. General information is available 7 a.m.-8 p.m., as well as campground permits, basic food and beverages and a lost-and-found (907-683-9275).

Continue on **Park Road**, the east-west roadway that runs through the park along the Alaska Mountain Range. The first 15 miles of road into the park passes through lower elevations filled with what's known as **taiga**, areas with acidic soils that host few plant species. This part of the park is loaded with evergreens and smaller pockets of aspen, balsam poplar and paper birch. Gradually, the taiga gives way to midelevation treeless tundra. Moist tundra can often be brushy with short willow and birch trees, while drier areas are spongier and

can host a tangle of small plants, including lacy reindeer moss and crowberries.

At Mile 14.8, the **Savage River** is the perfect place to observe the effects of glacier movement. To the south, a vast, U-shaped, rolling valley shows how a giant glacier carved out the area before stopping and eventually retreating 10,000–14,000 years ago. To the north, the melting rains and snows from other distant glaciers contributed to the river, which in turn eroded this V-shaped canyon.

At Mile 16, just beyond the point where only shuttle and camper buses are allowed, plan time to enjoy the emerald green hills and Alaska Range from **Primrose Ridge**. Rising 1,500 feet above Park Road, the ridge is often covered in wildflowers and serves as an excellent viewing perch for sheep sightings.

Continuing along Park Road and the Alaska Range, you'll find the **Teklanika River** (Mile 29) running through **Igloo Forest** and flanked by a wide gravel bar. Several glaciers in the mountain range feed the river as it flows through the valley past surrounding spruce forests and wet tundra. Directly to the south, in the distance, **Cathedral Mountain**'s steep, 4,900-foot slopes are visible.

Past Igloo Creek and Igloo Mountain, further south and west along the road, **Sable Pass** rises 3,895 feet—a moderate elevation when compared to the massive 6,000-foot Sable Mountain with

DENALI

★
★
★
☆

its peak on the north side of the pass. Be on the lookout for grizzlies, since this section of the park attracts these bears with its dense supply of edible plants.

About five miles further down the Park Road, one of the most majestic views is from **Polychrome Overlook** on the steep Polychrome Pass. The sweeping vistas of the Alaska Range contrast with the alluvial terraces, known as the **Plains of Murie**, lying far below and the Polychrome Glaciers resting snugly against the southern hills.

The road travels to its highest point at Highway Pass (3,980 ft) to the **Stony Hill Overlook**. This is the best place to glimpse Mt. McKinley, still some 40 miles away.

Originally a tent camp, the present day **Eielson Visitor Center** (Mile 66) is a new building that just opened in June 2008. Basic orientation information, bathrooms and shelter are available 24 hours a day. After passing steep cliffs, the road slopes down and passes near the 35-mile-long **Muldrow Glacier** before heading to its westernmost endpoint, the old gold town **Kantishna** at Mile 92.

WHAT TO DO

FLIGHTSEEING

For a true bird's eye view of Denali, many travelers get their bearings with a flightseeing expedition. Most flights take off 60 miles south of the park entrance in Talkeetna. Talkeetna Air Taxi (907-733-2218, 800-533-2219; www.talkeetnaair.com) uses local pilots who specialize in glacier landings and offer numerous flying options, including a 20,000-foot trip to circumnavigate Mt. McKinley's summit. For a more complete flight, the 1.5-hour Denali-wide tour passes Mt. McKinley and even includes an aerial wildlife tour. Other flightseeing companies in Talkeetna include K2 Aviation (907-733-2291, 800-764-2291; www.flyk2.com) and Talkeetna Aero Services (907-733-2899, 888-733-2899; www.talkeetnaaero.com).

HIKING

Not knowing where to start in such a big park is no excuse to pass up an unforgettable hiking experience.

─────── **EASY** ───────

Horseshoe Lake Trail
3 miles round-trip
Trailhead: Mile 1.0 on Park Road at intersection with Alaska railroad tracks.
This trek meanders through an aspen and spruce forest and ends at Horseshoe Lake.

Mount Healy Overlook Trail
4.5 miles round-trip
Trailhead: Same as Horseshoe Lake Trail, but take Taiga Trail to the left for about 1 mile, then look for Mount Healy Trail to branch off to the right.

DENALI

Rising above the timberline to 1,700 feet, this walk guarantees killer vistas of the fast-flowing Nenana River and majestic peaks of the Alaska Range.

—— **MODERATE TO STRENUOUS** ——

Denali offers several different 11-person Discovery hikes. These moderate to strenuous excursions—from exploring a moose trail to tundra walks—are ranger led and vary from three to five hours plus travel time to parkwide destinations. (Check schedules and destinations at the visitor center or at www.nps.gov/dena/planyourvisit/walks-and-hikes.htm.)

PARK SHUTTLE BUS

Since only the first 15 miles of Park Road is open to private vehicles, one of the best ways to see Denali is via the park's shuttle bus service that was created in the 1970s to keep traffic down and the park in pristine condition. Travel times and fares depend how far along the 92-mile Denali Park Road you want to travel (Kantishna at the end of the road is a 13-hour round-trip for $43.75). You can stay on the shuttle the entire ride and enjoy the sights or get off to hike through the backcountry and catch the next bus when you're ready to move on. Passes are available for purchase at the visitor center and free shuttles run continuously around the visitor center area and to the sled dog demos. Shuttle rides are not offi-

cially guided, but often drivers will stop for any animal sightings (often after a passenger shouts "Grizzly!" or "Moose!"), point out interesting sights and answer questions. Mid-May to mid-September, daily 5 a.m.-6 p.m.

RAFTING

Flowing to the north, the Nenana River is the setting for some of the most beautiful rafting in the United States. Most trips start from near Denali Park's entrance, and levels vary from peaceful floats toward the south of the park to stretches of class III to IV whitewater rafting in the northern sections. Trips can last anywhere from a couple of hours to multiday excursions. Some popular outfitters include Denali Raft Adventures (Mile 238 on George Parks Highway, 907-683-2234, 888-683-2234; www.denaliraft.com), Nenana Raft Adventures (Mile 238 on George Parks Highway, 907-683-7238, 800-789-7238; www.alaskaraft.com) and Denali Outdoor Center (Mile 240 on George Parks Highway or Mile 0.5 on Otto Lake Road—turn west at Mile 247 on George Parks Highway, 907-683-1925, 888-303-1925; www.denalioutdoorcenter.com).

BIKING

Bicycling is another favored activity. Bikes may be transported on the Park Road shuttle bus, allowing for a one-way bike ride to the center of Denali followed by a

DENALI

one-way bus ride back to the visitor center. Bikes can be rented at Denali Outdoor Center (Mile 240 on George Parks Highway, 907-683-1925, 888-303-1925; www.denalioutdoorcenter.com).

MOUNTAINEERING

For those seeking to test their mettle, Mount Foraker rises 17,400 feet, and Mount McKinley stands as one of the most difficult climbs in the world. While not technically difficult, bitterly cold temperatures, fierce winds and 16,000 feet of snowline make for a daunting expedition. All climbers must register 60 days in advance of their planned climb. (Call 907-733-2231 for more information on registration and mountaineering.)

WILDLIFE

The national park and preserve was created originally to protect the area's abundant wildlife, which still remains one of the park's biggest draws. Luckily, the warmer tourist season corresponds to animals' most active time as they gather food and prepare for the harsh Alaskan winter. The preserve is home to 37 species of mammals, including lynx, porcupine and foxes, while golden eagles, short-eared owls and raptors are just a few of the 160 species of birds that soar through the region. But it's the so-called "big five" (moose, caribou, Dall sheep, wolves and grizzly bears) that most visitors hope to catch sight of.

Horned Dall Sheep: The horned Dall sheep often appear as tiny white dots on mountainsides. These relatives of bighorn sheep favor roaming the rocky steep precipices, where they can graze on evergreen shrubs, grasses and moss and stay far from wolves and other predators. The animals are more visible at lower elevations in early summer, but they tend to climb higher as the snows melt.

Caribou: Caribou, like the Dall sheep, travel in herds. These antlered animals are often on the go and migrate great distances depending on the season. The approximately 1,700 caribou that roam the park are often found on the tundra above the timberline.

Moose: Standing almost eight feet tall, the moose can weigh up to about 1,400 pounds. During the autumn mating season, or the rut, a bull may gather a "harem" of cows. Calves are born in late spring and stay with their mothers for up to two years. Most moose can be found in the wooded taiga area feasting on grass, willow, aspen or birch.

Wolf: The wolf hunts a variety of the area's animals, from arctic ground squirrels and hare to caribou and moose. Unfortunately, wolves are the most difficult of the "big five" to spot, since only around 100 inhabit the entire park.

Grizzly Bear: Probably the most awe-inspiring Denali resident, the grizzly bear can be found throughout the park and can often be seen

DENALI

★

★

★

☆

☆

lumbering around Sable Pass and on the tundra. The omnivores, who often eat Arctic ground squirrels, caribou, moose calves and carrion, can also be found feasting on berries, roots and other small plants. Each October, Denali's roughly 300 grizzlies enter their dens to hibernate, emerging sometime in spring. As adults, the grizzlies typically weigh between 300 and 650 pounds.

BIRDS

Like most nature preserves, Denali hosts dozens of bird species, depending on the season and available food sources. From the common **least sandpiper** that resides in the lowlands to the **northern pintail** and **green-winged teal** in the wetlands, there is no shortage of bird-watching in the park. Check birding resources online (such as www.adfg.state.ak.us/pubs/notebook/notehome.php) or at any of the visitor centers for bird species listings, including seasonal abundance.

WHERE TO STAY

CAMPING

Campers wishing to strike off on their own within the park need to obtain a backcountry camping permit in person at the Backcountry Information Center for one of the park's 87 subdivisions, called "units." Stays are limited to seven consecutive days in one unit and a maximum of 30 days in the park. Many units have quotas for how many people can camp at a time, so be prepared to be flexible if you can't get your first choice. You can also choose from the six campgrounds within the park (stays are limited to 14 days per year). Most are open late May to early September, depening on the weather, except where noted.

Igloo Campground: This 5-site campground is located at Mile 35 on Park Road. A chemical toilet is available but no potable water, hook-ups or other amenities. Accessible via camper bus. Fees: $5 reservation plus $9/night.

Riley Creek Campground: These 147 sites just inside the park entrance are open year-round. Toilets, showers and drinkable water are available. The Riley Creek Mercantile Camper Convenience Store is located nearby. Accessible by private vehicle. Fees: $20/night drive-in, $12/night walk-in.

Sanctuary Campground: These seven sites are at Mile 23. Chemical toilets are available, but no drinkable water, hook-ups or other amenities. Accessible by camper bus. Fee: $5 reservation plus $9/night.

Savage River Campground: Located at Mile 13 on Park Road, Savage River has 33 sites, including three for groups of nine to 20 people. Toilets and drinkable water are available but no hook-ups or other amenities. This campground can accommodate RVs and tents. Accessible by private vehicle. Fee: $20/night.

DENALI

Teklanika River Campground:
At this 53-site ground at Mile 29 on Park Road, toilets and drinkable water are available but no hook-ups or other amenities. RVs up to 40 feet and tents can be accommodated. Accessible by private vehicle. Fee: $5 reservation plus $16/night (three-night minimum stay).

Wonder Lake Campground: This 28-site campground is at Mile 85. Toilets and drinkable water are available; no hook-ups or other amenities. Accessible by Camper Bus. Fee: $5 reservation plus $16/night.

HOTELS

★★**Denali Crow's Nest Log Cabins**
Mile 238 on the George Parks Highway, Denali National Park and Preserve, 907-683-2723, 888-917-8130;
www.denalicrowsnest.com
Sleep in a log cabin atop Sugarloaf Mountain within walking distance of the park entrance. After a hard day's hike, what could be better than relaxing in a hot tub surrounded by stunning vistas? The accommodations are clean and quiet—perfect for the traveler who can't wait to get up early to tackle the park.
39 cabins. Closed early September to mid-May. Restaurant, bar. $

★★**Denali Princess Wilderness Lodge**
Mile 238 on the George Parks Highway, Denali National Park and Preserve,
907-683-2282, 800-426-0500;
www.princesslodges.com
From the dramatic two-story rock and wood beam main building, completed in 2004, to the rustic, elegant log buildings that house the guest rooms, this lodge is perfect for those who want to experience nature without roughing it. Terraces wrap around the lodge for spectacular views, while a soak in one of the outdoor hot tubs can help relieve the aches and pains of a long day's hike. Shuttle service is available to the park, and staff can arrange tours, helicopter flightseeing or horseback riding.
661 rooms. Closed mid-September to mid-May. Four restaurants, bar. Fitness center. $$

★★**Grande Denali Lodge**
Mile 238 on the George Parks Highway, Denali National Park and Preserve,
907-276-7234, 800-276-7234;
www.denaliparkresorts.com
Perched at the top of a mountain, this upscale lodge has sweeping views of the Alaska Range and Nenana River Canyon just north of Denali National Park's entrance. Stay in one of the main lodge's guest rooms or in a log cabin that boasts its own private deck. Staff is happy to help arrange a variety of activities.
163 rooms, 6 cabins. Closed mid-September through mid-May. Restaurant, bar. $$

★★McKinley Chalet Resort

Mile 239 on the George Parks Highway, Denali National Park and Preserve,
907-276-7234, 800-276-7234;
www.denaliparkresorts.com

A mile from the park entrance, this upscale resort has the feel of a Swiss chalet with its cedarwood lodges nestled in a spruce forest on the Nenana River. Guided nature walks and twice-daily informational talks given by naturalists familiar with the wildlife and geology of the park are just a few of the complimentary perks. The centerpiece of the stunning lobby is a large, three-dimensional topographical map of the Denali area, which serves as a useful aid in understanding just how big and untamed the park really is.

345 rooms. Closed mid-September to mid-May. Two restaurants, bar. $$$

★★Mt. McKinley Princess Wilderness Lodge

Mile 133 on the George Parks Highway, Denali National Park and Preserve,
907-733-2900, 800-426-0500;
www.princesslodges.com

Travelers to Denali will appreciate this self-described "true wilderness retreat" that sits just 41 miles from Mt. McKinley on 146 acres. Guests can easily take an excursion into the park or hike the lodge's own network of trails before capping off the day in a hilltop whirlpool, one of the onsite restaurants or the cozy sitting room.

460 rooms. Closed mid-September through mid-May. Wireless Internet access. Three restaurants, bar. Fitness center. Business center. $$

—— ALSO RECOMMENDED ——

Earthsong Lodge

Stampede Road, 4 miles off George Parks Highway, Healy,
907-683-2863;
www.earthsonglodge.com

Run by a former Denali National Park Ranger and his wife, this off-the-beaten-path lodge 17 miles north of the park is one of the few places open in both summer and winter. Guests stay in their own log cabins set above the tree line on the open tundra. Explore on your own or take one of the lodge's unforgettable organized winter dogsledding trips.

11 cabins. Open year-round. Coffeehouse. $

Kantishna Roadhouse

Denali National Park and Preserve, 800-942-7420;
www.kantishnaroadhouse.com

The Kantishna Roadhouse, originally a gold miners' tent camp, is now a full-service lodge in the heart of the park, owned and staffed by Native Americans of Athabaskan descent. Guests stay in quiet, deluxe cabins. A main building provides a place to relax, a saloon and an activities desk so guests can plan daily guided or independent adventures.

32 cabins. Closed mid-September to early June. Breakfast, lunch, dinner included. Bar. $$

★
★
★
★

North Face Lodge

Denali National Park and
Preserve, 907-683-2290;
www.campdenali.com

Set on rolling, emerald green
hills, the comfortable rooms all
have private bathrooms, and the
inn has an inviting living area
with fireplace and dining room
for delicious meals prepared with
ingredients from the greenhouse
garden. Each day, the bakery also
serves up piping hot bread, flaky
pastries and delicious cookies and
desserts, perfect to stash in your
backpack. Minimum three-night
stay.

15 rooms. Closed mid-September
to early June. $

WHERE TO EAT

42

★★Alpenglow Restaurant

George Parks Highway, Denali
National Park and Preserve,
907-683-8500, 866-683-8500;
www.denalialaska.com

Set on the edge of a cliff, this restaurant greets diners with good
service and even better views of the
Denali Canyon and Alaska Range
from a two-story wall of windows.
The spacious dining room has
sloped wood beam ceilings, giving it a true alpine lodge feel. The
American menu uses the freshest
ingredients available and serves
American dishes like beef brisket,
as well as regional favorites.

American menu. Breakfast, lunch,
dinner. Closed mid-September
through mid-May. Bar. Children's
menu. Casual attire. Reservations
recommended. $$$

★★★Nenana View Grille

Mile 239 on the George Parks
Highway, Denali National Park
and Preserve, 907-276-7234,
800-276-7234;
www.denaliparkresorts.com

Located at the McKinley Chalet
Resort with sweeping views of the
Nenana River, this sophisticated
eatery offers some of the best fine
dining in the area. Featuring an
open kitchen and a large stone
pizza oven, the dining room is
filled with beautiful wood furni-
ture and striking artwork, giv-
ing it an air of rustic elegance.
The menu is a mix of haute cui-
sine, popular Alaskan dishes and
lighter fare—all complemented by
a primo wine selection.

American menu. Lunch, dinner,
late-night. Closed mid-September
through mid-May. Bar. Children's
menu. Casual attire. Reservations
recommended. Outdoor seating.
$$$

★★Overlook Bar and Grill

Mile 238 on the George Parks
Highway, Denali National Park
and Preserve, 907-683-2723,
888-917-8130;
www.denalicrowsnest.com

Boasting "the largest beer selection in all of Alaska," this lively
bar and grill at the Denali Crow's
Nest Log Cabins has become an
area institution known for its good
food and fun atmosphere. Alaskan halibut and salmon, burgers,
chili and other kinds of pub grub
are served in its scenic dining area
or on the sun deck.

American menu. Lunch, dinner. Bar. Children's menu. Casual attire. Outdoor seating. $

★★The Perch

Mile 224 on the George Parks Highway, Denali National Park and Preserve, 907-683-2523, 888-322-2523; www.denaliperchresort.com

Part of the Denali Perch Resort, this hilltop restaurant specializes in fine-dining cuisine with an emphasis on popular Alaskan seafood and steak dishes. Multiple bay windows offer dramatic, unobstructed views of the wilderness outside, while the restaurant's rustic architecture and open kitchen provide visual interest inside. Everything here is made from scratch, from the loaves of bread served with meals to the soups, salad dressings and desserts prepared fresh each day. The restaurant also has a full bar featuring Alaskan beers and an extensive wine list.

American menu. Dinner. Bar. Children's menu. Casual attire. Outdoor seating. $$

43

DENALI

EVERGLADES NATIONAL PARK

LOOKING DECEPTIVELY LIKE AN OPEN PRAIRIE, EVERGLADES NATIONAL Park is actually more than 1.5 million acres of wetlands. Although much smaller than it once was—it previously covered the bottom third of the state—today the Everglades encompasses the southernmost tip of Florida and is the lower 48 states' third-largest national park. Unfortunately, it's probably one of the most difficult of the national parks to explore—much of it is impenetrable, and an experienced guide is often necessary to point things out while navigating its tangled labyrinth of waterways via boat.

Creating what's known as the "River of Grass," large swathes of the park are blanketed with saw grass, a plant with barbed blades and needle-sharp edges that shoot up ten feet from the water. Only clusters of trees and dense vegetation, called hammocks, break up these grassy glades, which eventually give way along the coast to huge, shadowy mangrove swamps interlaced with tranquil, winding water lanes. The Everglades, considered to be the largest subtropical wilderness in the United States, contains a number of fragile ecosystems and boasts more than 300 animal and 700 plant species.

Humans, beginning with Paleo-Indians, have inhabited the Everglades area since 10,000 B.C. From 1500-1750 A.D., five separate tribes and as many as 20,000 Native Americans dominated South Florida. Their numbers dissipated to only several hundred with the arrival of Spanish explorers, and when the English took control of the area in 1763, the remaining few eventually fled to Cuba. With the indigenous populations absent and with European settlers encroaching further north, migrating tribes of Creek and proto-Seminoles roamed the area to hunt, fish and evade the foreigners settling Florida.

Unfortunately, by the late 1800s the Everglades region began to change shape when early settlers and developers deemed the area useless swamp and began to drain the wetlands. At the beginning of the 20th century, land created by dredging, including areas like Miami and Fort Myers, led to even more loss of the fragile wetlands ecosystem. Species that once thrived in the Everglades began to dwindle and the threat of extinction became a reality for animals like the Florida panther, the American crocodile and the West Indian manatee, among many others.

The idea for saving the Everglades was first proposed and lobbied for by landscape architect Ernest Coe. His efforts were successful, and in

★
★
★
★
★

1934, Congress approved the creation of Everglades National Park. It was finally established on December 6, 1947.

Today the Everglades is one of the most threatened national parks. Alterations to paths of flowing water from Lake Okeechobee and population growth have caused the disappearance of more than 50 percent of the original Florida wetlands. Rare and endangered species that can't be found anywhere else in the world still face extinction, and large areas of sea grass beds are dying. Strict conservation is this park's only hope.

40001 State Road 9336, Homestead, Florida, 305-242-7700; www.nps. gov/ever

WHAT TO SEE

The most popular time of year to visit Everglades National Park is Florida's dry season in winter, as the summer wet season brings flooding, making much of the park challenging to navigate. The park is best traveled by car or boat, and because of its large size, you'll first want to decide which of the four main visitor centers and main entries will be your starting point. The Everglades contains four visitor centers: The Gulf Coast Visitor Center welcomes travelers on the northwest coast of the park, the Shark Valley Center on the northeast corner is closest to Miami, Earnest Coe Center serves the East Coast and abuts Florida City, and the coastal Flamingo Visitor Center to the south looks onto a plethora of tiny keys.

Starting in the northwest corner of the park and heading south toward Flamingo will allow for sights along the main park road. The park's main entrance, just southwest of Homestead, is the **Ernest F. Coe Visitor Center and Park Headquarters** (40001 Route 9366, 305-242-7700; November-April, daily 8 a.m.-5 p.m.; May-

October, daily 9 a.m.-5 p.m.), where guests can get oriented to the surrounding sites and history through a short film. Next, take the 38-mile main park road, Route 9366, to the **Royal Palm Center** (check for daily walks and other schedules) at Mile 4. Explore the **freshwater slough** (along the **Anhinga Trail**) to get a lesson on saw grass marsh or to see some of the Everglades' abundant wildlife. There are also great opportunities here to stop and see the trees that populate the park—gumbo limbo, strangler figs and hardwood hammocks (**Gumbo Limbo Trail**)—and the slash pines that once covered modern-day Miami and other towns, visible at the **Pinelands** at Mile 7. At Mile 12, you can explore the park's **dwarf cypress** trees, so named because of their stunted stature due in large part to shallow soils. For a more elevated view of the Everglades, **Pa-hay-okee Overlook** at Mile 13 is a two-story wooden tower that sits on the saw grass prairie and offers views of these shallow grassy waters for as far as the eye can see. Further along at Mile 20, **Mahogany Hammock** boasts mahogany

EVERGLADES

and poisonwood trees as well as the United State's only paurotis palm trees, typically found solely in Cuba and Central America. At the end of the road, the **Flamingo Visitor Center** (239-695-2945; mid-November to mid-April, daily 8 a.m.-4:30 p.m.) is a wild and remote part of the southern Everglades that serves as access to Cape Sable and Florida Bay. Traverse the waterfront to observe an array of Everglades wildlife at this marine nursery.

If you choose to begin your tour of the park in the northeast region and head west, toward the opposite coast and a completely different ecosystem, you'll want to navigate along **Tamiami Trail** (US 41), which will take you from Shark Valley Visitor Center to Gulf Coast Visitor Center. On the northeastern boundary of the park, US 41 passes by **Shark Valley Visitor Center** (36000 SW Eighth St., Miami, 305-221-8776; mid-December to mid-April, daily 8:45 a.m.-5:15 p.m.; mid-April to mid-December, daily 9:15 a.m.-5:15 p.m.). This home base and starting point for those visiting from Miami or other East Coast cities sits in the valley named for the Shark River, which runs from the middle of the Everglades to the Gulf of Mexico, where sharks are known to congregate at its mouth. Just past the Visitor Center, look for the 15-mile scenic **Loop Road** that leads to a **65-foot observation tower** where you'll be treated to a stunning 360-degree view of the surrounding saw grass prairies that are filled with birds and

alligators. Continuing on US 41 past the **Big Cypress Visitor Center** and the **Florida National Scenic Trail** (which leads into the 2,400-square-mile **Big Cypress National Preserve** just north of the Everglades), head five miles down Highway 29. Just past Everglades City, the **Gulf Coast Visitor Center** (800 S. Copeland Ave., Everglades City, 239-695-3311; mid-November to mid-April, daily 8 a.m.-4:30 p.m.; mid-April to mid-November, daily 9 a.m.-4:30 p.m.) is the gateway to the **Ten Thousand Islands**, a mangrove archipelago that sits on the Gulf of Mexico. These "islands" are formed by accumulating deposits of leaves and other plant debris that collect in the waterways flowing around mangrove roots, creating the ever-changing number of small land formations that comprise the southwest Florida coast.

WHAT TO DO

HIKING

Because the Everglades Park is largely made up of wetlands and lacks the mountain peaks of many other national parks, the trails here are easy. Because of the park's huge geographic coverage, it's best to navigate hiking and biking trails by distinct area within the park. Each hurricane season can bring damage to the trails, which close until repairs can be made.

Shark Valley Trails

★
★
★
☆
☆

Bobcat Boardwalk Trail

1 mile round-trip

Trailhead: Off Tram Road behind the Shark Valley Visitor Center.

In the park's northeast region, explore the 0.5-mile Bobcat Boardwalk Trail. This self-guided tour cuts through the area's saw grass prairie and tropical hardwood forest. Wheelchair accessible.

Otter Cave Hammock Trail

0.5 miles round-trip

Trailhead: Off Tram Road a half mile behind the Shark Valley Visitor Center.

Summer rains can cause this rough limestone trail to flood, but when conditions are good, it leads through a quarter mile of tropical hardwood forest.

Pine Island Trails

Mahogany Hammock Trail

0.5-mile loop

Trailhead: 20 miles west of the Ernest Coe Visitor Center.

The Mahogany Hammock Trail is an elevated boardwalk that wanders through mahogany trees and other lush vegetation. Don't miss the world's largest living mahogany tree, seen on this trail. Wheelchair accessible.

Pineland Trail

0.5-mile loop

Trailhead: 7 miles west of the Ernest Coe Visitor Center.

The paved Pinelands Trail meanders through palmettos, pines and perky tickseed and ruellia wildflowers, which grow on a thin layer of soil covering porous limestone bedrock. A handful of jaunts shoot off the Main Park Road. Wheelchair accessible.

Flamingo Trails

Bear Lake Trail

3.2 miles round-trip

Trailhead: 2 miles north of the Flamingo Visitor Center.

At the southernmost tip of the Everglades, Bear Lake Trail takes hikers past 50 types of trees before coming to the lake. This hike is a treat for bird-watchers.

Christian Point Trail

3.6 miles round-trip

Trailhead: 1 mile north of the Flamingo Visitor Center.

This trail traverses several ecosystems. See airplants (bromeliads) and coastal prairie before reaching Snake Bight. A long trail, it's best to reserve a half or full day if you plan to walk the entire thing.

TRAM TOURS

Shark Valley Tram Tours (305-221-8455; www.sharkvalleytramtours.com) conducts two-hour guided environmental and educational tours year-round along the 15-mile loop through the "River of Grass." Park-trained naturalists point out wildlife, including woodstorks, red-shouldered hawks and alligators, while explaining the Everglades' fragile ecosystem. The tour culminates with a stop at the park's 45-foot observation deck—the perfect perch for 360-degree panoramic

47

EVERGLADES

views of the Everglades. Rates are $15.25 for adults, $9.25 for children 3–12.

BOATING

Boating, kayaking and canoeing are great ways to take advantage of what the park has to offer since more than one-third of the Everglades consists of water. All equipment can be rented at various points in the park for excursions down trails like the Turn River Trip's cypress swamp or the 99-mile Wilderness Waterway Trail. For guided boat tours, the Everglades National Park Boat Tours (Gulf Coast Visitors Center, 239-695-2591; year-round, daily) has a narrated excursion that travels through the Ten Thousand Islands area. For that quintessential swamp experience, the Everglades Alligator Farm (40351 SW 192 Ave., Florida City, 305-247-2628, 800-644-9711; www.everglades.com) has airboat rides year-round through the farm's "back 40" everglades. Admission is $19 for adults, $12 for children 4–11, includes access to the farm (see below); the airboat ride alone is $13.50 and $8.50, respectively.

FISHING

Both freshwater and saltwater fishing for grouper, sea trout, bass, mackerel and other edible species are popular in the park. The best fishing is on the many water flats, channels and mangrove keys, while shore fishing is somewhat limited. Prime spots for freshwater angling can be found from Nine Mile Pond north and along the Main Park Road. Separate freshwater and saltwater licenses are required for park visitors over 16. The best saltwater fishing is along the Everglades' western coast in Monroe County, in Florida Bay to the south and Ten Thousand Islands to the northwest. Check the visitor centers for information on charter excursions.

ALLIGATOR FARM

To see alligators up close without risking life or limb, the Everglades Alligator Farm (40351 SW 192 Ave., Florida City, 305-247-2628, 800-644-9711; www.everglades.com; year-round, daily) is home to more than 2,000 of the reptiles ranging from newly hatched to fully grown. Stop by during an alligator feeding demonstration or go to the farm's Wildlife Shows, where you can hold baby alligators and snakes.

WILDLIFE

Insects, especially mosquitoes, thrive in the Everglades in huge numbers. But don't let them distract you from enjoying the diversity of animals that roam this biological wonderland.

American alligators and crocodiles: South Florida is the only place in the world where alligators and crocodiles live together. Most people confuse the two similar-looking reptiles, but the difference is simple: adult American alligators are blackish in color, have a broad snout and only their upper teeth stick out when their jaw is closed; American crocodiles are olive brown, have narrower snouts and sport both upper and lower protruding teeth with a closed mouth. The alligator, once in danger of disappearing from the Everglades due to poaching, can easily be spotted, especially in the marl prairies, while crocodiles thrive in the mangrove swamps.

Florida panther: The larger Everglades mammals, like bobcats, coyotes and bears, are often harder to spot because of their elusive nocturnal natures. Among the rarest of the protected mammals in the park, the Florida panther is numbered at just 30-50 cats. These endangered animals are a subspecies of the mountain lion and mostly make the areas in or around Big Cypress National Preserve their home.

West Indian manatee: Aquatic life thrives in the Everglades' waters, including more than 300 species of fish in the park's marine coastlines and freshwater areas. One of the best places to spot these animals is in Florida Bay—home to dolphins, sea turtles and the endangered West Indian manatee. This wrinkled and whiskered marine mammal can weigh as much as one thousand pounds and consume 10 to 15 percent of its body weight daily in sea grasses and other plants that grow in the bay.

Birds: Despite the fact that many of the Everglades' birds were slaughtered in the early 20th century for their plumes—wading birds'

populations have been reduced by 90 to 95 percent—almost 400 species of birds still pass through or live in the Everglades today. **Bald eagles**, **warblers** and **barred owls** are active in the Mahogany Hammock vicinity; **roseate spoonbills** flit about the Paurotis Pond mangroves; and **red-shouldered hawks**, **painted buntings** and other transient birdlife are found at Eco Pond.

WHERE TO STAY

CAMPING

There are two campgrounds in the Everglades: Long Pine Key (six miles from the Ernest Coe Visitor Center, 305-242-7873) has 108 sites with restrooms and water available but no showers or hookups, and Flamingo (end of the main park road near the Flamingo Visitor Center) has 234 drive-in sites, three group sites and 40 walk-up sites with cold-water showers available but no hookups. Both have 14-day limits November-May and a 30-day limit the rest of the year. Both are open year-round and charge nightly fees of $16 during the dry season. Long Pine Key is first-come, first-served only; reservations can be made at Flamingo (877-444-6777; www.recreation.gov). There are 47 designated backcountry camping sites throughout the Everglades that can be reached by hiking or via boat, but beware that camping in the Everglades during the wet season may be uncomfortable. Backcountry sites are not available by car, and a backcountry permit is required (Ernest Coe, Flamingo or Gulf Coast Visitor Centers, 239-695-2945).

HOTELS

Marco Island

★★★Hilton Marco Island Beach Resort
560 S. Collier Blvd., Marco Island, 239-394-5000, 800-445-8667; www.marcoisland.hilton.com
Outdoors enthusiasts visiting the Everglades will appreciate the large variety of water sports at this hotel, including sailing, parasailing and jet skiing, as well as tennis onsite and golf close by. Or rest up after a day at the park by relaxing in the pool or a tropical-motif suite.
275 rooms, 22 suites. High-speed Internet access. Two restaurants, bar. Fitness center. Tennis. Pool. Beach. Spa. Business center. $$

★★★Marco Beach Ocean Resort
480 S. Collier Blvd., Marco Island, 239-393-1400, 800-715-8517; www.marcoresort.com
This property is located on Marco Island's white sand Crescent Beach about 30 miles from Everglades Park. Each suite is exquisitely furnished and includes a multitude of luxury appointments, including marble showers, fully equipped kitchens, and floor-to-ceiling sliding glass doors—perfect for pampering oneself after a long day amongst the mosquitos.
98 rooms, all suites. High-speed Internet access. Three restaurants,

three bars. Fitness center. Pool. Beach. Spa. $$$

Miami

★★Circa 39 Hotel
3900 Collins Ave., Miami, 305-538-4900, 877-824-7223; www.circa39.com
Circa 39, an Art Deco hotel built around 1939, is just steps from the beach and about a half hour from Everglades National Park. This boutique hotel features a contemporary lobby with a relaxed feel, as well as guest rooms with mounted flat-screen TVs, Aveda bath products and relaxing blue and white color schemes to match the Miami sky and water. The bustle of the city serves as a contrast to those exploring the Everglades by day.
71 rooms, 15 suites. High-speed Internet access. Complimentary continental breakfast. Bar. Fitness center. Pool. $

★★Doubletree Grand Hotel Biscayne Bay
1717 N. Bayshore Drive, Miami, 305-372-0313, 800-222-8733; www.doubletree.com
A short drive from the northeast corner of the Everglades preserve, this hotel offers contemporary guest rooms overlooking the bay, as well as an outdoor pool, jogging track and fitness center. The one- and two-bedroom condo units have fully equipped kitchens.
96 rooms, 56 condo units. High-speed Internet access. Five restaurants, bar. Fitness center. Tennis. Pool. Business center. $

50

EVERGLADES

★★★★Four Seasons Hotel Miami

1435 Brickell Ave., Miami,
305-358-3535, 800-332-3442;
www.fourseasons.com

This contemporary hotel is located in downtown Miami's newly buzzing Brickell neighborhood. Guest rooms and suites are decorated with cool earth tones and distinctive art, and after a long day in the Everglades, the 50,000-square-foot Splash Spa at the onsite Sports Club/LA offers guests ten treatment rooms and a unique menu of pampering options. The hotel features a fine dining restaurant, Acqua, which serves up Latin-inspired fare, and two lounges, including the skytop, poolside Bahia, where locals and travelers alike gather for cocktails.

182 rooms, 39 suites. Wireless Internet access. Restaurant, two bars. Fitness center. Pool. Spa. $$$$

★★★Marriott Miami Biscayne Bay

1633 N. Bayshore Drive, Miami,
305-374-3900, 800-228-9290;
www.marriott.com

Just minutes from Miami International Airport and less than 30 miles east of the Everglades, this waterside tower in the center of the downtown arts and entertainment district overlooks Biscayne Bay. The terrace is perfect for an afternoon outdoor meal with views of the ocean and the port of Miami.

580 rooms, 21 suites. Wireless Internet access. Two restaurants, bar. Fitness center. Pool. $$

★★★Mayfair House Hotel

3000 Florida Ave., Miami,
305-441-0000, 800-433-4555;
www.mayfairhotelandspa.com

Nestled in the heart of Miami's famous Coconut Grove, Mayfair House is located in an avant-garde building featuring a lush, central courtyard where the plethora of plant species that thrive in southern Florida is represented. Each suite features a unique name, character and design, as well as hand-carved mahogany furniture and a Japanese-style hot tub or Roman tub. Stained glass windows and antique artwork decorate this 12,000-square-foot space.

179 rooms, all suites. Wireless Internet access. Restaurant, bar. Fitness center. Pool. Spa. Pets accepted. $$

★★★The Mutiny Hotel

2951 S. Bayshore Drive, Miami,
305-441-2100, 888-868-8469;
www.mutinyhotel.com

Towering over Sailboat Bay, many of the rooms here have private balconies with excellent views of the bay or city. Deluxe suite accommodations include bedroom, bathroom, living room and a fully equipped kitchen for those who prefer the comforts of home. This is a good base for trips to the Everglades and for taking in the sailing, fishing, beaches and everything else Miami has to offer.

120 rooms, all suites. Restaurant, bar. Fitness center. Pool. $$$

51

EVERGLADES

★★★★The Ritz-Carlton Coconut Grove

3300 SW 27th Ave., Coconut Grove, 305-644-4680, 800-241-3333; www.ritzcarlton.com

This world-class hotel is recognized for its impeccable service—technology, travel, bath and even pet butlers cater to your every need. Its Miami location makes it a good upscale choice for visitors to the Everglades, just 30 miles west of the hotel. And once you return from the park, you won't have to leave the Ritz grounds: the lobby lounge serves cocktails and afternoon tea, while Bizcaya Grill serves steaks prepared to perfection each evening.

97 rooms, 18 suites. High-speed Internet access. Restaurant, bar. Fitness center. Pool. Spa. Business center. $$$$

WHERE TO EAT

Marco Island

★★Café De Marco

244 Palm St., Marco Island, 239-394-6262; www.cafedemarco.com

Opened in 1983, this bistro is known for its diverse seafood menu including black grouper de Marco, Chilean sea bass and the house specialty, jumbo prawns. For non-seafood lovers, Café De Marco also serves landlubber favorites such as pasta and filet mignon.

Seafood menu. Dinner. Closed Sunday (off-season). Children's menu. Casual attire. Outdoor seating. $$

★Snook Inn

1215 Bald Eagle Drive, Marco Island, 239-394-3313; www.snookinn.com

Located on the Marco River, this restaurant is named for the snook fish that congregate right off the dock. Setting a true island vibe, daily live music welcomes boaters (who can park in one of Snook Inn's docking spots). Seafood, steaks and sandwiches are served both indoors and waterside underneath the Chickee Bar's thatched roof. If you've caught and cleaned your own fish, the chefs will prepare it for you.

Seafood, steak menu. Lunch, dinner. Bar. Children's menu. Casual attire. Outdoor seating. $$

★Su's Garden

537 Bald Eagle Drive, Marco Island, 239-394-4666

A longtime Marco Island favorite, this restaurant has a menu largely comprised of Mandarin-style Chinese dishes. The light sauces and vegetarian choices make for many health-conscious options, and the price is right on both Su's lunch and dinner entrées.

Chinese menu. Lunch, dinner. Casual attire. $$

Miami

★★★★Azul

500 Brickell Key Drive, Miami, 305-913-8358; www.mandarinoriental.com

Mediterranean and Asian flavors come together at Azul in the Mandarin Oriental Miami hotel, where chef Clay Conley crafts a menu made from the day's fresh catch

★

★

★

★

★

and seasonal ingredients. Miso-marinated hamachi is accompanied by edamame rice, shrimp dumplings and sake butter sauce, while a grilled lamb chop might rest alongside a harissa-marinated lamb loin with smoked eggplant. An ample wine list offers pairings for any of Azul's menu choices.

Japanese, Mediterranean menu. Lunch (Monday-Friday), dinner. Closed Sunday. Bar. Children's menu. Business casual attire. Reservations recommended. Valet parking. Outdoor seating. $$$

★★★Baleen
4 Grove Island Drive, Miami, 305-857-5007; www.groveisle.com

Baleen's focus is on eclectic, contemporary, seafood-centered fare. This serene oasis is set in a vista of plush outdoor greenery, complete with waterfront views. Inventive fish dishes accompany menu items including Vietnamese-style sugarcane pork skewers and a maple- and soy-roasted chicken.

International menu. Breakfast, lunch, dinner, Sunday brunch. Bar. Business casual attire. Reservations recommended. Valet parking. Outdoor seating. $$$

★Café Med
3015 Grand Ave., Miami, 305-443-1770; www.cafemedmiami.com

This Italian restaurant boasts great people watching from its Mediterranean-style patio as well as a hefty menu of traditional pasta dishes, pizzas and sandwiches. You'll also find many seafood-heavy preparations and the house specialty: a mixed seafood linguini dish.

Italian menu. Lunch. Bar. Children's menu. Casual attire. Outdoor seating. Valet parking. $$

★★Café Tu Tu Tango
3015 Grand Ave., Miami, 305-529-2222; www.cafetututango.com

The original location of a chain of four restaurants, this Coconut Grove restaurant was inspired by the rich history of artists in the Miami neighborhood and has been serving an international fusion menu since 1993. Paying homage to the artists, the restaurant's small plates are meant to be enjoyed by several people.

International/fusion menu. Lunch, dinner, late-night. Bar. Children's menu. Casual attire. Outdoor seating. $$

★★News Cafe
800 Ocean Drive, Miami Beach, 305-538-6397; www.newscafe.com

After a day getting down and dirty in the Everglades, why not show your celeb side? With a see-and-be-seen oceanfront spot in South Beach, News Café regularly makes the news with A-list star sightings, although the news in the name officially refers to an in-house bookstore and newsstand. In addition to salads, soups, sandwiches, pizzas, and a smattering of Middle Eastern dishes, such as falafel and tabbouleh salad, the café serves breakfast round-the-clock.

International menu. Breakfast, lunch, dinner, late-night. Bar.

EVERGLADES

Casual attire. Valet parking. Outdoor seating. $$

★★★Shibui
7101 SW 102nd Ave., Miami, 305-274-5578;
www.shibuimiami.com
Though fans rave about the freshness of the fish, Shibui's real claim to fame is its menu: if you can get past the 45 different sushi rolls, you'll find a vast array of traditional Japanese appetizers, combos and entrées.
Japanese menu. Dinner. Children's menu. Reservations recommended. $$$

★Tobacco Road—
Blues Bar and Restaurant
626 S. Miami Ave., Miami, 305-374-1198;
www.tobacco-road.com
Established in 1912, Tobacco Road is Miami's oldest bar. With a history that covers nearly a century, it has seen Miami through Prohibition as well as some sweeping music trends. Today it still serves up an ample bar menu (including outstanding burgers) as well as live music seven nights a week.
American menu. Lunch, dinner, late-night. Bar. Casual attire. Valet parking. Outdoor seating. $$

★Versailles
3555 SW Eighth St., Miami, 305-444-0240;
Diners appreciate the authenticity of the dining experience as well as the affordable cuisine. With a long menu of Cuban staples and a family-friendly atmosphere, Versailles isn't fancy, but it does offer an opportunity to refuel on yellow rice, beans and seafood after a day spent exploring the Everglades.
Cuban menu. Breakfast, lunch, dinner, late-night, Sunday brunch. Casual attire. Reservations recommended. $$

EVERGLADES

GLACIER NATIONAL PARK

VAST, RUGGED, PRIMITIVE AND MAJESTIC, GLACIER NATIONAL PARK IS nature's unspoiled domain. This is the place for a midsummer snowball fight, honing photography skills with a lens trained on glacier-wrapped peaks, enjoying the pure solitude on a wilderness trail bordered by alpine wildflowers and then settling in for all the tranquility that a remote campsite on a fir-fringed lake affords. This is the place to come simply to gawk at nature and gain an appreciation for everything that created it. The park is a living textbook in geology from 800 million-year-old rocks that show millions of years of sea patterns and marine environments to stromatolites, ancient fossils of blue-green algae that give evidence of the earth's earliest physical and chemical compositions. Next to those, all of human history sounds like yesterday, even the findings from recent archaeological surveys that show evidence of humans in the Glacier area dating back more than 10,000 years.

When the first European explorers arrived here, several Native American tribes inhabited the region. Fur trappers came to the area in the early 1800s looking for beaver. And in 1806, the Lewis and Clark Expedition passed within 50 miles of the present-day park boundary. The westward migration of homesteaders eventually pushed the Native American tribes out of the park and onto reservations. Soon settlers began seeing the value the land had as well, and by the late 1890s the tourism industry had been born. It was then that George Bird Grinnell, an early explorer of Montana, pioneered the movement to win the region protection with national park status. President Taft granted his wish and declared Glacier a national park on May 11, 1910.

Glacier National Park is linked to 204 square miles of Canada, known across the border as Waterton Lakes National Park. The two countries share the protected region, known collectively as the Waterton-Glacier International Peace Park. Glacier National Park wasn't named for any of the 37 small glaciers that remain in the park today but instead for the mile-deep ice that once filled the area and, over time, shaped the park's peaks and valleys as it continually melted and refroze. Unfortunately, those 37 remaining patches of ice represent less than a quarter of the glaciers that were in the park just 150 years ago, and experts say that if current warming trends continue, there will be no glaciers left in their namesake park in just 30 years. This wild wonderland boasts more than 200 lakes, 1,400 varieties of plants, 63 species of animals—from mice to moose—and 272 varieties of birds. Spectacular views of the park can be glimpsed while driving, particularly when crossing the Continental Divide on the precarious Going-to-the-Sun Road. The awe-inspiring 50-mile-long road's construction was an unrivaled engineering feat when it was completed in 1932 and is still a marvelous sight today. Most of the park, however, including the glaciers, is accessible only by trail. There are 732 miles of maintained trails penetrating the far-flung wilderness areas, making this park an adventurous backpacker's paradise. Whether you're going by foot or on horseback, magnificent and isolated parts of Glacier await discovery.

West Glacier, Montana, 406-888-7800; www.nps.gov/glac

WHAT TO SEE

The primary entry point for exploring Glacier National Park is **West Glacier**, a northwestern Montana town with coffee houses, restaurants, all kinds of camping and mountaineering supplies—basically everything a visitor needs before heading into the wild. Glacier National Park has one main thoroughfare, the 50-mile-long **Going-to-the-Sun Road**. A trip on this road gives visitors a little taste of the park's majesty right from the seats of their cars—or, better yet, from one of the park's new shuttles. The system, initiated in 2007, operates free biodiesel-powered shuttles through the park on Sun Road during July and August with stops at key facilities, campgrounds and trailheads to reduce the environmental impact of summer's heavy tourist traffic. The frequent shuttles come approximately every 15-30 minutes from 7:15 a.m.-7:00 p.m., and there are 17 shuttle stops.

If you're entering the park from the west on Highway 2, you'll travel two miles before arriving at the **Apgar Visitor Center**, **Backcountry Office** and **Transit Center**, the park's main information hub. Apgar Village is situated at the foot of **Lake McDonald**, the largest lake in the park at 10 miles long and 472 feet deep. Experts estimate that the glacier that sculpted the Lake McDonald valley was around 2,200 feet thick. Boat and canoe rental facilities are here, as well as a number of independent tour operators.

From Apgar Village, take Going-to-the-Sun Road to explore the park. Hugging the shoreline of Lake McDonald, Sun Road is 50 miles long and one of the most magnificent drives in the world (open approximately mid-June to mid-September). It's 32 miles from the Apgar Village to the **Logan Pass Visitor Center** and another 18 miles from the pass down to the **Saint Mary Visitor Center** at the park's East Entrance. Saint Mary Visitor Center offers similar services as Apgar Village, including trip-planning information, rangers on hand to answer questions, parking lots for shuttle

★
★
★
★
★

riders and a shuttle stop. Driving all 50 miles without stopping at any of the scenic viewpoints takes about two hours. The road winds continuously up the mountain edge, making for an unforgettable ride and linking the east and west sides of the park. At **Logan Pass**, enjoy a 100-mile view from an elevation of 6,646 feet. Note that vehicles longer than 21 feet (including trailers) and wider than eight feet (including mirrors) are prohibited on Going-to-the-Sun Road between Avalanche and Sun Point (roughly the middle third of the road). The park also began an 8- to 10-year renovation of the road in June 2008; expect short delays because of the construction during the summer months.

Along Sun Road, you will pass many trailheads, offering countless day hiking opportunities, wildlife (especially mountain goats and bighorn sheep in the area surrounding Logan Pass), campgrounds, picnic areas, and numerous mountain streams and waterfalls. A few specific points of interest: The **Lake McDonald Lodge**, a historic location on the west side of the park, offers lodging, restaurants, a camp store and a plethora of activities ranging from boat tours to horseback riding. There are several designated scenic pullout spots (though the whole drive is breathtaking), including the **Jackson Glacier Overlook** on the east side, which imparts views of glaciers right from Sun Road, and one over **Sunrift Gorge**, also on the east side,

which offers views of a striking gorge cut by the melt from Sexton Glacier. Finally **Saint Mary Lake**, near the East Entrance to the park, has a dock with tour boat operators at **Rising Sun** on the east side.

Sun Road connects Highway 2, to the west of the park at West Glacier, to Highway 89, to the east of the park at Saint Mary. Highway 89, called the Blackfeet Highway, extends from Browning, Montana, past the park to Canada. The road to **Many Glacier Valley** branches from Highway 89, nine miles north of Saint Mary. The Many Glacier area offers a ranger station, lodging, camping, fishing, boating, horseback riding and hiking access to a number of lovely lakes, waterfalls and the Grinnell Glacier, one of the largest in the park. Farther south, the road to **Two Medicine Lake** leaves Highway 49 four miles north of East Glacier Park town. The Two Medicine area offers a ranger station, fishing (brook, rainbow trout), boating, camping and several trailheads for hiking access to remote waterfalls and alpine lakes surrounded by deep valleys and towering peaks. To the north, Chief Mountain International Highway (Highway 17) leads to **Waterton Lakes National Park** in Canada.

★

★

★

★

★

BACKPACKING

Glacier National Park is a backpacker's realm and consistently ranks as one of the most popular destinations for backcountry camping. Sun Road offers just a taste of what the Glacier wilderness holds, and the greedy, or adventurous, depending on how you see it, want more: a pristine alpine lake all to themselves, endless mountain vistas with no one but their friends and to spot a mountain lion not just from the road but to pay it a visit at home. Of course, there are some inherent risks when you leave developed areas of the park for the wilderness, from contending with river crossings and steep snowfields to having close encounters with dangerous wildlife and unexpected severe weather. The Park Service asks that everyone entering the backcountry start by fully reading the *Backcountry Guide,* found at www.nps.gov/glac/planyourvisit/backcountry.htm and at visitor centers in the park. You can download the permit application and submit it by fax or mail. For more information, call the Backcountry Reservations Office (406-888-5819).

BIKING

Pedaling up Sun Run is becoming more popular every year. For the safety of riders and to ease congestion on the already busy road, the park has instituted some restrictions for the busiest times in the park. From June 15th through Labor Day, 11 a.m.-4 p.m., bicycles are prohibited from Apgar Campground to Sprague Creek Campground in both directions and from Logan Creek to Logan Pass in the eastbound/uphill direction. Bicycles are restricted to roadways, bike trails and parking lots in Glacier National Park; they are prohibited on trails.

BOATING

There are quite a few options in the park for boating, whether you take a private motorboat out on a lake for a weekend of waterskiing, rent a canoe for an hour or two or take a boat tour deep into the park. Motorboats are allowed on the following lakes: McDonald, Sherburne, Saint Mary, Two Medicine and Waterton. All motorboats and sailboats from Montana 12 feet or longer must be registered, but boats from elsewhere can be used temporarily without registration. Boat rentals are available from the Glacier Boat Company at Apgar Village, Lake McDonald Lodge, Rising Sun Dock, Many Glacier and Two Medicine. Boat tours are yet another way to go. The Glacier Park Boat Company also operates the park's guided boat tours, a great way to see and learn about this big-lake-filled region. For more information, contact the Glacier Park Boat Company (406-257-2426; www.glacierparkboats.com). Keep in mind that the waters in the park are cold and hypothermia is a danger year-round.

BUS TOURS

Two independent tour operators offer guided bus trips in Glacier National Park. Glacier Park, Inc. (U.S.: 406-892-2525, Canada: 403-236-3400; www.glacierpark-inc.com) takes you on various park tours in vintage red motor coaches with convertible tops that were first used in the park in 1936. These tours are both scenic and informational. Sun Tours (406-226-9220, 800-786-9220; www.glaciersuntours.com) provides trips with a Native American perspective. On the tour over Going-to-the-Sun Road, learn all about Native American spiritual and philosophical beliefs and nutritional and medicinal plants in the park, among other topics. Sun Tours uses air-conditioned 25-passenger buses.

FISHING

You don't need a permit or license to fish inside the park. However, all anglers must stop at a visitor center or ranger station for a copy of the current fishing regulations before casting a line.

HIKING

Day hikes are a great way to see a little more of the park than possible from Sun Road and experience its terrain. Here are a few sugges-

tions for hikes of various difficulties in the area.

─────── **EASY** ───────

Hidden Lake Overlook
3 miles round-trip
Trailhead: Logan Pass Visitor Center
This trail drops 460 feet from Logan Pass to a viewpoint over the lovely Hidden Lake. Look for high-altitude residents like bighorn sheep and mountain goats on this trail.

Johns Lake Loop
3-mile loop
Trailhead: East of Lake McDonald Lodge on Going-to-the-Sun Road.
This short loop passes serene Johns Lake and offers views of the valley below. The hike has a 160-foot elevation gain.

Trail of the Ceders
0.7-mile loop
Trailhead: Avalanche picnic area on Going-to-the-Sun Road.
This flat, self-guided nature walk provides visitors with information on the surrounding features and crosses a bridge over Avalanche Gorge.

─────── **MODERATE** ───────

Apikuni Falls
2 miles round-trip
Trailhead: 1.1 miles east of Many Glacier Hotel in Many Glacier Area.
This short trail with a 700-foot elevation gain takes hikers to a scenic overlook above Many Gla-

59

GLACIER

cier Valley and the base of a lovely waterfall.

Grinnell Lake
6.8 miles round-trip
Trailhead: Grinnell Glacier
Trailhead in Many Glacier Area
This relatively flat hike takes visitors into the wilderness for stunning views over pristine Grinnell Lake.

Virginia Falls
3 miles round-trip
Trailhead: Saint Mary Falls
This short trail drops 260 feet and then climbs 285 feet through a lush forest to the base of a rushing waterfall.

—— **STRENUOUS** ——

Grinnell Glacier Viewpoint
11 miles round-trip
Trailhead: Grinnell Glacier
Trailhead in Many Glacier Area
This hike, with a 1,600-foot elevation gain, affords a more intimate look at one of the park's biggest glaciers.

Piegan Pass
9 miles round-trip
Trailhead: Piegan Pass Trailhead, east of Logan Pass on Going-to-the-Sun Road.
This hike meanders through meadows as it climbs 1,750 feet and delivers overlooks of remote pristine alpine lakes.

Ptarmigan Lake
8.6 miles round-trip
Trailhead: Iceberg Ptarmigan
Trailhead in Many Glacier Area

GLACIER

This trail travels through picturesque meadows past the stunning Ptarmigan Falls (a good turnaround point for a shorter hike) and up to this splendid alpine lake surrounded by striking vistas. Elevation gain is 1,700 feet.

HORSEBACK RIDING

Guided trail rides are available inside the park during the summer through Swan Mountain Outfitters (September 15-May 15, 800-919-4416; May 16-September 16, 877-888-5557) at Many Glacier, Lake McDonald and Apgar.

RAFTING

Several companies offer river-rafting trips in the area on the fast-flowing Flathead River:
Glacier Raft Co. (406-888-5454, 800-235-6781; www.glacierraftco.com); Great Northern Whitewater Raft & Resort, (406-387-5340, 800-735-7897; www.gnwhitewater.com); Glacier Guides & Montana Raft Company (406-387-5555, 800-521-7238; www.glacierguides.com); Wild River Adventures (406-387-9453, 800-700-7056; www.riverwild.com).

SKIING

Whitefish Mountain Resort
County 487, Flathead National Forest, Whitefish, 406-862-2900, 800-858-4152;
www.skiwhitefish.com
World-class skiing is available daily from early December to

early April at this ski resort with a double, four triple, two quad and three high-speed quad chairlifts; two T-bars; a Magic Carpet conveyer; and ski patrol. The longest run is 3.3 miles, and the vertical drop is 2,500 feet. Cross-country trails are also available. Adventure-seekers can test their skills on bowl and tree skiing as well. Summer (late June-early September) activities include hiking, mountain biking, bungee jumping and concerts.

Advanced cross-country skiers may want to tackle the trails, mostly unmarked, within the park itself. Register at the trailhead registration boxes—just be aware of the potential for severe or sudden changing weather and avalanches.

WILDLIFE

This vast, unsullied wilderness provides a habitat for a whole empire of wildlife, from bats to bighorn sheep, garter snakes to grizzly bears, and lake trout to lynx. There are 62 species of mammals living in the park. Thanks to the park's early establishment and vast area, these animals have enjoyed a generous, protected habitat for nearly a century, and flourished. A trip to Glacier will give you a closer look at the animal kingdom. Here are some of the interesting creatures you may meet on the trail.

Bighorn sheep: Their preferred homes are at the top of the peaks along the continental divide. Look for them near Logan Pass.

Black bear: Ranging in color from blond to black, these bears are smaller than grizzlies and have shorter claws.

Dipper (water ouzel): These unique birds may be seen bobbing in a stream, often McDonald Creek. They actually swim with their wings underwater instead of wading. Their eyes have special membranes and their nostrils special flaps to allow them to stay underwater for up to 30 seconds.

Grizzly bear: Like the black bears, these bears' colors also range from light to dark. They can be distinguished by the slope in their face, unlike the black bear's straighter profile, and by the muscular hump between their shoulders. Glacier is home to one of the largest remaining grizzly populations in the lower 48 states. Their diet mostly consists of grasses, glacier lilies and huckleberries. Scientists have recently begun studying the bears using DNA from their hair and scat. Their research shows the current population is somewhere around 300 bears.

Harlequin duck: Glacier is one of the best places to find these pretty birds with feathers in an elaborate pattern of gray, orange, black and white that looks painted on. Their call sounds a little like a bark. Look for them in McDonald Creek.

Lynx: Considered a threatened species, these big cats have a gray-and beige-mottled coat.

Mountain goat: These sure-footed animals like to make their homes in the steep terrain along the Continental Divide and are frequently seen near Logan Pass.

Western painted turtle: These colorful turtles have orange and yellow markings on their shells and yellow-streaked skin. Visitors may spot them lazing around lakes on the west side of the park at lower elevations.

WHERE TO STAY

CAMPING

There are 13 campgrounds—six of them along Sun Road, one at Many Glacier, one at Two Medicine and the other five at various entry points to the backcountry along the perimeter of the park. The camping limit is seven days. Most campgrounds are available on a first-come, first-served basis. Fish Creek and Saint Mary campgrounds may be reserved ahead of time (877-444-6777; www.recreation.gov). Visitors planning to camp overnight in Glacier's backcountry must obtain a Backcountry User Permit and camp in designated sites.

Glacier National Park

★★Lake McDonald Lodge
Lake McDonald, Going-to-the-Sun Road, Glacier National Park, 406-892-2525 (U.S.), 403-236-3400 (Canada); www.glacierparkinc.com

This Swiss-style lodge perched on the shores of the park's biggest lake was built in 1913-14, just a few years after the park was established. It is convenient for boat-

ing, hiking, horseback riding or just sitting back and enjoying the views. The accommodations are rustic but comfortable.

100 rooms. Two restaurants, bar. $

★Village Inn at Apgar
Apgar Village, Going-to-the-Sun Road, Glacier National Park, 406-892-2525 (U.S.), 403-236-3400 (Canada); www.glacierparkinc.com

Scenically set on the shores of Lake McDonald, this '50s throwback motor inn offers a retro Americana ambiance that fits perfectly in this classic American family vacation destination. Some rooms offer kitchenettes or additional bedrooms.

36 rooms. $

— ALSO RECOMMENDED —
Many Glacier Hotel
Swiftcurrent Lake, Many Glacier Area, Glacier National Park, 406-892-2525 (U.S.), 403-236-3400 (Canada); www.glacierparkinc.com

Construction of this historic hotel began the same year that Glacier became a national park. At the base of Mount Grinnell and on the shores of Swiftcurrent Lake, this Swiss-themed hotel's picturesque setting lends itself to convenient hiking, horseback riding, boating and more. And when guests return in the afternoon, there's fondue for dipping fun.

214 rooms. Restaurant, two bars. $

Rising Sun Motor Inn

Saint Mary Lake, Going-to-the-Sun Road, Glacier National Park, 406-892-2525 (U.S.), 403-236-3400 (Canada); www.glacierparkinc.com

This rustic inn sits on the shores of dazzling Saint Mary Lake, surrounded by stunning mountain peaks. Just out the door is all the recreation the lake has to offer, from boat rentals and tours to hiking around its shore. There's also a camping store and restaurant onsite.

72 rooms. Restaurant. $

West of Glacier National Park
Whitefish

★★Grouse Mountain Lodge

2 Fairway Drive, Whitefish, 406-862-3000, 800-321-8822; www.grmtlodge.com

This chicly decorated inn has a tasteful and rustic ambience punctuated by a host of modern amenities, including a video arcade, tennis and volleyball courts and more.

145 rooms. Wireless Internet access. Three restaurants, bar. Fitness center. Pool. Airport transportation available. Business center. $$

★★Kandahar The Lodge at Big Mountain

3824 Big Mountain Road, Whitefish, 406-862-6098, 800-862-6094; www.kandaharlodge.com

This casual mountain lodge just 34 miles from the park delivers cozy comfort in a wide variety of forms, from single motel rooms to apartment-style suites. Furnishings are basic, but the overall character is snug.

49 rooms, 11 suites. Closed mid-April to May, October-late November. Wireless Internet access. Complimentary full breakfast. Restaurant, bar. Fitness center. $$

Kalispell

★★Izaak Walton Inn

290 Izaak Walton Inn Road, Essex, 406-888-5700; www.izaakwaltoninn.com

This unique inn should create a memorable family vacation for guests who end up in its caboose lodging—four rooms are housed in former train cabooses. They don't lack any amenities, though. The owner remembers everything from hot showers to hot chocolate and cider. Complimentary wireless access is available in the lounge.

33 rooms. Complimentary continental breakfast. Restaurant, bar. $

East of Glacier National Park

★Glacier Park Lodge

Midville Drive, East Glacier Park, 406-892-2525 (U.S.), 403-236-3400 (Canada); www.glacierparkinc.com

This grand old lodge just outside the park ushers guests inside through its 40-foot-tall Douglas fir pillars supporting the roof above the impressive lobby. Guest rooms are Montana-style rustic with craftsman-style furniture and western charm. The heated

GLACIER

outdoor pool sparkles under the big sky for which Montana is known.

161 rooms. Closed October to mid-May. Restaurant, bar. Golf. Pool. Spa. $$

★★Saint Mary Lodge & Resort
Highway 89 and Going-to-the-Sun Road, St. Mary,
406-732-4431, 888-788-6279;
www.stmarylodgeandresort.com

With seven lodging facilities plus cabins, this resort has accommodations to meet any guest's desire from budget basics to choice refinement with highlights like granite countertops, mini wet bars, stone fireplaces, leather sofas, Jacuzzi tubs, gas barbecue grills and private decks. New 17-foot-tall, 700-square-foot tipis are available with cedar floors, fire pits and Jacuzzis.

122 rooms, suites, cottages, and tipis. Closed mid-October to April. Wireless Internet access. Two restaurants, bar. Pets accepted. $

WHERE TO EAT

Glacier National Park
★★Snowgoose Grille in the Saint Mary Lodge
Highway 89 and Going to the Sun Road, Saint Mary,
406-732-4431, 888-788-6279;
www.stmarylodgeandresort.com/restaurants

This upscale park eatery offers gourmet western specialties all day long, from the Montanan breakfast omelet with bacon, jack cheese and apples to the roast buffalo on a baguette served au jus at lunch to the sautéed rainbow trout dusted in cornmeal at the end of the day.

American menu. Breakfast, lunch, dinner. Closed mid-October to April. Bar. Children's menu. Casual attire. $$

— ALSO RECOMMENDED —
Ptarmigan Dining Room
Many Glacier Hotel, Many Glacier Area, Glacier National Park,
406-892-2525;
www.glacierparkinc.com

The stars of this restaurant are the stunning peaks out the window, which diners might mistake for the Alps, given their surroundings. The warm Swiss ambience of the dining room coupled with a frosty cold Montana microbrew welcomes hikers back from the trail as they are.

American, Continental menu. Breakfast, lunch, dinner. Closed October-May. Casual attire. $

West of Glacier National Park

— ALSO RECOMMENDED —
Buffalo Cafe
514 Third St., Whitefish,
406-862-2833;
www.buffalocafewhitefish.com

This family-run café is where the locals head for a hearty breakfast. From the pancakes and cinnamon French toast to the dozen-plus excellent egg dishes, the menu covers all the bases. Try the first-rate homemade biscuits and gravy for a bit of traditional comfort food.

American menu. Breakfast, lunch.
$

Café Kandahar
3824 Big Mountain Road,
Whitefish, 406-862-6247;
www.cafekandahar.com

A 22-year-old fine dining tradition in Whitefish, this creative contemporary restaurant draws locals and return tourists alike. This is a place that's great for special occasions—or turning any night into one. A meal here could start with the Glacier salad, a marinated Flathead Valley pork tenderloin, Terrapin Farms arugula and field greens, local goat cheese and toasted pine nuts tossed with a huckleberry vinaigrette, before moving on to the grilled beef tournedos with an oyster-mushroom and smoked-shallot bordelaise alongside tasso-maytag-bleu grits and string beans. The sommelier's wine choices don't disappoint either.

Contemporary American menu. Breakfast, dinner. Closed mid-April to mid-June, mid-September to Thanksgiving. $$

MacKenzie River Pizza Co.
9 Central Ave., Whitefish,
406-862-6601;
www.mackenzieriverpizza.com

This Montana-born pizza chain started in Bozeman in 1993, aiming to bring "crazy" combinations like basil, sun-dried tomatoes, artichoke hearts and almonds onto the slices of a state that didn't deviate from pepperoni. It didn't take Montanans long to come around to these gourmet pizzas, though; in just 15 years, that one pie shop turned into a chain of 12, all serving a variety of pizzas, fresh salads, sandwiches and pasta. Pizza menu. Lunch, dinner. $

Pescado Blanco
235 First St., Whitefish, 406-862-3290; www.pescadoblanco.com

This Mexican eatery fuses traditional cuisine from south of the border with local high-altitude flavors, using only fresh, local, seasonal ingredients and making everything by hand—from salsas to tortillas. Try the Mountain Mexican Sliders appetizer, seared carnitas or beef served with guacamole and pico de gallo on mini torta buns, or the Elk Chorizo Taco, the chef's own local elk chorizo sautéed with carmelized onions, crimini mushrooms and roasted sweet chilis, then served on handmade corn tortillas with cheese, baby arugula and Mexican crema.

Mexican fusion menu. Dinner. Children's menu. $

Tupelo Grille
17 Central Ave., Whitefish,
406-862-6136;
www.tupelogrille.com

This warm and welcoming little eatery has garnered accolades from all over the country for its inventive take on Cajun cuisine. Visitors who can get a table might enjoy something like cumin-grilled sea scallops on chorizo black lentils with ancho crème fraiche to start, followed by grilled

65

GLACIER

★
★
★
★
★

shrimp served on a garlic-cheddar-grit cake with a tasso cream sauce and, of course, complemented by a wine from Tupelo's commended and extensive wine list.

Cajun, Italian, seafood menu. Dinner. $$

East of Glacier National Park

★★ Glacier Village Restaurant

304 E. Highway 2, East Glacier Park, 406-226-4464

A family-owned and operated joint for more than 50 years, this is the place for a hearty pre-hike breakfast or to refuel after a long day on the road. In the morning, don't miss the pancakes—any of them. Later in the day, reliable western menu choices range from local fish to chicken fried steak to buffalo ribs, all to be washed down with one of the many wine offerings or a local microbrew.

American menu. Breakfast, lunch, dinner. Closed late September-early May. $$

— ALSO RECOMMENDED —

Serrano's Mexican Restaurant

29 Dawson Ave., East Glacier Park, 406-226-9392

One of the few restaurants on this side of the park, this little place draws quite a crowd for its homemade authentic Mexican cuisine. Guests should arrive early if they don't want to wait for their chili rellenos and margaritas.

Mexican menu. Dinner. Closed fall-spring. $

Two Sisters Cafe

Highway 89, four miles north of Saint Mary, Babb, 406-732-5535; www.twosistersofmontana.com

Regarded by many as the best restaurant on the east side of the park, this funky little café can be spotted from miles away, thanks to local artists who've bestowed the place with a hodgepodge of murals. It's a no-frills menu here, but it's homecooking as it should be. Try a burger or chicken-fried steak and make sure to save room for the huckleberry pie.

American menu. Breakfast, lunch, dinner. Closed October-May. $

★
★
★
★
★

GRAND CANYON NATIONAL PARK

THIS IS NOT QUITE THE IMAGE OF AN ALPINE WONDERLAND THAT YELLOW-stone, Glacier and Rocky Mountain national parks conjure. Grand Canyon National Park is simply a big hole in the middle of the desert—and teeming with tourists at that. But look out over the great expanse of the Grand Canyon, and the awe-inspiring vistas reveal a spectacular desert landscape. Rocks in this great chasm change colors from sunrise to sunset and hide multiple ecosystems of wildlife.

It's not surprising that nearly 5 million visitors travel to see this world wonder and World Heritage site every year. (Compare that to the 44,173 tourists the park welcomed in 1919, when it was established.) People from all over the globe come here to hike the trails, travel down to the base by mule, camp, backpack, raft the Colorado River or simply stare in admiration from the rim. The entire park is 1,904 square miles in size, with 277 miles of the Colorado River running through it. Draining water systems have carved dramatic canyons throughout the walls, making every rock in every direction worthy of a look. Forests descend from upper elevations at the rim and give way to desert basins below. At its widest point, the north and south rims are 15 miles across, with average elevations of 8,000 feet and 7,000 feet, respectively. The canyon averages a depth of one mile. At its base, 2 billion-year-old rocks are exposed.

Not quite as old as those rocks, but pretty ancient, are the 12,000-year-old human artifacts found in the park. Archaeologists say that people have used and occupied the area since that time, known as the Paleo Indian period. Nomadic groups hunted animals like mountain goats and bison and gathered plants around the Canyon. Over centuries, environmental changes forced them to adapt, and they began experimenting with horticulture around 3500 B.C. and eventually developed a more sedentary, agricultural lifestyle. People of this period left behind split-twig figurines representing animals of the Canyon; some are on display at the Tusayan Museum. In 500 A.D., there were the first suggestions of villages. By 1300, there is evidence that other groups of seminomadic, nonpuebloan people, the Pai and Paiute, also occupied the area in the river corridor. These were the ancestors of the present-day Hualapai and Havasupai people, who still live in and near the Canyon today.

Other current residents of the Canyon include approximately 355 bird species, 89 mammals, 47 reptiles, 9 amphibians, 17 fish, and thousands of aquatic and terrestrial invertebrates. The canyon accommo-

GRAND CANYON

dates a vast diversity of habitats, including every one that is present in the United States, except alpine tundra, thanks to such dramatic variance in elevation and the differing exposures to sunlight on various slope faces. Such habitats are home to unique species, such as the black-bellied, white-tailed Kaibab squirrel, not found anywhere but on the Kaibab plateau on the North Rim of the park. One-of-a-kind animals, unrivaled views and extraordinary experiences with nature make a trip to this peerless national park an unmatched experience.

Grand Canyon National Park (South Rim), approximately 80 miles northwest of Flagstaff, Arizona, via Highway 180, 928-638-7888; www.nps.gov/grca

WHAT TO SEE

Grand Canyon National Park essentially encompasses two distinct parks: the South Rim and the North Rim. The two sides of the canyon are only about 10 miles apart as the crow flies, but for us grounded creatures, they are realistically a five-hour drive, or 215 miles, from each other—and very different places at that. The scenery, climate and vegetation are all noticeably different between the two sides of the canyon because of the contrast in elevation. Visitors should be aware that it takes a bit of extra planning to visit both Rims in one trip to the Grand Canyon. Most visitors fly into Phoenix or Flagstaff, Arizona, or Las Vegas, Nevada. The drive to the South Rim from Flagstaff is about 80 miles, and there are three possible routes: I-40, Highway 180 or Highway 89 to Highway 64. From Phoenix, the drive is 231 miles, taking I-17 north to I-40 west to Highway 64 north into the park. From Las Vegas, it's 278 miles, taking Highway 93 south to I-40 east to Highway 64 north.

The South Rim, open year-round, is 60 miles north of Williams, Arizona, and has many more tourist services than the North Rim, including day and overnight mule trips, horseback riding and air tours. In addition, there are a variety of museums and facilities on the South Rim. A good starting point is the **South Rim Grand Canyon Village**, which is the park headquarters and heart of park activity and transportation. Heading north on the South Entrance Road, you will reach a curve toward the left (west) near the rim of the canyon and find the **Canyon View Information Plaza**, a short walk from **Mather Point**. This visitor center provides information, a bookstore and outdoor exhibits and is the transportation hub for free shuttle bus tours of the South Rim. They go in both directions from the visitor center, hit all of the hot spots and are a convenient way for families to get around. The West Rim and East Rim drives out from the Village are equally rewarding. Less than a mile west of the visitor center

★

★

★

★

and Mather Point is the **Yavapai Observation Station**. The museum offers scenic views, geological exhibits and a bookstore. It's open daily 8 a.m.-8 p.m. A couple miles further west on the paved trail hugging the rim leads past gift shops and lodging to the **Kolb Studio** in the Village Historic District at the Bright Angel Trailhead, which features art displays and a bookstore. It was once the home and business of the Kolb brothers, who were pioneering photographers here at the turn of the 20th century. West of Bright Angel Trailhead are a number of scenic viewpoints along the rim overlooking the canyon. From March to November, this road is closed to private vehicles west of Hopi Point. The free Hermits Rest shuttle and a walkable trail (about 5 miles long) access these western overlooks.

Heading east from the Canyon View Information Plaza and continuing that way on **Desert View Drive**, you will pass a couple of the park's most magnificent vistas at **Grandview Point** and **Desert View**. About 25 miles west of Grand Canyon Village on Desert View Drive, visitors will find the **Tusayan Museum**. This museum displays exhibits on prehistoric people in the southwest using artifacts like pottery, jewelry, corncobs and arrowheads to shed light on the ancient culture. There's also an excavated pueblo ruin (circa 1185) with a self-guided trail nearby. The museum is open daily 9 a.m.-5 p.m., weather permitting, and offers ranger-led tours daily at 11 a.m. and 1:30 p.m. Continuing east from the museum, head toward the **Desert View Visitor Center**, which houses a book store and information center. Also in the area is the **Watchtower**, a historic replica of an ancient pueblo tower. It was designed in 1932 by Mary Colter, the primary architect of the park's rustic southwestern-style buildings along the South Rim. A climb to the top of the tower delivers 360-degree views, and the walls inside display murals by Hopi artist Fred Kabotie.

Directly south of the South Rim is tourist-centered **Tusayan**, offering camping, lodging, restaurants, souvenirs, an IMAX theater, various tours of the canyon, car rentals and service stations.

It is a 215-mile drive from the South Rim to the **North Rim** around the east side of the park on Highway 89 and Highway 67. A shuttle is available between the two sides (Trans Canyon Shuttle, Tusayan, 928-638-2820). However, the road is blocked by heavy snows in winter and is only open from mid-May to mid-October. Mule trips are available during the summer from the North Rim, as they are from the South. The **North Rim Visitor Center** near Bright Angel Point offers information, exhibits and a bookstore during the summer season. Facilities besides these on the Bright Angel Peninsula are few and far between. There are trailheads and a few picnic areas along the main road. If you're visiting the North Rim, the 23-mile trip from Bright

GRAND CANYON

★

★

★

★

Angel Point to **Cape Royal** is a must. You'll encounter several good viewpoints along the way, and many say the view from here is better than from the South Rim. Archaeology and geology talks are given here in summer and fall.

North Rim visitors with a little extra time or adventurous energy would do well to spend it traveling to **Tuweep**, a remote area on the northwest rim of the Grand Canyon that's best accessed via the Sunshine Route (BLM Road #109) from Highway 389 about seven miles west of Fredonia, Arizona. Although this, the most reliable route to the area, is often quite dusty and rough, the overlook from 3,000 feet above the Colorado River is jaw-dropping. Down the river is the Lava Falls Rapid, which is not only visible but easily audible from the viewpoint. Volcanic features and the sheer vertical drop make this a dramatic, awe-inspiring destination and every bit worth the rugged and challenging trek to reach it.

WHAT TO DO

BACKPACKING

Fall and spring, when the park is less crowded, are the best times to trek into the canyon. Fifteen main trails provide access to the inner canyon. Even experienced hikers should allow extra time and come prepared for the canyon's extreme conditions. Be sure to carry plenty of food and water—in fact, much more than you might think you

need. Consider the dramatically steep descent from high elevation (with a heavy backpack), little shelter from the harsh desert sun, and of course, the climb all the way back up (which takes twice as long). In other words, it's harder than you think. For more information, call 928-638-2125. Submit requests for backcountry permits as early as possible, about four months in advance. (The park service receives about 30,000 requests for backcountry permits a year but only issues 13,000.) Guided backcountry trips are also available through the Grand Canyon Field Institute (866-471-4435).

MULE TRIPS

South Rim mule trips into the Canyon are offered year-round and may be booked up to 13 months in advance through Xanterra Parks & Resorts (303-297-2757, 888-297-2757; www.grandcanyonlodges.com). They fill up early so try to plan far ahead—preferably booking one year in advance. Some restrictions apply. North Rim trips are offered mid-May to mid-October. Because the North Rim trips start from a higher elevation, they do not go all the way to the river. Trips range in length from one hour around the North Rim to two nights/three days from the South Rim, staying overnight at Phantom Ranch inside the Canyon. For reservations or more information on the available North Rim trips, contact Grand Canyon Trail Rides (435-679-8665; www.canyonrides.com).

HIKING

It's best not to hike to the base and back up in a day. Here are a few shorter hikes to try:

---------- EASY ----------

Bright Angel Point Trail
0.5 miles round-trip
Trailhead: Near North Rim Visitor Center.

This short, paved trail leads to a remarkable viewpoint. Self-guided nature trail pamphlets are available at the visitor center.

Rim Trail
0.3–12.5 miles one-way; many starting and stopping points
Trailhead: Pick up the trail from any viewpoint from Pipe Creek Vista to Hermits Rest, South Rim.

This hike is a great way to see the canyon from various viewpoints along the South Rim, and you can hike as little or much as you want, with many shuttle stops interspersed at viewpoints along the easy, flat trail.

---------- MODERATE ----------

Cedar Ridge
1.5 or 3 miles round-trip
Trailhead: South Kaibab Trail, south of Yaki Point on Yaki Point Road, South Rim; access by shuttle bus only.

Some of the best views of the canyon available to day hikers are on this trail. Just 0.75 miles into the canyon, you'll understand why Ooh-Aah Point is so named when the trail opens up to the stupendous panoramic view. This is a good turn-around point. Hikers who wish to continue to Cedar Ridge at the 1.5-mile mark will reach even more impressive overlooks before heading back to the rim. It is not recommended to hike below Cedar Ridge on a day hike during summer.

Supai Tunnel
4 miles round-trip
Trailhead: North Kaibab Trail, North Rim

This is a good day hike on the only maintained trail that goes into the Canyon from the North Rim. It reaches stunning viewpoints and offers a different perspective from hiking around the rim. Hikers looking for a full day's adventure can continue on the trail to Roaring Springs; start out before 7 a.m.

Bright Angel Trail to Three Mile Resthouse
6 miles round-trip
Trailhead: West of Bright Angel Lodge, South Rim

This very popular trail affords tremendous views all the way, starting out easier and getting steeper after the first switchback. At the 1.5-mile mark, there is a resthouse with toilets, an emergency phone and water available during summer. For many hikers, this is a good turnaround point. The trail gets even steeper after the 2-mile mark. At 3 miles, you'll find another resthouse with water (seasonally) and an emergency phone. The total elevation change is 1,948 feet.

GRAND CANYON

★
★
★
★

─── STRENUOUS ───

Coconino Saddle

2.2 miles round-trip
Trailhead: Grandview Trail at
Grandview Point, 12 miles east
of village on Desert View Drive,
South Rim.

This hike is for experienced desert hikers only. Hiking boots are recommended on this narrow, steep, rocky and strenuous trail, which is not maintained. There is no water along this trail so you should carry plenty of your own. It is not recommended to hike beyond the Coconino Saddle point as a day hike during the summer, as the trail gets steeper and rockier beyond this point. The elevation change is 1,165 feet.

HORSEBACK RIDING

Apache Stables (928-638-2891, 928-638-3105), just outside the park's south entrance, offers one- and two-hour trail rides at the South Rim. Twilight campfire and wagon rides are also available.

RAFTING

Rafting the Colorado River through Grand Canyon National Park requires reservations far in advance of your intended visit. Trips with commercial outfitters vary in length from a half day (which may not be in the National Park) to 18 days. Trips of 3 to 18 days, often reserved one or even two years in advance, are offered by more than a dozen guiding companies. For a list of all of the available outfitters to find the best trip for you, see www.nps.gov/grca/planyourvisit/whitewater-rafting.htm. For one-day white-water raft trips, contact Hualapai River Runners (928-769-2210, 800-622-4409; www.destination-grandcanyon.com/runners.html). For half-day smooth-water raft trips, call Colorado River Discovery (800-522-6644; www.raftthecanyon.com). Private, or independent, river trips are also possible on a 52-mile stretch of the Colorado that starts at Diamond Creek and takes two to five days to raft. Permit requests for private trips are not accepted earlier than one year in advance and are then taken on a first-come, first-served basis. For more information, contact the River Permits Office (800-959-9164).

RANGER PROGRAMS/ OUTDOOR EDUCATION

The Park Service presents various free informational outdoors programs throughout the year at many South Rim locations. Educational Junior Ranger Programs are available for children of various ages. Get details on both at a visitor center upon arrival. Adults looking for an immersive educational experience should consider a "class" with the Grand Canyon Field Institute (928-638-2485; www.grandcanyon.org/fieldinstitute), which offers everything from educational day hikes to weeklong backpacking trips, and teaches not only backcountry skills but also specified subjects like geology, natural or human history, archaeology or botany related to the Canyon.

AIR TOURS

Both fixed-wing and helicopter tours are available daily through several local companies based outside of the park. The Grand Canyon Chamber of Commerce (928-638-2901, 888-472-2696; www.grandcanyonchamber.com) can provide visitors with a list of air operators.

IMAX

The **Grand Canyon IMAX Theatre** (928-638-2468; www.explorethecanyon.com) in the National Geographic Visitor Center in Tusayan, just south of the South Entrance, shows a 34-minute large-screen film highlighting features of the Grand Canyon. The movie is shown hourly on the half hour: March-October, 8:30 a.m.-8:30 p.m.; November-February, 10:30 a.m.-6:30 p.m.

WILDLIFE

With an elevation difference of as many as 8,000 feet from the highest points on the North Rim to the bottom of the gorge, a great diversity of habitats in Grand Canyon National Park support a wide variety of wildlife. Here are some of the animals that you may be lucky enough to see:

Bald eagle: Look for them in the river corridor in the winter, especially late December and early January, when they nest there to feast on the abundant trout in the Colorado River.

Bats: One of the Canyon's most common mammals, both migratory and resident bats roost in the inner gorge's multitudinous caves. Humans exploring these nooks and crannies can disturb maternity colonies of bats.

Bighorn sheep: At one time, these Rocky Mountain mammals had nearly disappeared from the area, but after a population of wild burros was removed from the Canyon in the 1980s, the bighorn sheep population was restored. They typically live at higher elevations along the South Rim but may be seen at the bottom of the Canyon in the river corridor seeking food and water.

Black bear: These bears live in the coniferous forest at the park's higher elevations on the Kaibab plateau on the North Rim.

California condor: The largest land bird in North America, these giants have a wingspan of 9.5 feet and weigh up to 22 pounds. They're grayish-black with some white beneath the wings that makes them easily identifiable from below. One of the rarest birds in the world, there are only about 60 of them in Arizona. You may spot them soaring overhead looking for food to scavenge— dead animals such as deer, cattle, rabbits and rodents.

Kaibab squirrel: This unique squirrel lives only on the Kaibab Plateau at the North Rim of the park. It has a black belly and white tail and can't be found anywhere else in the world.

Mule deer: These mammals may be seen throughout the park. They typically live in the coniferous forest at the park's higher elevations on the Kaibab plateau on the North Rim and in the Upper Sonoran Zone of the South Rim, but they descend from the rim into the river corridor when food and water sources are scarce above.

Rattlesnakes: Six species of rattlesnakes have been identified in the park. Two of these are rarely seen: the southwestern speckled rattlesnake and the northern black-tailed rattlesnake. The four common rattlesnakes are all subspecies of the western diamondback rattlesnake: the Grand Canyon pink rattlesnake, Great Basin rattlesnake, Mojave green rattlesnake, and Hopi rattlesnake. The Grand Canyon pink are the most common and they are found in the inner canyon scrubland and also in the Colorado River corridor where their prey, lizards, are more available.

WHERE TO STAY

CAMPING

Reservations are accepted for only two of the park's campgrounds and one RV park: the Mather Campground on the South Rim, the adjacent Trailer Village and the North Rim Campground. You can make reservations up to six months in advance. The sites tend to book up quickly, so plan ahead. (Tent sites: 877-444-6777; www.

recreation.gov. RV sites: same-day: 928-638-2631, advance: 888-297-2757.) The Desert View Campground on the South Rim has 50 sites on a first-come, first-served basis. Also near the South Rim, the U.S. Forest Service operates the Ten-X Campground just outside the park on a first-come, first-served basis, and the Forest Service also allows camping at large in the National Forest outside of the National Park boundaries. For more information and the Forest Service's requirements, call 928-638-2443. Additional accommodations for RVs are available at Camper Village (928-638-2887) in Tusayan, seven miles south of the park. Near the North Rim outside of the park, two additional campsites are operated by the Forest Service—DeMotte Campground and Jacob Lake Campground (closed for upgrading in 2008)—and dispersed camping is also allowed.

HOTELS

South Rim

★★**Bright Angel Lodge**
On the South Rim, Grand Canyon, 928-638-2631, 888-297-2757;
www.grandcanyonlodges.com
This Registered National Historic Landmark is a Grand Canyon standby. Designed by the park's renowned Mary E. J. Colter, the rustic southwestern-style lodge has been housing travelers since 1935. The world-famous Grand Canyon Mule Rides leave from

here, and a Canyon tour service is offered. The lodge has two restaurants and operates an old-fashioned ice cream fountain in the summer. Some rooms have canyon views (but no TVs).

89 rooms and cabins. Two restaurants, bar. $

★★★El Tovar

On the South Rim, Grand Canyon, 928-638-2631, 888-297-2757; www.grandcanyonlodges.com

The premier lodging facility at the Grand Canyon, El Tovar Hotel—named in honor of the Spanish explorer Don Pedro de Tovar, who reported the existence of the Grand Canyon to fellow explorers—opened its doors in 1905 and was said to be the most expensive log house in America. Just 20 feet from the edge of the Canyon's South Rim, the building is charming and rustic. The hotel features a fine dining room, a lounge and a gift shop highlighting Native American artists. With so much to do right at your doorstep—hiking, mule rides, train excursions, interpretive walks, cultural activities—El Tovar offers the best of the Grand Canyon, combining turn-of-the-century lodge ambience with the highest standard of service. Advance reservations are recommended, especially for the summer season, which is usually booked up a year in advance.

78 rooms and suites. Restaurant, bar. Airport transportation available. $

★★Yavapai Lodge

Half mile from the South Rim, 928-638-2631, 888-297-2757; www.grandcanyonlodges.com

Set in a piñon and juniper forest, the Yavapai is the park's largest lodge. The comfortable motel rooms include TVs in addition to the basic necessities. Right next to the Market Plaza, the location is convenient to a general store, bank and post office—plus it's only a half mile from the park visitor center.

358 rooms. Closed two weeks in mid-November, three weeks in early December, January-February. Restaurant. $

Inner Rim

— ALSO RECOMMENDED —

Phantom Ranch

Inner Rim, Grand Canyon, 928-638-2631, 888-297-2757; www.grandcanyonlodges.com

The only lodge below the Canyon's rim, this ranch is planted at the bottom of the Canyon beside the Bright Angel Creek on the north side of the Colorado River. It is only reachable by mule, foot or raft. Completed in 1922, the ranch features rustic cabins for overnight mule trips and a stone lodge with dormitory-style accommodations for backpackers. There is also a Park Service campground nearby, which requires a backcountry permit. The Phantom Ranch Canteen is a popular destination for hungry hikers, but reservations must be made well in advance. The first of each month, the Ranch begins taking reserva-

GRAND CANYON

tions for that entire month for the following year; thus, reservations are accepted up to 13 months in advance.

20 dormitory bunks, separated by gender; 11 cabins. Restaurant. **$**

Tusayan, AZ

★★Best Western Grand Canyon Squire Inn

100 Highway 64, Tusayan, 928-638-2681, 800-622-6966; www.grandcanyonsquire.com

A great place to stay with the family, this hotel offers a number of amenities. For kids, there are more entertainment options after they've exhausted those in the park—a swimming pool, pool tables, bowling and arcade games. There's an onsite salon for adults as well as a massage therapist who can rub away any aches and pains from hiking.

250 rooms. Wireless Internet access. Three restaurants, two bars. Airport transportation available. Fitness center. Tennis. Pool. Spa. **$**

Williams, AZ

— ALSO RECOMMENDED —

FireLight Bed and Breakfast

174 W. Mead, Williams, 928-635-0200, 888-838-8218; www.firelightbandb.com

Poised and polished might be the best words to describe this elegant Tudor-style home that the owners renovated into a refined bed-and-breakfast. Each room's stunning décor imparts an ambience of warm sophistication with gas fireplaces and luxurious furnishings and bathrooms. But beyond the aesthetic appeal, the owners also present their guests with generous amenities: a pool table, a ping-pong table, a restored historic shuffleboard table, video games, board games and a weight machine.

4 rooms. Wireless Internet access. Complimentary full breakfast. **$$**

North Rim

★★Grand Canyon Lodge

On the North Rim, Grand Canyon, 928-638-2611

This rustic lodge at Bright Angel Point has been named a National Historic Landmark. It is the only lodging available in the National Park on the North Rim side. The comfortable accommodation options range from standard motel rooms to two-bedroom cabins.

214 rooms and cabins. Closed mid-October to mid-May. Restaurant, bar. **$**

WHERE TO EAT

South Rim

★★Arizona Room

South Rim, Grand Canyon Village, 928-638-2631; www.grandcanyonlodges.com

This full-service restaurant attempts to serve a little of Arizona with every meal. The specialty is the chipotle baby-back ribs, but fish and chicken dishes like a sautéed rainbow trout with lemon sage butter and an oven-roasted half chicken with ancho-pistachio dry rub are delicious as well.

American, southwestern menu. Lunch, dinner. $$

★★★El Tovar Dining Room
**1 Main St., South Rim,
928-638-2631;
www.grandcanyonlodges.com**
Considered the premier dining establishment at the Grand Canyon, this restaurant provides a memorable experience thanks to the spicy regional cuisine and spectacular Canyon views. The atmosphere is casually elegant with native stone fireplaces, Oregon pine vaulted ceilings, American Indian artwork and mission-style accents. Diners can select from a well-rounded menu that blends regional flavors and contemporary techniques and offers many vegetarian options. There's also an extensive wine list.
Southwestern menu. Breakfast, lunch, dinner. Children's menu. Reservations recommended. $$

— ALSO RECOMMENDED —
Bright Angel Restaurant
**South Rim, Grand Canyon;
www.grandcanyonlodges.com**
This casual park restaurant serves three meals a day, but breakfast is the one you shouldn't miss with such creations as the Rim to Rim Skillet—a corned beef hash, three eggs and diced red pepper over potatoes topped with jalapeno cream cheese and jack cheese. The portions are big enough to keep you hiking all day.
American menu. Breakfast, lunch, dinner. $

Inner Canyon

— ALSO RECOMMENDED —
Phantom Ranch Canteen
**Inner Canyon, Grand Canyon,
303-297-2757, 888-297-2757;
www.grandcanyonlodges.com**
What beats a cold beer in the middle of the wilderness after a four-hour hike? Maybe a steak dinner or hearty bowl of stew or vegetarian chili alongside it. The restaurant at Phantom Ranch requires reservations far in advance, same as the lodging. Meals are served at specified times, and diners must be there for their reserved seating. The Canteen also serves breakfast with two seating times and sells sack lunches the rest of the day.
American menu. Breakfast, sack lunches, dinner. Reservations required. $$

Williams, AZ

— ALSO RECOMMENDED —
Old Smoky's Restaurant and Pancake House
**624 W. Route 66, Williams,
928-635-1915**
This authentic Route 66 roadside restaurant went through many incarnations before becoming the popular breakfast spot it is today. Stop here for a big pancake or omelet breakfast and you won't be sorry.
American menu. Breakfast, lunch. $

Red Raven Restaurant

135 W. Route 66, Williams,
928-635-4980;
www.redravenrestaurant.com

For an old Route 66 stop of a town like Williams, this is finer dining than most expect. The atmosphere is casual; however, the food preparation is anything but. The menu features mostly traditional fare with several steaks, some seafood, many pastas and several salads. Some creativity finds its way onto the menu with dishes like tenderloin of pork scallopini—thin slices of white wine and olive oil–braised pork tenderloin served in a slow-roasted tomato sauce with seasonal fresh vegetables on a bed of angel hair pasta.

Steak, seafood menu. Lunch, dinner. Closed Monday. $$

Kanab, UT

— ALSO RECOMMENDED —

Escobar's Mexican

373 E. 300 South, Kanab,
435-644-3739

This is authentic Mexican food the way it's supposed to be served: warm, crisp chips with homemade salsa to greet you and fresh ingredients used throughout the repertoire of traditional dishes on the menu. This is a favorite of the locals, and vacationers will quickly understand why.

Mexican menu. Breakfast, lunch, dinner. $

★
★
★
☆
☆

Rocking V Cafe

97 W. Center St., Kanab,
435-644-8001;
www.rockingvcafe.com

This is not your average road trip food. The Rocking V takes pride in serving only carefully prepared dishes made from scratch from the freshest ingredients. The innovative menu features entrées such as a southwestern blue cornmeal–crusted trout topped with green chili and tomatillo salsa over a bed of wild rice and fresh vegetables, or there are the risotto cakes, a combo of tomato sauce, vegetables and risotto crusted with Parmesan cheese and served over a bed of sautéed vegetables and greens with a spicy tomato sauce. And definitely don't miss the dessert.

International menu. Lunch, dinner. Hours change seasonally. $$

GREAT SMOKY MOUNTAINS NATIONAL PARK

HALF IN NORTH CAROLINA AND HALF IN TENNESSEE (WITH THE STATE line smack in the middle), the Great Smoky Mountains National Park is renowned for its diversity of both flora and fauna. More than 95 percent of the park is covered in trees, and dense deciduous and spruce-fir forests blanket the area's valleys and ancient peaks, which range from 875 to 6,643 feet. The thick mixture of all this brush and trees creates a haze from the water and hydrocarbons thrown off by their leaves, resulting in a "smoky" appearance. These emerald-green stretches are dotted with numerous roaring waterfalls that help make every season—even winter—beautiful. More than 800,000 square miles became a National Park in 1934; they were designated an UNESCO World Heritage Site in 1983 and an International Biosphere Reserve.

The mountains were formed between 200 and 300 million years ago. As recently as the year 10,000 B.C., northern glaciers ground away the lands but stopped short of the Smokies, providing refuge for hundreds of different plant and animal species that can still be found here today. The Cherokee Nation first inhabited the region, and mountain people, whose ancestors came from England and Scotland, followed in the late 1700s. Remnants of their time here, including cabins, barns and mills, are still scattered throughout the park.

Whether to discover the historic abandoned buildings, hike, or just take in the dazzling fall foliage and amazing views, it's no wonder 9 million visitors come here each year, making the Great Smoky Mountains one of America's busiest national parks.

Gatlinburg, Tennessee, 865-436-1200; www.nps.gov/grsm

SMOKY MOUNTAINS

★

★

★

★

WHAT TO SEE

A trip to the vast park is best begun at one of three main visitor centers. Serving the western corner of the park, the **Cades Cove Visitor Center** sits on the Caves Cove Loop. To the north, the **Sugarlands Visitor Center** (Newfound Gap Road, 865-436-1291; open June-August, 8 a.m.-7 p.m.; April-May and September, 8 a.m.-6 p.m.; March and October, 8 a.m.-5 p.m.; November-February, 8 a.m.-4:30 p.m.) is near Gatlinburg, Tennessee, and next to **Park Headquarters** (107 Park Headquarters Road. Gatlinburg, 865-436-1200; www.nps.gov/grsm). The **Oconaluftee Visitor Center** (828-497-1904; open daily 8 a.m.-7 p.m.; off-season schedule varies) by Cherokee, North Carolina, provides access to the park from the south. In addition, there are four other visitor centers outside of the park in the towns of Gatlinburg, Sevierville and Townsend. Depending on your starting point, you can choose from two major loops through the park that give a great overview and allow you to see a numerous sites: Cades Cove Loop Road and Newfound Gap Road.

If you begin at the Sugarlands Visitor Center, the **Cades Cove Loop Road** runs 11 miles west through forests and valleys to Cades Cove. The road has a number of stop-off sites that provide a glimpse of the rich history of the area through its buildings. The **John Oliver Place** is the first

stop. Don't miss your chance to explore an early 19th-century log cabin nestled in a large valley. The white-frame Primitive Baptist Church and graveyard, Methodist Church and Missionary Baptist Church are good examples of pre–Civil War churches, and the Rich Mountain Road has great views of Cades Cove. The John Cable Mill is near the Cades Cove Visitor Center, where you can examine a wide variety of artifacts and learn about the history of early Great Smoky settlers.

The **Newfound Gap Road** runs about 45 miles southeast from the Sugarlands Visitor Center in the north to the Oconaluftee Visitor Center in the south. Passing from lowland cove hardwood pine-oak and northern hardwood forests to thick spruce-fir forests, don't be surprised if your ears pop as you ascend nearly 4,000 feet. Be sure to stop at the **Chimney Tops Overlook,** where the Sugarland Mountains' steep, tree-covered peaks jut up through fog-laced valleys. In the middle of the park, the Appalachian Trail cuts through the 5,048-foot **Newfound Gap** that sits on the Tennessee-North Carolina border. A trip from the visitor center to the gap is said to be equivalent to traveling from Georgia to Maine in terms of ecosystem variety. From climate to elevation to wildlife, the journey offers many different habitats along the way. A seven-mile detour on **Clingmans Dome Road** off the Newfound Gap Road is worth the trek, as it brings you to a half-mile trail that reaches the lookout tower at **Clingmans Dome**. Take in the amazing 360-degree views from here, the highest point in the park at 6,643 feet. It also has the distinction of being both the highest point in Tennessee and the third-highest mountain east of the Mississippi River.

Off the beaten paths of the north and western Smokies, the **Cataloochee Valley** lies in the rugged Balsam Mountains in the park's far eastern section. Soaring 6,000-foot peaks look down on this picturesque valley, which was once home to farms, orchards and early settlements. Today, visitors who make the long trip down the well-maintained gravel roads can see the remaining historic buildings as well as wildlife, including elk and bears.

Whether you're driving, hiking or biking the trails of the park, you will want to stop to view at least one of the many waterfalls. The Great Smokies' 85 inches of yearly rainfall and steep elevations make for spectacular falls and smaller cascades. Waterfalls are located throughout the park (maps are available at visitor centers and www.nps.gov/grsm/planyourvisit/waterfalls.htm), and most, like the popular **Ramsey Cascades** (the tallest waterfall in the park at 100 feet), are accessed by hiking trails. If you're not in the mood to walk, **Meigs Falls** (Little River Road, 13 miles west of Sugarlands Visitor Center) and **Place of a Thousand Drips** (Roaring Fork Motor Nature Trail, stop 15) are both accessible by car.

WHAT TO DO

HIKING

Hiking is extremely popular throughout the park, and there are more than 900 miles of trails and 170 miles of roads to explore, including 70 miles of the Appalachian Trail. For information on backcountry hiking, call 865-436-1297.

─────────── **EASY** ───────────

Laurel Falls
2.6 miles round-trip
Trailhead: From Sugarlands Visitor Center, turn toward Cades Cove on Little River Road and drive 3.5 miles.

This very popular paved trail will take you to the 80-foot waterfall. The trail is bordered by the evergreen laurel shrub, which blooms in May.

Andrews Bald
3.6 miles round-trip
Trailhead: Follow Clingmans Dome Road to the end (20 miles from Gatlinburg). Just before the restrooms, the Andrews Bald trailhead drops to the left.

This trail provides you with stunning views of the Smokies from one of only two grassy balds in the park, perfect for an afternoon picnic surrounded by sky. Just don't skimp on the carbs as the return trip requires a slight uphill climb.

─────────── **MODERATE** ───────────

Rainbow Falls
5.4 miles round-trip
Trailhead: Drive on Historic

SMOKY MOUNTAINS

Nature Trail past the Noah "Bud" Ogle homesite to the clearly signed Rainbow Falls parking area.

This spectacular and popular trail climbs 1,500 feet to reach the 80-foot Rainbow Falls, whose mist creates a rainbow on sunny days. The adventurous can take the trail another four miles to Mount Le Conte.

———— **STRENUOUS** ————

Alum Cave Bluffs Trail
10.4 miles round-trip
Trailhead: Alum Cave Bluffs parking area, approximately nine miles south of the Sugarlands Visitor Center or four miles north of Newfound Gap.

This trail follows the steepest path up Mount Le Conte. It climbs gently through old-growth forest until reaching the Arch Rock landmark. Continuing more steeply along rocky footing, which gets slick when wet, it also passes Gracie's Pulpit, named for Gracie McNichol who hiked this trail on her 92nd birthday. On the 6,000-foot plateau is the Le Conte Lodge and spur trails to the four peaks of Le Conte. The Alum Cave Bluffs Trail joins the Rainbow Falls trail at this point.

Charlie's Bunion
12.8-mile loop
Trailhead: Newfound Gap parking area.

A 1925 wildfire that razed the slopes of this promontory, named for a hiker's inflamed big toe, created an exceptional view. The total elevation gain is over 4,500 feet, so you'll want to start early and dedicate a day to this trail, but the panoramas are worth it.

Chimney Tops
4 miles round-trip
Trailhead: Chimney Tops parking lot off Newfound Gap Road.

This trail starts gently but becomes rugged as it takes you on a 1,350-foot ascent to a breathtaking view—and a rock face, which is the Chimney. The daring and fit can use hands and knees to climb a crack in the Chimney and reach the summit.

HIKING AND NATURE STUDY ADVENTURES

Want to take an overnight backpack trip with experienced guides or have a scientist point out and explain black bears and other wildlife? A great way to learn about the park is through programs offered by the Great Smoky Mountains Institute at Tremont (9275 Tremont Road, Townsend, TN, 865-448-6709; www.gsmit.org) or the Smoky Mountain Field School (313 Conference Center Building, Knoxville, TN, 865-974-0150; www.ce.utk.edu/smoky). Both offer programs and classes for adults, and kids will love the multiday summer youth camps with hands-on activities from canoeing to field research.

★

★

★

★

FISHING

More than 2,115 miles of streams and 40 species of fish make for superb angling in the Great Smoky Mountains National Park. From coldwater smallmouth bass streams to headwater trout streams, fishing is allowed year-round in most waters. Fishing is permitted from 30 minutes before sunrise to 30 minutes after sunset; check visitor centers for off-limits areas. Tennessee or North Carolina fishing permits are required for anglers over 12 in Tennessee and over 15 in North Carolina and are available in area towns.

HORSEBACK RIDING

Riding is allowed on 550 miles of trails within the park. Five horse camps (Anthony Creek/Cades Cove, Big Creek, Cataloochee, Round Bottom and Towstring) provide easy access to backcountry trails April to mid-November, 10 a.m.-10 p.m. Reservations are required (877-444-6777). For visitors without their own animals, the Cades Cove Riding Stables offers guided horseback tours ($15 an hour) as well as hay and carriage rides April to October (10018 Campground Drive, Townsend, 865-448-6286). Horses can also be rented from Smoky Mountain Riding Stables (Highway 321 four miles east of Gatlinburg, 865-436-5634; www.smokymountainridingstables.com) and the Sugarlands Riding Stable (1409 E. Parkway, Gatlinburg, 865-436-3535).

BIKING

While there are no mountain biking trails in the Great Smoky Mountains, cycling is permitted on the gravel Gatlinburg Trail, Oconaluftee River Trail and Lower Deep Creek Trail. The Foothills Parkway, 11-mile one-way Cades Cove Loop Road and Cataloochee areas also offer decent routes. You can bring your own bike or rent one from the Cades Cove Store (near Cades Cove Campground, 865-448-9034).

WILDLIFE

Smoky the Bear never actually lived here (the bear who inspired the safety campaign was from New Mexico), but plenty of other black bears reside in the park. You may even see some elk. The Great Smoky Mountain region is also a top destination for birdwatchers.

Bears: Perhaps the animal most associated with the Smokies is the black bear. Up to about six feet in length, the females usually weigh around 100 pounds and males about 250, but both can double their weights as they prepare for winter. Black bears are omnivores, and 85 percent of their diet consists of plants, berries and nuts. There are currently about 1,600 living throughout the park. Bears in this region usually re-emerge from their slumbers in late March or early April and remain most active through the spring and summer months. You have the best chance of spotting a

SMOKY MOUNTAINS

black bear in open areas like Cades Cove or Cataloochee Valley.

Fish: Fishing is a popular sport in the park, but surprisingly, only about 800 out of the 2,100 miles of streams here actually contain fish. There are more than 60 species represented, including **bass**, **suckers** and **lampreys**. The park has one of the few remaining wild trout habitats left in the eastern United States, and an aggressive park initiative has restored the **native brook trout.**

Elk: Weighing in at up to 700 pounds, elk are the park's biggest mammals. They mostly inhabit the Cataloochee area, where they feed on grasses, bark, buds and leaves. Until 2001, these animals hadn't been seen in the Great Smoky Mountains for nearly 200 years, but thanks to an experimental release program, more than 50 elk were brought to the park. (**River otters** and **peregrine falcons** are two other examples of animals that the National Park Service has successfully reintroduced to the area.) The best time to try to see an elk is in the early morning or late evening.

BIRDS

About 240 species of birds have been spotted in the park. Of those, 60 live in the park year-round, 120 breed here and the remaining species use the forested region as a layover on their migratory routes. Because the mountain chain's upper ridges so closely resemble Canada's boreal for-ests, the region's **saw-whet owls**, **Canada warblers**, **black-capped chickadees** and **winter wrens**, among other birds, use the spruce and fir trees as breeding grounds. The middle and lower elevations are the best places to see birds. **Downy woodpeckers**, **American goldfinches**, **song sparrows** and **belted kingfishers** are just a few species that flit through the hard-woods, while **red-tailed hawks**, **wild turkeys** and **eastern meadowlarks** prefer the park's open fields.

WHERE TO STAY

CAMPING

There are ten campgrounds scattered throughout the park. Smokemont, Elkmont, Cades Cove and Cosby take reservations (mid-May to October, 877-444-6777; www.recreation.gov), while the other seven are first-come, first-served. Each has restrooms and water but no showers. Stays are limited to seven days in summer and fall and 14 days off-season. Fees range from $14 to $23 per night. Backcountry camping is permitted with reservations and permits, which are available at ranger stations and visitor centers (865-436-1231, daily 8 a.m.-6 p.m.). Check www.nps.gov/grsm/planyourvisit/carcamping.htm for more information.

★
★
★
★
★

HOTELS

Gatlinburg

Gatlinburg is just minutes from the Great Smoky Mountains National Park, and many hotels offer trolley access to area attractions.

★★Buckhorn Inn

2140 Tudor Mountain Road, Gatlinburg, 865-436-4668, 866-941-0460;
www.buckhorninn.com

This relaxing inn, opened in 1938, is a perfect romantic getaway that's just one mile from the park and a short drive from downtown Gatlinburg. Looking across meadows of wildflowers, the inn has fantastic views of the Great Smoky Mountains. The décor is elegant but comfortable with soft tones, floral arrangements and beautiful accent pieces. Take a stroll around the pond and through the pine and hemlock forests or snuggle into a wicker rocker on the covered porch with an iced tea and a good book. The grounds also include a rugged self-guided nature trail and a large meditation labyrinth.

10 rooms, 10 cottages. Children over 12 only in inn rooms. Complimentary full breakfast. Restaurant. $$

★★The Edgewater at the Aquarium

402 River Road, Gatlinburg, 865-436-4151, 800-423-9582;
www.edgewater-hotel.com

Activities and attractions are just steps away from the Edgewater Hotel, situated on the banks of the Little Pigeon Forge River where you can fish for trout. Guest room balconies overlook water or mountain views, and the pool area is the perfect place to lounge while lapping up the scenery.

205 rooms, 3 suites. Wireless Internet access. Complimentary continental breakfast. Bar. Fitness center. Pool. Business center. $

★★★Eight Gables Inn

219 N. Mountain Trail, Gatlinburg, 865-430-3344, 800-279-5716;
www.eightgables.com

In a tranquil wooded setting, this welcoming country bed and breakfast suits romantics and adventure-seekers alike. Explore nearby attractions, including fly-fishing, golf and whitewater rafting, or just relax on the porch and admire the grounds. Guest rooms are quaintly furnished with feather-top beds; suites have fireplaces and two-person whirlpool tubs. In addition to a five-course breakfast, the Magnolia Tea Room serves lunch and candlelight dinners of regional Southern cuisine three nights a week.

19 rooms and suites. Children over 10 only. Complimentary full breakfast. Restaurant. Spa. $$

★★Garden Plaza Hotel

520 Historic Nature Trail, Gatlinburg, 865-436-9201, 800-435-9201;
www.4lodging.com

LeConte Creek winds through this mountain retreat located just two blocks from downtown Gatlinburg and adjacent to the Great Smoky Mountain National

SMOKY MOUNTAINS

★
★
★
★

Park. Hop the convenient trolley for a short ride to Dollywood, music shows, theaters and shops. Kids can keep busy with onsite activities such as volleyball, horseshoes, video games, indoor and outdoor pools and a children's playground.

399 rooms. Wireless Internet access. Complimentary full breakfast. Two restaurants, bar. Fitness center. Pool. Pets accepted. $

Townsend

Townsend, located at the gateway to Great Smoky Mountains National Park, offers convenient lodging options for those visiting the park and other east Tennessee attractions.

★★★Richmont Inn B&B
220 Winterberry Lane, Townsend, 865-448-6751, 866-267-7086; www.richmontinn.com
In the shadow of Rich Mountain and just ten minutes from the park entrance, this charming inn affords an elegant respite. The comfort and coziness of the rustic accents, such as wide-planked and slate floors, high exposed-beam ceilings and country furniture, are enhanced by the formal, attentive service.

14 rooms. Children over 12 only. Wireless Internet access. Complimentary full breakfast. Restaurant. Business center. $

Newport

★★★Christopher Place: An Intimate Resort
1500 Pinnacles Way, Newport, 423-623-6555, 800-595-9441;
www.christopherplace.com
Tucked away on 200 forested acres in the scenic mountains, this antebellum inn has been restored to its original splendor. Enjoy the romantic candlelit ambience of the Mountain View dining room while savoring four-course menus selected daily by the chef. And whether they have an unfettered view of the gardens, a cozy sitting area or wood-burning fireplace, all rooms are large and nicely furnished.

8 rooms, 1 suite. Children over 12 only. Complimentary full breakfast. Fitness center. Tennis. Pool. $$

WHERE TO EAT

Gatlinburg
★★Maxwell's Steak and Seafood
1103 Parkway, Gatlinburg, 865-436-3738; www.maxwells-inc.com
Maxwell's is a nice change of pace from the chain restaurants that dominate the area. Seafood fans will appreciate the Smoky Mountain rainbow trout, a local favorite, while beef lovers can choose from a wide selection, including prime rib, charbroiled filet mignon and rib-eye steak. Desserts include homemade cheesecake.
American menu. Dinner. Bar. Children's menu. Casual attire. Reservations recommended. $$

★★The Park Grill Steakhouse
110 Parkway, Gatlinburg, 865-436-2300;

SMOKY MOUNTAINS

★
★
★
★
★

www.parkgrillgatlinburg.com

This rustic yet elegant log cabin–style restaurant is located on the main street in downtown Gatlinburg. Its whimsical decorations include antler fixtures, bird sounds and an outdoor waterfall. The menu mostly focuses on steaks and seafood, including area favorites like ribs and trout. There is also an impressive salad bar for diners to peruse while listening to the live piano music (offered six nights a week).

American menu. Dinner. Bar. Children's menu. Casual attire. $$

★★The Peddler Restaurant
820 River Road, Gatlinburg, 865-436-5794; www.peddlergatlinburg.com

Literally constructed around the cabin of one of Gatlinburg's first pioneer families, this restaurant is within the park boundaries. The dining room has a cozy atmosphere, with cedar paneling and furniture, and covered porch seating gives diners extra-special views of the river. The menu offers favorites such as steaks, ribs, chicken and trout, all in generous portions. Be sure to leave room for the monstrous mud pie or hot blackberry cobbler for dessert.

American menu. Dinner. Bar. Children's menu. Casual attire. $$

Pigeon Forge
★Old Mill
164 Old Mill Ave., Pigeon Forge, 865-429-3463; www.old-mill.com

Located in an old mill on a river (ask for a window seat), this popular tourist restaurant is conveniently located off a parkway in the heart of Pigeon Forge with specialty shops nearby. The charming and cozy interior features wood floors and ceiling beams, antique furniture and accents and an open kitchen. The extensive menu includes a great selection of Southern-style homemade meals.

American, Southern menu. Breakfast, lunch, dinner. Children's menu. Casual attire. $$

Sevierville
★Applewood Farmhouse Restaurant
240 Apple Valley Road, Sevierville, 865-428-1222; www. applewoodfarmhouserestaurant.com

Acres of apple trees and a wraparound porch with comfortable rockers greet diners at this downtown Sevierville restaurant. The interior features a country-cozy décor with double fireplaces, oak tables and chairs, and other antiques. Fritters and juleps are served when seated—a preview of the delicious Southern country cuisine to come. It's a great choice for authentic down-home cooking.

American, Southern menu. Breakfast, lunch, dinner. Children's menu. Casual attire. $

SMOKY MOUNTAINS

JOSHUA TREE NATIONAL PARK

IT IS SAID THAT MORMONS PASSING THROUGH THIS AUSTERE DESERT region in the 19th century were so taken by the yuccas' giant outstretched arms, which seemed to beckon them onward toward the Promised Land, that they named them "Joshua" trees after the Hebrew prophet. Even today, the Joshua tree—a member of the lily family that thrives in the desert heat and can reach heights of 40 feet and live to 300 years—remains an impressive symbol of this park.

Covering more than 1,200 square miles, Joshua Tree National Park preserves one of the most unique sections of western U.S. desert. In the middle of the park, the wetter and higher Mojave Desert butts up against the arid Colorado Desert. The Mojave in the northern and western part of the park is wetter and more vegetated due to its higher elevation, more than 3,000 feet. In comparison, to the south and east, the Colorado Desert, part of the Sonoran Desert, is much sparser and hotter with elevations less than 3,000 feet. Twisted rock attests to the powerful geological forces at work here. Giant granite boulders and stony canyons showcase the powerful tectonic activity and the force of erosion on the desert's features. Hundreds of faults web Joshua Tree, including the famous San Andreas Fault that borders the park to the south region and the Cut Fault in the park's center.

The Joshua Tree area has been inhabited for at least 5,000 years, starting with the Pinto culture at the end of the Ice Age and followed by the Serrano, Chemehuevi and Cahuilla Indians. In the 1800s, cattlemen used the grassy areas to graze their cattle, and prospectors dug tunnels to mine gold. By the early 1900s, homesteaders even built cabins and planted crops here. Eventually, though, the inhospitable desert won and all hope of permanent settlement was abandoned.

A desert plant lover named Minerva Hoyt lobbied to protect the area from exploitation by landscapers who were removing cacti and other plant species to use in Los Angeles gardens. In 1936, her efforts paid off and 825,000 acres of land were made into the Joshua Tree National Monument. Although that was reduced by 265,000 acres in 1950, on October 31, 1994, the Desert Protection Bill elevated the Joshua Tree Monument to park status and enlarged it to 794,000 acres. Joshua Tree is America's newest and one of its most distinctive national parks.

74485 National Park Drive, Twentynine Palms, California, 760-367-5500; www.nps.gov/jotr

★
★
★
★
★

WHAT TO SEE

Joshua Tree is geographically split into two main parts: the Mojave Desert to the north and west, the Colorado Desert to the south and east. Both sections have their own visitor centers outlining attractions with area maps.

When entering the park from the northwest, on the Mojave Desert side, start at one of three visitor centers for information on park geology, plants, animals and other topics. The **Black Rock Canyon Nature Center** (Yucca Valley, from Highway 62, take Joshua Tree Lane south, take a right onto Black Rock Rd., 760-367-3001; October-May, closed Friday, open 8 a.m.-4 p.m.) or the **Joshua Tree Visitor Center** (6554 Park Blvd., Joshua Tree, 760-366-1855; open daily year-round, 8 a.m.-5 p.m.) is a good place to begin before heading to the West Entrance Station (off Route 62 at Joshua Tree; $5 entry fee per person or $15 per vehicle, good for seven days). From the northeast, stop at the Oasis Visitor Center (74485 National Park Drive, Twentynine Palms, 760-367-5500; open daily year-round, 8 a.m.-5 p.m.) before heading to the North Entrance Station.

One of two main park roads, **Park Boulevard** runs from the West Entrance east to Pinto Basin Road and is an essential landmark when navigating Joshua Tree attractions. Take Park Boulevard south from the West Entrance to **Hidden Valley**, a large, rock-enclosed area that provided cattle rustlers with the perfect place to hide stolen cattle in the 1800s. Today, it is one of the best sections to see dense forests of the park's namesake Joshua trees.

If you're ready for higher elevations, **Keys View** is further south, 21 miles from the West Entrance, rising 5,185 feet in the Little San Bernardino Mountains. You'll find beautiful panoramas of the Coachella Valley and the bone-dry desert basin below. To the left, the **Salton Sea**, 230 feet below sea level, is sometimes visible glittering in the distance. To the right are the **Santa Rosa Mountains**, the 10,800-foot **San Jacinto Peak** and the 11,500-foot **San Gorgonio Mountain**. The 700-mile San Andreas Fault is due south, and with luck (and good air quality). Signal Mountain is sometimes visible further south in Mexico.

Take Park Boulevard east, where a sandy desert plateau gives way to the odd **Jumbo Rock** formations, which occur throughout the park and are concentrated in some areas. Popular with climbers, these giant granite rocks are believed to have formed 100 million years ago as a result of earthquakes and molten liquid oozing up from the earth's crust. Eons of erosion have worn these rocks into today's strange formations that seem to be literally melting back into the earth.

One such formation just off Park Boulevard is **Skull Rock**. This giant granite rock is a popular attraction due to its resemblance to a human skull. The large holes are the result of erosion after rainwa-

JOSHUA TREE

★
★
★
★
★

ter accumulated in small holes and began to wear away the granite, resulting in large "eye sockets."

While Park Boulevard covers much of the northern portion of Joshua Tree Park, **Pinto Basin Road** runs south from the Mojave Desert's North Entrance to the Cottonwood Visitor Center in the Colorado Desert. Head south on Pinto Basin Road and find **Oasis of Mara.** Here, at one of five spring-fed oases in Joshua Tree, the Serrano Indians were the first settlers to set up camp and take advantage of the oasis's much-needed water and large desert fan palms. They named it Mara, meaning "the place of little springs and much grass."

The Pinto Basin Road gradually descends from the edges of the Pinto Mountains into the vast arid Pinto Basin that was once an ancient lakebed. At this point, **Wilson Canyon** marks the desolate transition zone between where the Mojave and the Colorado Desert meet.

The park's Colorado Desert section allows visitors arriving from the south to enter the park through the Cottonwood Visitor Center (off I-10 at Route 95 at Cottonwood Springs, 760-367-5500; open year-round 9 a.m.-3 p.m.). This part of the park has few roads and is served mainly by the Pinto Basin Road.

One mile from the Visitor Center, you'll find **Cottonwood Springs**. Formed by intense earthquake activity, this beautiful hidden gem has a number of hiking trails, and the cottonwood trees and fan palms make it one of the best bird-viewing spots of the park. An adjoining trail leads to the equally beautiful **Lost Palms Oasis**.

For plant enthusiasts, Joshua Tree offers two distinct natural "gardens." Look for the **Ocotillo Patch,** filled with gray spikelike ocotillo plants that suddenly burst with red flowers after March and April rain showers. Further north on the Pinto Basin Road, near where the Mojave and Colorado deserts meet, lies the **Cholla Cactus Garden**—a grove of crooked spiny cacti in the Pinto Basin.

WHAT TO DO

HIKING

Joshua Tree has a large network of trails ranging from short loop trails that can be trekked in an hour to overnight hikes. Most trails offer spectacular mountain views as well as a good chance to come across some of the park's wildlife and rare plant life. Look out for rock formations and the avid climbers upon them. However, while the natural walls and cliffs at Joshua Tree make it a popular climbing destination, there is also of plenty of stable terrain for the hiker. For maps and a complete listing of trails, visit www.nps.gov/jotr/planyourvisit/hiking.htm.

Hidden Valley Nature Trail

1-mile loop
Trailhead: Hidden Valley
picnic area

The Hidden Valley Nature Trail in the northeast Mohave portion of the park is a circular trail that travels through the odd assortment of rocks that enclose the area. A nice option for inexperienced hikers, this trail's elevation remains fairly constant and photo opportunities abound.

Barker Dam Trail

1.3-mile loop
Trailhead: Just north of the Barker Dam parking area.

The Barker Dam Trail is an extremely popular option, rewarding hikers of the short loop with views of interesting petroglyphs (ancient rock drawings and carvings) as well as proximity to the park's only lake.

— MODERATE TO STRENUOUS —

Lost Horse Mine Trail

8 miles round-trip, 10.2-mile loop
Trailhead: Terminus of Lost Horse Mine Road or far side of Big Trees Loop Trail.

For a more difficult walk, trek this four-mile trail to the top of Ryan Mountain (535-foot elevation change) to see the Lost Horse, Queen and Pleasant Valleys. Take the same trail back or continue on around the loop.

Lost Palms Canyon

7.4 miles round-trip
Trailhead: Cottonwood

Spring Trailhead

The Lost Palms Canyon Trail, where an underground spring supports a palm oasis, is an ideal place to spot wildlife including bighorn sheep. Keep in mind that you'll climb 700 feet on your return trip to get back to the trailhead.

California Riding and Hiking Trail

4, 6.7 or 11 miles round-trip
Trailhead: Various points

The 35-mile California Riding and Hiking Trail, from Black Rock Canyon Campground in Yucca Valley to the park's North Entrance Station, takes two to three days to travel in its entirety or can be intercepted at various points for a shorter trip. It passes through a wide variety of terrain, from juniper and Joshua tree forests to desert lowlands. The flatter sections of the trail can involve hiking over moderately deep sand, which slows your pace, so plan accordingly.

MOTOR TOURS

To see the wide variety of park landscapes, motorists (except those in campers, trailers and motor homes) can take the self-guided Geology Motor Tour that begins near Jumbo Rocks Campground on Park Boulevard. Maps are available at the beginning of the route (check visitor centers for more information), which takes you down a dirt road and makes a series of 16 stops. Most cars will have to turn around at stop #9,

Squaw Tank, but four-wheel drive vehicles can continue.

ROCK CLIMBING

Joshua Tree is a rock-climbing mecca for enthusiasts of almost any level. The massive boulders at Hidden Valley and Jumbo Rocks offer challenging climbs, but with more than 400 climbing formations and 8,000 climbing route options, you're sure to find something that suits your skill level (for climbing maps, check out www.nps.gov/jotr/planyourvisit/maps.htm). For guided climbing, Uprising Adventure Guides (888-254-6266; www.uprising.com) offers private or group classes and park climbing outings for everyone from rock rookies to advanced climbers.

RANGER PROGRAMS

From taking a guided walk around the Oasis of Mara or exploring rock formations and learning how they were formed to listening to a lecture about wildflowers, there are a number of ranger-led activities (check visitor centers for options or call 760-367-3011). One popular option is the Keys Ranch guided walking tour (0.5 mile, 1.5 hours). Located in the high desert, this remote national historic site includes the still-standing ranch house, school, store and workshop of William F. Keyes and his homesteading family (reservations recommended).

WILDLIFE

Joshua Tree, with its scarce water supply and scorching sun, may seem inhospitable to wildlife, but take a closer look. The best time to see the park's animals is at dawn, when birds, lizards and ground squirrels are out, or at dusk, when snakes, bighorn sheep and coyotes roam. Most of Joshua Tree's 52 species of mammals are relatively small due to the lack of food.

Amphibians: Surprisingly, despite its arid climate, Joshua Tree has three types of amphibians—animals that begin life in water before transitioning to living on land as adults. The **California tree frog** is found only in southern California; hikers can sometimes spot them in the watery areas around the Pinto Fault. The **red spotted toad** can be found everywhere in the park, while the **California toad** resides in Oasis of Mara, the Morongo Basin and in Little Morongo Canyon.

Arthropods: There are thousands of tiny multilegged creatures scurrying around the desert, and Joshua Tree is no exception. Perhaps one of the most famous—and feared—is the **tarantula**, which can be spotted around Oasis of Mara, Split Rock and Wilson Canyon. This two- to three-inch, brown-to-black spider has eight eyes and is covered in fine hair, which it uses to detect the movement of prey. Contrary to popular belief, a tarantula's bite is no more harmful than a bee sting. The **giant hairy scorpion** is a five-inch, yellow-brown poisonous predator that kills insects, lizards and snakes with a sting of its tail.

Bats: Bats are widespread, with more than a dozen species in the region. These creatures tend to live in rock crevices, caves and other dark areas but come out of hiding at dawn and dusk.

Bighorn Sheep: Some of the larger park animals, about 250 bighorn sheep live inside the park and can often be found grazing on cacti and bounding along the steep cliffs in rockier areas. About 120 live in the Eagle Mountains to the east, 100 dwell in the Little San Bernardino Mountains and the rest stick around the Wonderland of Rocks. The Bighorns' only predator in the park is the mountain lion, which often attacks the sheep while they are drinking from the springs that flow through narrow canyons.

Desert Kit Fox: Often spotted in the sand dunes or on the open desert, the desert kit fox is most recognizable by its long ears and foxlike looks. It is carnivorous and feeds mainly on kangaroo rats, while its own only known predator is the desert coyote.

Reptiles: Perhaps the easiest animals to see are the many reptiles, due mainly to their ability to thrive in dry environments, survive on limited food and live on little water. There are 18 types of lizards, including desert banded geckos and northern desert iguanas, that call the park home. Twenty-five species of snakes, including Mojave rattlesnakes, Colorado Desert sidewinders and harmless California kingsnakes slither through the region.

BIRDS

More than 240 species of birds have been spotted in Joshua Tree. Many are migratory birds making pit stops in the park, but 78 species nest here and use the desert as their permanent home. Keep a lookout for the famed **roadrunner** or a **golden eagle** on the hunt.

WHERE TO STAY

CAMPING

With no lodging available within the park, staying in one of the nine campgrounds spread throughout Joshua Tree is a popular option. Between September and Memorial Day, reservations (877-444-6777; www.recreation.gov) are recommended for the campgrounds at Black Rock, Sheep Pass and Indian Cove (famous for its nearby waterfalls). Belle, Cottonwood, Hidden Valley, Jumbo Rocks, Ryan and White are all first-come, first-served (Black Rock, Cottonwood and Indian Cove only during the summer months). Tip: Because of their high elevation, Sheep Pass at 4,500 feet and Jumbo Rocks at 4,400 feet are often not as hot as the other campgrounds.

Backcountry camping is allowed, but overnight visitors must register at one of the 13 backcountry registration boards located around the park. All camps must be set up at least one mile from the road and 500 feet from trails.

HOTELS

Outside Joshua Tree

★Best Western Garden Inn & Suites

71487 29 Palms Highway, Twentynine Palms, 760-367-9141, 800-780-7234; www.bestwestern. com/gardeninnsuites

This hotel is located just five miles outside the park and even closer to many of the area's dining and entertainment options, including a nearby drive-in theater. Native palm trees adorn the hotel grounds, which include an outdoor pool.

72 rooms, 12 suites. Wireless Internet access. Complimentary continental breakfast. Fitness center. Pool. $

★Oasis of Eden Inn & Suites

56377 29 Palms Highway, Yucca Valley, 760-365-6321, 800-606-6686;

www.oasisofeden.com

For travelers not willing to make the 30-minute drive to nearby Palm Springs, this hotel offers a quirky lodging choice near the park. Standard rooms are simply furnished with no fancy frills, while the 14 suites come with different special themes–everything from the Rockin' '50s suite (the bed is in a '59 Cadillac) to the Cave room (it even boasts stalactites designed by a Hollywood prop man).

39 rooms and suites. High-speed Internet access. Complimentary continental breakfast. Pool. $

— ALSO RECOMMENDED —

Joshua Tree Inn

61259 29 Palms Highway, Joshua Tree, 760-366-1188; www.jtinn.com

This Hacienda-style inn, built in 1950, is just five miles from the park entrance. The cozy dining room features a large stone fireplace, and the veranda is covered in vines—all giving Joshua Tree Inn a one-of-a-kind eccentric feel. All rooms have private patios, perfect for enjoying the mountain views or gazing at the stars.

10 rooms, 2 suites. Complimentary continental breakfast. Pool. $

Palm Springs

Just 50 miles from Joshua Tree, Palm Springs offers plenty of dining and lodging options within an hour's drive of the park. The city also hosts the closest airport in the area, making it a good landing point and place to stay for out-of-town park visitors.

★Ballantines Hotel

1420 N. Indian Canyon Drive, Palm Springs, 760-320-1178, 800-485-2808;

www.ballantineshotels.com

This 1950s modernist-style hideaway once attracted the celebrated likes of Gloria Swanson and Marilyn Monroe. Today, its well-preserved midcentury accommodations draw romantics and escape-seeking adults. Vibrantly colored guest rooms (picture lemon-colored walls) are done up in individual Old Hollywood themes, including '50s musicals, as well as the Douglas Fairbanks and Audrey Hepburn rooms. All have private patios, high-end retro furnishings and kitschy kitchenettes with functional period appliances. A day spa and a massage room are available, and the party-ready pool area is replete with a bar, a fire pit and hot tub.

14 rooms. No children allowed. Complimentary continental breakfast. Bar. Pool. Spa. $$

★★★Hyatt Regency Suites

285 N. Palm Canyon Drive, Palm Springs, 760-322-9000, 800-223-1234; www.palmsprings.hyatt.com

This Hyatt property is set in a prime downtown location overlooking the San Jacinto Mountains. Spacious guest rooms, tastefully decorated in a swath of desert colors, feature separate sitting areas with a pullout sofa and a dining table if you're traveling with a pack. Furnished balconies give way to views of the mountains, pool or city, and you'll find jogging and bike paths to warm up on before you hit the park, in addition to a heated pool and a putting green.

193 rooms, all suites. Wireless Internet access. Restaurant, bar. Airport transportation available. Fitness center. Pool. Spa. Pets accepted. $$

★★★Rancho Las Palmas Resort and Spa

41-000 Bob Hope Drive, Rancho Mirage, 760-568-2727, 866-423-1195; www.rancholaspalmas.com

This charming, family-friendly hotel, which recently underwent a major renovation, is situated in the heart of Rancho Mirage on 240 acres surrounded by mountains, lakes and gardens. Activities include a 25-court tennis center, world-class European spa and a Ted Robinson–designed 27-hole course. The warm and bright Spanish-style guest rooms feature plush bedding and French doors that open onto furnished patios or balconies overlooking the breezy, flower-filled grounds. After a day in the park, cool off in the resort's new two-acre water park with its own innertubing river, two 100-foot long waterslides, pool and sandy beach.

444 rooms, 22 suites. High-speed Internet access. Four restaurants, bar. Fitness center. Pools. Tennis. Golf. Spa. $$

★★★Viceroy Palm Springs

415 S. Belardo Road, Palm Springs, 760-320-4117, 800-670-6184; www.viceroypalmsprings.com

Built in 1929 and updated to reflect the Hollywood Regency style popular during the city's original glamour era, this boutique hotel located in the historic district is the chicest way to spoil yourself on a trip to Joshua Tree. Rooms, which look like they jumped out of the pages of a magazine, are decorated with black and white drapes, bright yellow upholstered reading chairs and lantern-style lighting. The hotel's spa offers aromatherapy and an array of body treatments in cabanas sur-

★

★

★

★

rounding the pool, and the onsite restaurant is a treat.

64 rooms, suites, and villas. High-speed Internet access. Restaurant, bar. Fitness center. Pool. Spa. Pets accepted. $$

★★★The Willows Historic Palm Springs Inn

412 W. Tahquitz Canyon Way, Palm Springs, 760-320-0771; www.thewillowspalmsprings.com

Built in 1924, this legendary Mediterranean-style inn in the heart of Old Palm Springs has hosted everyone from Albert Einstein to Clark Gable and Carole Lombard, who spent part of their honeymoon here. It's a great choice if you're looking for something small and intimate. The inn only has eight rooms, each with its own style, from the slate flooring (and an actual boulder) in the Rock Room to the coffered ceiling in the Library (where Gable and Lombard stayed). The hillside gardens overlook the Coachella Valley and Little San Bernardino Mountains.

8 rooms. Wireless Internet access. Complimentary full breakfast. Restaurant service. Pool. $$$

WHERE TO EAT

Outside Joshua Tree

— ALSO RECOMMENDED —

Crossroads Cafe and Tavern

61715 29 Palms Highway, Twentynine Palms, 760-366-5414; www.crossroadscafeandtavern.com

Half bar, half restaurant, this lively

café attracts a fun crowd of locals and Joshua Park enthusiasts. The staff serves all the typical breakfast fare as well as lunch and dinner favorites like the Grilled Coyote, a large sandwich made from grilled chicken breast, peppered bacon and avocado topped off with the house sauce.

American menu. Breakfast, lunch, dinner. Closed Wednesdays. $$

The Rib Co.

72183 29 Palms Highway, Twentynine Palms, 760-367-1663; 56193 29 Palms Highway, Yucca Valley, 760-365-1663; www.theribco.com

From babyback ribs to beef ribs and Jack Daniels ribs, this restaurant has ribs! And it has two locations near Joshua Tree National Park. For more adventurous palettes, it even serves kangaroo, alligator and rattlesnake.

American, barbeque menu. Lunch, dinner. $

Route 62 Diner

55405 29 Palms Highway, Yucca Valley, 760-365-6311; www.hutchinshd.com

Located at the Harley Davidson dealership, this breakfast, lunch and dinner spot is a fun place to pull into and grab a stool. Typical diner dishes are named after different bikes, and there's a daily breakfast special for just $3.99. They also make a mean milkshake.

American menu. Breakfast, lunch. Closed Monday. $

Palm Springs

★★Blue Coyote Bar & Grill
445 N. Palm Canyon Drive,
Palm Springs, 760-327-1196;
www.bluecoyote-grill.com

After a day at the park, this lively Mexican spot may be just the ticket. You gotta love a restaurant that calls itself "the home of the Wild Coyote margarita." Gold tequila, orange curacoa and fresh lime juice are used to create the potent concoction, which you can enjoy under the desert sky on the large outdoor patio while munching on southwestern-style baby back ribs or meatloaf, among a host of Mexican-inspired dishes. Southwestern, Mexican menu. Lunch, dinner. Outdoor seating. $$$

★★★Europa
1620 S. Indian Trail,
Palm Springs, 760-327-2314;
www.villaroyale.com

Housed in the Villa Royale Inn, this restaurant is beloved by locals for its delightful Continental cuisine, inspired by the sun-basked countries of Southern Europe, and its strong wine list. Dine on duck confit or osso bucco poolside by the fountains or enjoy a bottle of wine fireside in the cozy dining room. Continental menu. Dinner. Closed Monday. Bar. Business casual attire. Reservations recommended. Outdoor seating. $$$

★Great Wall
362 S. Palm Canyon Drive,
Palm Springs, 760-322-2209;
www.greatwallrestaurant.com

This family-run Chinese restaurant serves up all the traditional favorites from Mandarin, Cantonese, Hunan and Szechuan cuisines. Hungry hikers will love the all-you-can-eat Mongolian barbeque menu that a chef prepares on the restaurant's signature circular grill. Chinese menu. Lunch, dinner. Casual attire. $$

★★Kaiser Grill
205 S. Palm Canyon Drive,
Palm Springs, 760-323-1003;
www.kaisergrille.com

There's a reason why this bustling downtown restaurant decorated in warm desert hues is a Palm Springs favorite. From a classic Caesar salad to wood oven–fired pizzas and lasagna to house specialties like Greek steak, chicken schnitzel and shrimp pancetta, you'd be hard-pressed to find something you don't like. The open-air exhibition kitchen adds to the lively atmosphere, making it a big draw for group gatherings. American menu. Lunch, dinner. Bar. Children's menu. Casual attire. Reservations recommended. Outdoor seating. $$

★★Palmie
44491 Town Center Way,
Palm Springs, 760-341-3200

This cozy Palm Springs bistro is filled with Art Deco posters of French seaside resorts that give it

JOSHUA TREE

a relaxed yet romantic vibe, and is the perfect little spot for some pampering after roughing it in the park. The menu focuses on traditional French cuisine, all prepared by chef Alain Clerc with the strictest attention to the tiniest details. Lobster ravioli is garnished with caviar, while a trio of petite crème brûlées is flavored with ginger, vanilla and Kahlúa.

French menu. Dinner. Closed Sunday. Bar. Business casual attire. Reservations recommended. Outdoor seating. Valet parking. $$$

★★★St. James at the Vineyard
**265 S. Palm Canyon Drive,
Palm Springs, 760-320-8041;
www.stjamesrestaurant.com**

The lively décor at this downtown Palm Springs restaurant should clue you into the menu: wine buckets and golden Buddhas from Nepal, natural brick from Mexico, and masks and fabrics from India, Thailand and Morocco inspire the cuisine. The food here steals flavors from the Mediterranean, Morocco, the Pacific Rim and California. Signature curries are offered alongside dishes like baked vegetarian cannelloni, bouillabaisse Burmese and grilled New York Steak, while the award-winning wine list offers choices from California, Hungary, Portugal, Italy and Australia. The bar is a popular spot for cocktails and features live music Wednesday through Sunday.

International menu. Lunch, dinner. Bar. Children's menu. Business casual attire. Reservations recommended. Outdoor seating. $$$

★

★

★

★

★

OLYMPIC NATIONAL PARK

CONTRASTS ABOUND IN THESE 1,442 SQUARE MILES OF RUGGED WIL-
derness: the wettest climate in the contiguous United States (averaging
140 to 167 inches of precipitation a year) and one of the driest; seascapes
and snow-cloaked peaks; glaciers and rain forests, elk and seals; unadul-
terated wilderness and extravagant hot springs resorts. This national
park shares the Olympic Peninsula due west of Seattle and Puget Sound
with Olympic National Forest, State Sustained Yield Forest No. 1, much
private land and several American Indian reservations.

An ancient spear tip indicates that hunter-gatherers roamed the region
at least 12,000 years ago. About 3,000 years ago, people began to settle in
villages and develop the maritime culture that is the heritage of today's
northwestern Native American tribes. In 1592, the Greek explorer Juan
de Fuca, sailing under a Spanish flag, was probably the first European
to spot the Olympic Peninsula. Englishman Captain William Barkley
reconfirmed the existence of the strait in 1787 and named it in honor
of de Fuca. Homesteaders started arriving in earnest in the mid-1800s.
Since then, generations of adventurous tourists have rediscovered Mount
Olympus, the highest peak in the Olympic Mountain range at 7,965 feet;
several other 7,000-foot-plus giants; and hundreds of ridges and crests
between 5,000 and 6,000 feet high. The architects behind these ruggedly
contoured mountains are glaciers, which have been etching these peaks
for thousands of years. They continue today, as nearly 60 glaciers work to
evoke these picturesque mountains.

Some 50 species of mammals inhabit this wilderness, including several thousand elk, Olympic marmots, black-tailed deer and black bears.
On the park's 60-mile strip of Pacific coastline wilderness, deer, bears,
raccoons and skunks can be seen, while seals sun on the offshore rocks
or plow through the water beyond the breakers. Mountain and lowland
lakes sparkle everywhere, including Lake Crescent which reigns among
the largest.

From approximately November through March, the west side of the
park is soaked with rain and mist, while the northeast side is the driest
area on the West Coast apart from southern California. The yearly del-
uge creates a rain forest in the western valleys of the park. Here, Sitka
spruce, western hemlock, Douglas fir, and western red cedar grow to
heights of 250 feet with eight-foot diameters. Mosses carpet the forest
floor and climb tree trunks. Club moss drips from the branches.

99

OLYMPIC

★
★
★
★

The peerless forests on the peninsula are not only stunningly statuesque but a valuable resource that has been a point of contention among differing groups in the park's history. As early as 1897, some Americans were becoming concerned about the disappearance of the country's forests, and in response, President Grover Cleveland designated most of the peninsula's land a national forest reserve. But the controversy didn't end there, and those in the forestry business eventually won a battle to cut the reserved acreage in half, opening up more of the lowland forest for harvesting. The two sides—one campaigning for a national park, the other defending the commercial value of such productive forest—continued to butt heads until President Franklin Roosevelt visited the area and felt inspired to sign the act in 1938 that established Olympic National Park.

Since then, the park has afforded the northwest's prodigious population of outdoors enthusiasts a local haven for hiking, biking, kayaking, fishing, camping, backpacking, mountaineering and more. Almost 40,000 people a year come to Olympic to go backcountry camping, and several hundred thousand a year enjoy day hikes. In 1981, the park was also designated a UNESCO world heritage site, securing a protected future for one of the country's most remarkable natural spaces.

600 E. Park Ave., Port Angeles, Washington, 360-565-3130, 800-833-6388; www.nps.gov/olym/

WHAT TO SEE

On the way to the park, visitors may cross the remarkable **Tacoma Narrows Bridge** (Highway 16), the fifth-longest suspension bridge in the United States. This bridge across the Puget Sound replaced one known as "Galloping Gertie," which collapsed in 1940, just four months and seven days after it had officially opened. At the Port Angeles park entrance are the park headquarters and the **Olympic National Park Visitor Center** (600 E. Park Ave., 360-565-3130; May-September, daily; October-April, Thursday-Monday), which has information, natural and cultural history exhibits, displays of American Indian culture, an orientation film and a hands-on children's room. The **Wilderness Information Center** (early April-late October) is here, too, offering information, trip-planning advice and permits.

From here, Heart o' the Hills Parkway leads 5 miles south through thick old-growth forest to the **Heart o' the Hills area**, which offers camping facilities, a ranger station, a few trailheads and Lake Darwin. Another 12 miles south lands you at **Hurricane Ridge** to which access is limited November through April, as the area receives 30 to 35 feet of snow each year that lingers into summer (call 360-565-3131 for current road conditions). The **Hurricane Ridge Visitor Center** (late June to mid-

★

★

★

★

★

September, daily; late December-late June, weekends) has an information desk and exhibits on the park's mountain habitats. The surrounding area includes two picnic areas and several trailheads. Going back through Port Angeles and then west, Highway 101 travels past turnoffs for the lush **Elwa** (30 miles) and **Sol Duc** (39 miles) lowland forest areas; both offer camping facilities and trailheads. Farther west, Highway 113 heads north toward Hoko-Ozette Road, which leads to **Lake Ozette** on the far northwestern reaches of the peninsula and where you'll find campgrounds, trailheads and beaches, and a ranger station.

Past the Highway 113 intersection, Highway 110 leads west to the **Mora area** (49 miles from Sol Duc). This rough coastal area provides 94 first-come, first-served campsites that are open year-round, as well as a ranger station, a few trailheads and several beaches, which make good wildlife-watching spots. Circling counterclockwise around the park, 47 miles later, Highway 101 intersects another turnoff on the left (east) for **Upper Hoh Road**, which winds through a remarkable giant conifer rain forest that's covered by mosses, ferns and other plants to the **Hoh Rain Forest Visitor Center** (mid-May to September, daily; October to mid-May, Friday-Sunday). This facility offers information, exhibits on the park's temperate rain forests and backcountry permits. The nearby campground has 88 sites.

There are also a few trailheads in the area for further exploration. The milky-blue Hoh River, originating from Mount Olympus's glacier, passes through the area before dropping 7,000 feet into the Pacific.

Past Upper Hoh Road, Highway 101 turns west and hugs the shore until reaching the **Kalaloch area** 40 miles later. This stretch is a good place to watch for marine mammals such as harbor seals and sea otters; even whales and dolphins are spotted here occasionally. Kalaloch, which means "a good place to land" in the native Quinault language, is situated between the Quinault and Hoh rivers. A ranger station, year-round lodge, two campgrounds, restaurant, coffee shop, stores, service station and more amenities are available. From here, Highway 101 curves back east for 33 miles toward the **Quinault Rain Forest**. This scenic forested valley, soaked by more than 12 feet of rain a year, is rich in alpine meadows, sparkling lakes, ferns, moss and other greenery. It's also where the historic Press Expedition of 1889 ended up. The Olympic Peninsula was largely unknown to the Euro-Americans in the area at the time, so the Seattle Press funded a trip for a group of explorers who left from Port Angeles and ended up six months later at Lake Quinault—a trip that backpackers do in four to five days now. The Quinault area offers a ranger station, picnic area, self-guided nature trails, two campgrounds and several trailheads.

OLYMPIC

★
★
★
★

Back around on the southeast side of the park, Highway 101 passes a turnoff for Highway 119 (about 125 miles from Quinault), leading into a thick, vast Douglas fir forest to the **Staircase area**. The road is closed November through early May; the area has a picnic area, campground, restrooms, fire rings, plenty of trailheads and a ranger station that is open intermittently throughout the summer. Back on 101, heading around north toward Port Angeles again, is a turnoff that heads 18 miles up a steep, narrow mountain road (the last 9 miles are gravel) to **Deer Park**. This road is closed from late fall till late spring. In the rain shadow of the eastern Olympics, this area is in stark contrast to the Hoh Rain Forest, which gets an average rainfall of only 18 inches a year. A ranger station, campground, picnic area and some trailheads are accessible from here.

From Port Angeles, you can see and go any number of places. There's a 90-minute ferry service to Victoria, BC (101 E. Railroad Ave., Port Angeles, 360-457-4491, 800-833-6388; www.cohoferry. com). Four trips are made daily mid-May to September; two trips most of the rest of the year, except January, with one trip. (Don't forget your passport.) Also, the **Merrill and Ring Tree Farm** (11 Pysht River Road, Clallam Bay, 38 miles west of Port Angeles on Highway 112, 800-998-2382; www.byways.org/explore) offers a self-guided trail that explains

resource management and reforestation of the land, and educates visitors about the clear-cuts along the SR 112 corridor. The original cabins built to house early twentieth-century loggers are still here, too. Hours vary, so call ahead for current information. At the **Joyce Depot Museum** (Joyce, 16 miles west of Port Angeles on Highway 112, 360-928-3568; www.joycewa. com; Thursday-Monday 10 a.m.-4 p.m.), located in a former railroad station, you can browse through general store items from the 1920s through the 1940s, logging gear and historical railroad equipment. Old photos of the area have been preserved, as well as articles from the former City of Port Crescent newspaper. And after you've had your fill of Olympic National Park, **Mount Rainier** might be calling.

WHAT TO DO

BACKPACKING

All overnight trips require wilderness permits. You can get them at the Wilderness Information Center (360-565-3100) in Port Angeles, the Quinault Wilderness Office, the Forks Recreation Information Station and the Staircase Ranger Station, as well as some self-registration trailheads. Permits cost $5 per group plus $2 per person (older than 15) per night. A U.S. Forest Service Northwest Forest pass is also required to park near trailheads that originate in Forest Service areas. Those

★
★
★
★
★

trailheads are Upper Dungeness, Duckabush and Lena Lake. Forest Service permits cost $5 per vehicle per day or $30 for an annual pass. There are numerous backcountry hiking and camping options in this park. For more information, call the Wilderness Information Center or visit www.nps.gov/olym/planyourvisit/wilderness-trip-planner.htm.

CROSS-COUNTRY SKIING AND SNOWSHOEING

The Hurricane Ridge area offers opportunities for both cross-country skiing and snowshoeing. The road is open only on weekends from late November through March, weather permitting. Call 360-565-3131 for current conditions. Also stop by the visitor center, open Thursday-Monday, for current avalanche conditions and a map of the unmarked and ungroomed routes in the area. A ski shop at Hurricane Ridge rents both skis and snowshoes. The park service also offers a 90-minute guided snowshoe walk on Saturdays and Sundays at 2 p.m. (snowshoes are provided). You can register at the information desk 30 minutes before the walk to reserve a spot. A $5 donation per person for the snowshoe walk is requested.

DOWNHILL SKIING

The mostly volunteer-run Hurricane Ridge Ski Area (360-565-3131 for current conditions; www.hurricaneridge.com) has one lift and two rope tows, which run from 10 a.m.-4 p.m. on weekends from late December through March. A ski school and groomed beginner and intermediate trails—and 400-plus inches of snow a year—make this a great family ski mountain. For the more advanced skier or snowboarder, steeps, bowls and glades are just a hike away.

FISHING

Streams and lakes have game fish, including salmon, rainbow, Dolly Varden, eastern brook trout, steelhead and cutthroat. No license is required in the park, but a permit or punch card is necessary for steelhead and salmon. Contact Park Headquarters for restrictions.

HIKING

Olympic National Park has more than 600 miles of trails. Maps and trail guides are available at visitor centers in the park. In addition, some ranger-guided walks are conducted in July and August. Be prepared for changeable weather, even on short hikes. Here are just a few suggestions:

─────── **EASY** ───────

Heart o' the Forest
4.6 miles round-trip
Trailhead: Heart o' the Hills campground loop E
This easy trail takes hikers through pristine old-growth forest and dense vegetation.

★
★
★
★
★

Hurricane Hill

3.2 miles round-trip
Trailhead: Hurricane Ridge area
at the end of Hurricane Hill Road.
This paved trail climbs 700 feet to a viewpoint offering panoramas of both mountains and saltwater.

Kestner Homestead

1.3-mile loop
Trailhead: Quinault River Ranger Station.
A self-guided tour along this trail teaches visitors about homestead life on the Olympic Peninsula.

─────── **MODERATE** ───────

Heather Park

12 miles round-trip
Trailhead: Heart o' the Hills; end of the road just north of the entrance station.
This steady climb, with a 3,150-foot elevation gain, lands hikers in the wildflower meadows around Heather Park. Another more difficult 2.2 miles and 800-foot elevation gain leads to Klahhane Ridge in the high country.

Klahhane Ridge

13 miles round-trip
Trailhead: Heart o' the Hills; end of the road just north of the entrance station.
This hike climbs steadily to reach the subalpine Lake Angeles, then continues to Klahhane Ridge, where mountain vistas begin to appear (and the climb gets stiffer), and ends at the junction with Mount Angeles Trail. The net elevation change is about 1,500 feet. For a 12.9-mile loop, take Mount Angeles Trail back to Heart o' the Hills.

─────── **STRENUOUS** ───────

Deer Park to Obstruction Point

14.8 miles round-trip
Trailhead: Deer Park area near ranger station.
The trail begins with a descent and then climbs steeply (a 1,270-foot elevation gain), winding through subalpine forests, mountain meadows and tundra and offering great views of glaciers, Mount Angeles and Mount Olympus. It traverses the bare slopes of Elk Mountain at about 6,600 feet above sea level before reaching Obstruction Point.

Wagonwheel Lake

5.8 miles round-trip
Trailhead: Staircase Ranger Station at the end of Forest Road 24.
This stiff hike, a 3,200-foot climb through forests offers occasional glimpses of mountains on its way up switchbacks to Wagonwheel Lake. The lake is stocked with cutthroat trout.

MOUNTAINEERING

Olympic National Park offers something for everyone, from the novice to the experienced climber. Register at a ranger station or visit the Wilderness Information Center for more information and guide contacts.

OLYMPIC

RAFTING AND KAYAKING

River rafting, whitewater kayaking, sea kayaking and canoeing are all options in Olympic National Park. The only outfitter permitted to operate is Olympic Raft and Kayak (123 Lake Aldwell Road, Port Angeles, 360-452-1443, 888-452-1443; www.raftandkayak. com), which offers rentals, as well as guided raft and kayak trips.

WILDLIFE

Thanks to its special geographic location on an isolated peninsula, Olympic National Park is home to a unique community of animals. There are 20 endemic species in Olympic, not found anywhere else in the world, including the Olympic marmot, Olympic chipmunk, Olympic snow mole and Olympic torrent salamander. But what's equally notable is that some common western mountain species that would be expected to be found here are actually absent, including the pika, ground squirrel, red fox, coyote, wolverine and grizzly bear. The peninsula's rare old-growth forest provides an invaluable habitat to a number of species (some endangered) like the northern spotted owls and marbled murrelets (small seabirds), who depend on it for refuge. Then there are the 3,310 square miles of water that make up the Olympic Coast National Marine Sanctuary just off the park's 73 miles of shoreline. This area harbors 29 species of marine mammals including whales, dolphins, sea lions, seals and sea otters, and sea birds like the marbled murrelet and tufted puffin. Here are just a few of the park's species to keep an eye out for:

Fishers: In January 2008, 11 fishers were reintroduced to Olympic National Park. These relatives of minks and otters disappeared from Washington state by the 1930s due to overtrapping for their valuable fur and habitat destruction. They have the distinctive skill of being able to prey on porcupines, despite the quills, limiting that species' destruction of commercial timber.

Gray whales: Another species that had once disappeared from the area, these whales have come back in such numbers that they're no longer considered endangered. Watch for their spouts and splotchy backs just off the coast from March to May when they are migrating north.

Mountain beaver: These rodents, special to the northwest, are not really beavers but get the name from their tendency to chew through wood and bark in the same fashion. These animals dig burrow systems in moist forests and spend much of their lives underground, coming up only to gather plants to store in their burrows.

Olympic marmot: This species of large ground squirrels, related to other marmots and groundhogs, is unique to the Olympic Mountains. Their coats are brownish with white patches and they can

★
★
★
★

sometimes be spotted indulging themselves in the sun on rocks near their burrows.

Roosevelt elk: About 5,000 of these big guys are protected in Olympic National Park. They are the largest mammal in the park, bigger even than their Rocky Mountain relatives, and the males can weigh as much as 1,000 pounds. Females and their calves can be seen grazing in valley fields on the west side of the park throughout the year. During the fall rut, the bulls' calls can be heard echoing through the valleys as they challenge each other for dominance and females. **Sea otters:** These cute, cuddly creatures' super-soft fur led trappers to hunt them to extinction off of Washington's coast by the early twentieth century. Some Alaskan otters were reintroduced to the Washington coastal area in 1969 and 1970. The recovery effort continues with success and has resulted in a population of 800 otters in the waters around the Olympic Peninsula. Look for their furry, round heads bobbing out of sea kelp forests offshore, where they feast on sea urchins. They may be spotted from overlooks in the Kalaloch, Mora and La Push areas.

WHERE TO STAY

CAMPING

There are plenty of options for campers, with 16 campgrounds providing 910 campsites in the park. And then, of course, there's

the backcountry. Most of the campgrounds can accommodate RVs up to 21 feet long. Kalaloch Lodge and Sol Duc Resort also both offer more campsites for tents and RVs. Fees vary between $10 and $18, and all campsites except for Kalaloch are first-come, first-served. Reservations for Kalaloch can be made online at www.recreation.gov.

HOTELS

Port Angeles
★★Red Lion Hotel
221 N. Lincoln St., Port Angeles, 360-452-9215, 800-733-5466; www.redlion.com
This comfortable motel overlooking the Port Angeles harbor provides all of the vacation amenities a family needs just outside Olympic National Park and only a block from downtown Port Angeles. The hotel offers free shuttle service to the airport, as well as a nearby casino. If you're in the mood for crab, the onsite restaurant is the place to feast.
186 rooms. Wireless Internet access. Restaurant, bar. Pool. Fitness center. Business center. Pets accepted. $

★★Sol Duc Hot Springs Resort
12076 Sol Duc Hot Springs Road at Highway 101, Port Angeles, 360-327-3583, 866-476-5382; www.visitsolduc.com
This cozy cabin resort boasts reasonable rates, three hot spring pools and a freshwater pool, and makes a convenient base for hik-

ing, fishing, beachcombing and wildlife watching. To help you get away from it all, there are no phones or TVs in the rooms.

32 cabins. Closed late October-late March. Complimentary breakfast buffet. Two restaurants. Pool. Pets accepted. $

Seattle

★Hampton Inn & Suites
700 Fifth Ave. N, Seattle, 206-282-7700; www.hamptoninn.com

Great for families or guests seeking a larger space in which to unwind, the Hampton Inn features suites with full kitchens, fireplaces, and balconies. Its location near the Seattle Center puts guests close to restaurants, shopping, the opera, ballet and theater, as well as the Space Needle. And if you didn't get your fill of exercise on the hiking trails, the onsite fitness center is sure to tucker you out.

199 rooms. High-speed Internet access. Complimentary continental breakfast. Fitness center. Business center. $$

★★★Inn at the Market
86 Pine St., Seattle, 206-443-3600; www.innatthemarket.com

Seattle's renowned creative spirit is perhaps best felt at the delightful Inn at the Market. This boutique hotel enjoys a prime location at the vibrant Pike Place Market, overlooking the pristine waters of Elliott Bay. Picturesque views and cultural attractions are just outside the door at this coun-try chic home-away-from-home. The spacious and stylish accommodations are the last word in comfort, with in-room massages to soothe over-hiked muscles and special Tempur-Pedic mattresses to ensure a restful sleep.

70 rooms. Wireless Internet access. Three restaurants, bar. Pets accepted. $$$

★★★ Renaissance Seattle Hotel
515 Madison St., Seattle, 206-583-0300; www.marriott.com

Located in the heart of Seattle, this hotel combines contemporary décor of marble and glass with earth-toned colors that convey a warm, rich ambience. Guests have magnificent city views from the 25th floor, where the indoor pool is located, and the 28th floor, where guests may dine on authentic Italian fare at Pellini. Nearly everything that defines Seattle is less than a mile away—Pike Place Market and the waterfront, Pioneer Square, Safeco Field (home of the Mariners), and Seahawks Stadium.

553 rooms. High-speed Internet access. Two restaurants, bar. Fitness center. Pool. Business center. $$

★★University Tower Hotel
4507 Brooklyn Ave. NE, Seattle, 206-634-2000

This boutique hotel offers beautiful panoramic views of the University of Washington campus, the Seattle skyline, Mount Rainier, and the Olympic and Cascade

OLYMPIC

★
★
★
★

mountains–perfect for a post-park recoup. Guests will feel right at home in the stylish and comfortable rooms which have down blankets, down pillows, high-loft comforters, and rich color palettes. If you're looking to sample the local fare, try the in-house restaurant, the District Lounge, which features a Northwestern eclectic, globally inspired menu. 158 rooms. Wirless Internet access. Complimentary continental breakfast. Restaurant, two bars. $$

WHERE TO EAT

Port Angeles

★★Bushwhacker
1527 E. First St., Port Angeles, 360-457-4113
This is a traditional seafood restaurant in one of the best places for it. Catering to vacationing families, the Bushwacker is a favorite of return travelers to the peninsula.
Seafood menu. Dinner. Bar. Children's menu. Casual attire. $$

★★★Toga's International Cuisine
122 W. Lauridsen Blvd., Port Angeles, 360-452-1952
The menu at this quaint, intimate restaurant shows influences from all over Europe while highlighting ingredients unique to the Pacific Northwest. The dining room is located in a remodeled 1943 home and boasts beautiful views of the Olympic Mountain Range.

The carrot soup (yes, carrot soup) wins raves.
International menu. Dinner. Closed Sunday-Monday; September. Bar. Children's menu. Reservations recommended. Outdoor seating. $$

Seattle
★★★Cafe Flora
2901 E. Madison, Seattle, 206-325-9100;
www.cafeflora.com
There are people who believe that the words "delicious" and "innovative" could never be used to describe vegetarian cuisine, but Café Flora proves them wrong. Since 1991, this Seattle gem has been turning out perfect plates of fresh and nutritious fare that consistently receives raves from both vegetarians and carnivores alike. Herbs from the restaurant's own garden are used in seasonal dishes like mushroom asparagus risotto with artichoke bottoms, pine nuts, scallions, mascarpone and parsley oil; and coconut-breaded tofu with basil, cilantro and sweet chili dipping sauce.
Vegetarian menu. Lunch, dinner, brunch. Closed holidays Children's menu. $$

★★★Etta's Seafood
2020 Western Ave., Seattle, 206-443-6000; www.tomdouglas.com
With an atmosphere as colorful as the food, Etta's brings in droves of hungry patrons both day and night. The casual seafood house, owned and operated by Seattle's renowned chef, Tom Douglas and

OLYMPIC

his wife, Jackie, is located just half a block from the popular Pikes Peak Market and is named after the owners' daughter, Loretta. Its large windows overlook the bustling farmers' market which supplies a majority of the fresh ingredients on the menu. There's something on the menu for everyone, from fish and chips to juicy crab cakes to Oregon country beef rib eye steak.

Seafood menu. Lunch, dinner, brunch. Bar. Childrens' menu. Casual attire. Reservations recommended. $$$

★★The Pink Door

1919 Post Alley, Seattle, 206-443-3241; www.thepinkdoor.net

To find this lively Italian-American restaurant, walk down "Post Alley," look for the pink door, open it and go downstairs. A warm, eclectic experience awaits. Live entertainment such as tap dancing, jazz ensembles, and a trapeze act are featured nightly. The outdoor patio offers incredible views of Elliott Bay and the Olympic Mountains.

American, Italian menu. Lunch, dinner, late-night. Bar. Casual attire. Reservations recommended. Outdoor seating. $$

OLYMPIC

POINT REYES
NATIONAL SEASHORE

FROM SUBLIME SAN FRANCISCO, AN HOUR-LONG SCENIC DRIVE OUT OF the city, across the Golden Gate Bridge and up the shore, leads to this captivating coastline in charming Marin Country. Point Reyes National Seashore was established in 1962 by President John F. Kennedy to preserve a bit of the western coastline, which was quickly disappearing because of overdevelopment. Since then, these 71,000 acres of dense pine and fir forests, active grassy ranchlands, rugged sea cliffs and 80 miles of unspoiled beaches have become a sanctuary not only for the area's natural ecosystems, plant and animal species but also for droves of urbanites who habitually make the short drive to explore and relax here.

The popular peninsula's history dates back about 5,000 years to the Coast Miwok people who inhabited the area north of the San Francisco Bay. The craggy peninsula wasn't discovered by Europeans until 1579, when it's believed that Sir Francis Drake first saw and claimed it for Queen Elizabeth. He's said to have made his camp on what is now his namesake beach. The first (of many) shipwrecks in California history happened in 1595 just off the foggy, cliff-buttressed coast in what is now known as Drakes Bay. Spanish explorer Sebastian Vizcaino was the first to add the peninsula to a map when he spotted it on January 6, 1603, on the Roman Catholic holiday known as Three Kings Day. He named it "la punta de los reyes," or the point of the kings.

The peninsula is the windiest place on the Pacific Coast and the second foggiest place in North America. It proved such a hazard to mariners on the popular shipping route from Asia that, in 1870, the Point Reyes Light Station was built at the westernmost point of the headlands in the hopes of reducing the number of shipwrecks. Still, seemingly endless fog during the summer often reduces visibility to mere hundreds of feet, and with the Point Reyes headlands jutting ten miles out to sea, they're still a threat to each ship that goes in and out of San Francisco Bay.

Another key part of Point Reyes' history began with its 19th-century settlers who found the cool, moist climate was near-perfect for raising dairy cows on the coastal prairie. By 1857, the San Francisco law firm Shafter owned 50,000 acres on the peninsula and proceeded to create a dairy empire that revolutionized the dairy industry from small, family-run businesses to industrial-scale operations. The remnants of Point Reyes' history dots its landscape today in the form of lighthouses, farmhouses, barns and creameries. In combination with the wilderness that

★
★
★
★
★

the National Park Service works to preserve as a habitat for marine mammals—including 24 threatened and endangered species—this rugged seashore is a fascinating place to undertake an adventure of discovery.

1 Bear Valley Road., Point Reyes, California, 415-464-5100; www.nps.gov/pore

WHAT TO SEE

From San Francisco, take U.S. Highway 101 north across the Golden Gate Bridge and onward to the Sir Frances Drake-San Anselmo exit (450B). Take Sir Frances Drake Blvd. west for 21 miles until it intersects Highway 1 at Olema. Turn right/north onto Highway 1, take the first left turn at Bear Valley Road and head west about 0.5 mile. Look for a big red barn on the left and a Seashore information sign on the right. Turn left past the barn and continue to the **Bear Valley Visitor Center** (415-464-5100), the primary park headquarters. You can access several trailhead starts here. The center also offers informational exhibits on the park's ecosystems and history. There's also a short path (0.8 miles) that will take you to **Kule Loklo**, a replica of an ancient Coast Miwok Indian village with signs explaining their culture and history. From the visitor center, four main roads lead to various points of interest in the park.

Sir Frances Drake Blvd., which heads northwest and ends at the historic lighthouse at the tip of the Point Reyes headlands, is 1.75 miles northwest on Bear Valley Road. Along the way are sights and several trailheads. The turn for **Mount Vision Road** is 6.7 miles

down Sir Frances Drake Blvd. From here, turn left (south) and continue for another 3 miles on a narrow, windy road to the Mount Vision parking lot. This scenic drive, providing views from 1,282-foot Mount Vision and 1,336-foot Point Reyes Hill, leads to a couple of trailheads. A few miles past the Mount Vision turnoff is a road leading to the **Drakes Bay Oyster Farm** (17171 Sir Francis Drake Blvd., Inverness, 415-669-1149; www.drakesbayfamilyfarms.com), an independently-owned business that has been operating on the property since 1957, which is popular for its fresh oysters. After another couple of miles, there is a turnoff on the right for **Point Reyes North Beach**, also known as the **Great Beach**. This 10-mile-long pristine shore offers drive-up access to dramatic surf. (Be very cautious here; sneaker waves—unexpectedly large, high, strong, far-reaching waves—have been known to drag people out to sea from this beach and others in the area.) Another few miles down is the turnoff for **Drakes Beach**, a popular, wide stretch of sand surrounded by dramatic white sandstone cliffs. Also here are **Drakes Beach Café** (4 Drakes Beach Road, Inverness, 415-669-1297) and the **Kenneth C. Patrick Visitor Center** (415-669-1250), which features exhibits highlight-

111

POINT REYES

ing maritime exploration, marine fossils and the marine environment, including a full-size minke whale skeleton. The final five miles of Sir Frances Drake Blvd. brings you to the parking lot for the historic **Point Reyes Lighthouse**. From the parking lot, you must walk 0.4 miles west down some 300 steps to the **Lighthouse Visitor Center** (415-669-1534); be sure to dress for the typically windy, rainy, foggy and cool conditions that can blow in suddenly. The visitor center offers exhibits on the history of the lighthouse, as well as whales, seals, sea lions, wildflowers, birds and maritime history. On the first and third Saturday evenings of the month, April through December, the park service offers an evening lighting program. The program is free, but reservations are required.

Pierce Point Road, traveling north in Point Reyes, lends access to a number of beaches. From the Bear Valley Visitor Center, take Bear Valley Road to Sir Frances Drake Blvd. Continue north on Sir Frances Drake for 5.6 miles to Pierce Point Road. About 1.25 miles later, a road on the right leads into **Tomales Bay State Park** (1208 Pierce Point Road, Inverness, 415-669-1140; www.parks.ca.gov), 1,018 acres of California state land featuring virgin groves of Bishop pine and more than 300 species of plants. There are opportunities here for swimming, fishing, hiking, biking and picnicking. **Heart's Desire Beach** is a sheltered cove on Tomales Bay, providing slightly warmer and safer swimming for families with small children. Just north of the entrance to Tomales Bay State Park is a dire road to the **Marshall Beach** trailhead. Getting to this beach on the Tomales Bay side of the peninsula involves a 2-mile drive to the parking area and then a 1.2-mile hike to the beach. About a mile past the Marshall Beach road is the **Abbotts Lagoon Beach** parking area. From there, it's a 1.5-mile walk through scrub and sand dunes to the beach. A couple miles further on Pierce Point Road is the **Kehoe Beach** trailhead; this half-mile trail will take you to an interesting beach dotted with giant dunes and backed by dramatic cliffs—both sandstone and granite. Follow Pierce Point Road for another 3.5 miles to reach **Pierce Point Ranch,** a historic dairy ranch dating back to 1858, which offers a self-guided tour. From there, the **McClures Beach** parking lot is 100 yards down the hill to the west. A short but steep hike down to the beach is rewarded by views of the intense surf punctuated by dramatic rocks. (Only venture around the corner during the outgoing low tide.)

After all of these magnificent beaches, head to the **Tule Elk Reserve**, a nearby wildlife refuge where you can best observe the herds. For a closer look, use binoculars or a telephoto camera lens. The best season to visit is during the elks' fall rut, or breeding season, which begins in July and lasts through November.

★
★
★
★
☆

Limantour Road offers quick access from the Bear Valley Visitor Center to a number of trailheads for hiking, biking and horseback riding. Highway 1 travels south from Bear Valley Road and provides access to many more trails and beaches, including **Palomarin Beach**, a good place for tidepooling, though the hike down the cliff to the beach is strenuous. Continuing on Highway 1 south toward Stinson Beach leads to another playground for San Franciscans and the birthplace of mountain biking, **Mount Tamalpais State Park** (801 Panoramic Highway, Mill Valley, 415-388-2070; www.parks.ca.gov). The stiff climb up Mount Tam's 2,571-foot peak ends with spectacular views of the entire Bay Area and can be approached via the winding road on a bike (the way mountain biking moguls like Gary Fisher got their start) or in a car—although you won't get the pleasure of careening back downhill. There are a number of parking lots off the main road with access to trailheads for a little hiking or picnicking.

Just outside Point Reyes National Seashore on Sir Frances Drake Blvd. is **Samuel P. Taylor State Park** (8889 Sir Francis Drake Blvd., Lagunitas, 415-488-9897; www.parks.ca.gov), which encompasses 2,800 acres of wooded countryside with many groves of coastal redwoods and a historic paper mill site. The park provides hiking and bridle trails and opportunities for mountain biking, horseback riding, picnicking and camping.

WHAT TO DO

BIKING

In the county where mountain biking was born, what better way is there to explore the coastal shrub, evergreen forests and beach bluffs? Bicycles, which can be rented at Point Reyes Station, are allowed only outside of wilderness areas in the National Seashore. The visitor centers have free bicycle maps.

HIKING

Point Reyes National Seashore contains about 150 miles of hiking trails. Below is a sampling of the hikes available.

——————— **EASY** ———————

Coast-Laguna Loop

5-mile loop

Trailhead: Take Limantour Road west, turn left at the junction signed for the Hostel and Education Center and continue past Hostel to the Laguna Parking Lot on the right.

This easy walk through coastal scrub and grassland offers big ocean views. It starts with a bit of a climb before heading downhill. Access the beach by turning left on the Coast Trail or continue around, heading northwest back to the trailhead.

Earthquake Trail

0.6-mile loop

Trailhead: Southeast corner of Bear Valley picnic area, across the street from the visitor center.

POINT REYES

★
★
★
★
★

Signs along this short, paved loop through the San Andreas Fault zone describe the geology of the area.

Woodpecker Trail
0.7-mile loop
Trailhead: Bear Valley Trailhead, at the south end of the Bear Valley parking lot.
This trail loops through forest and meadow ecosystems and offers informative signs along the way about some of the area's plants and animals.

——— MODERATE ———

Mount Wittenberg and Sky Camp
4.3 miles round-trip
Trailhead: 10 minutes from Bear Valley Visitor Center on Limantour Road.
The easier of two ways to reach the highest point on the peninsula, Mount Wittenberg, this trail climbs 750 feet. Take the Sky Trail, which provides ocean views, to the Horse Trail. Turn right on Z Ranch Trail, which leads to the eroded trail that goes to the top. The summit offers panoramic views of the area. Continue from the summit to the junction of Sky and Meadow Trails and turn north onto Sky Trail, which passes Sky Camp before returning to the trailhead.

Woodward Valley Loop
13-mile loop
Trailhead: Bear Valley Trailhead
Both Mount Wittenberg and Meadow Trail lead to Sky Trail. From there, hike this lush, green

trail to Woodward Valley. Continue on this trail until reaching the Coast Trail, which offers broad ocean views on the way to Arch Rock. The trail lends access to remote Sculptured Beach.

——— STRENUOUS ———

Tomales Point Trail
9.5 miles round-trip
Trailhead: At the end of Pierce Point Road, 40 minutes from Bear Valley.
The difficulty of this hike depends on the weather and trail conditions; fog and wind can limit visibility and increase the challenge, as can overgrown shrubs. Long pants and long sleeves are recommended. The trail travels through the Tule Elk Reserve, providing views of Tomales Bay, Bodega Bay and the Pacific Ocean, all the way to the Point for the best views in the National Seashore.

HORSEBACK RIDING

Most trails and beaches in Point Reyes allow horses. Check at a visitor center for details and a horse-specific trail map. Five Brooks Ranch (415-663-1570; www.five-brooks.com) offers guided trail rides.

KAYAKING

Tomales Bay offers 15 miles of uninterrupted and protected water for kayaking. There are four launch points for the bay: Miller County Park (415-499-6387) on the east side of the bay, north of Marshall off of Highway 1;

POINT REYES

Tomales Bay State Park (415-669-1140) at Millerton Point on the east side of the Bay north of Point Reyes Station and at Hearts Desire Beach on the west side of the Bay off of Pierce Point Road; Golden Hinde Inn and Marina (415-669-1389) on the west side of the bay three miles north of Inverness off Sir Frances Drake Blvd.; and Lawson's Landing (707-878-2443) in Dillon Beach on the east side of the Bay.

RANGER PROGRAMS

Park rangers lead a number of informative and educational programs on subjects such as the San Andreas Fault, the Coast Miwok people, flora, fauna and more. For details or to make a reservation for a group of 15 or more, call the Bear Valley Visitor Center at 415-464-5100.

WILDLIFE

Nearly 40 species of land mammals, at least a dozen marine mammals and nearly half of the bird species found in North America have been identified in the park. Here are a few of the interesting creatures to look out for in the National Seashore.

California gray whale: Making the longest migration of any mammal, these whales travel 10,000 miles a year from cold Alaskan waters to the warm ones of Baja California, passing right by Point Reyes on their way. Jutting 10 miles out into the Pacific, the point provides a prime view for observing the mammals' trip south in mid-January and north in mid-March.

Coho salmon: As they have for thousands of years, salmon and trout return to their birthplace in the West Marin streams every winter to spawn. January is typically the best month to see them, especially for the one to three days following rain. Look for them in Samuel P. Taylor State Park (415-488-9897) near Camp Taylor off of Sir Frances Drake Blvd.

Elephant seal: Point Reyes has been a thriving breeding ground for the once nearly extinct elephant seals since 1981. Point Reyes Headland is one of only 11 mainland breeding areas for northern elephant seals in the world. Their colony has been growing at the rapid annual rate of 16 percent on average and now numbers about 100. Elephant seals can dive up to a mile below the ocean's surface in search of food. To see them, head to the Elephant Seal Overlook near Chimney Rock above Drakes Bay.

Tule elk: These elk were virtually gone by 1860; 30 years ago the park service began working to restore the population. In 1978, two bulls and eight cows were brought from the San Luis Island Wildlife Refuge. By the summer of 1988, their population was 93, and by 2000, there were as many as 400, making Point Reyes home to one of the largest populations of tule elk. The best place to observe them is at the Tule Elk Reserve at Tomales Point, where they graze freely.

POINT REYES

★ ★ ★ ★ ★

BIRDS

Point Reyes draws birders from all over the states. Its more than 70,000 acres of habitat may be home to as many as 490 avian species. The area consistently reports one of the highest tallies in the country every year during the Christmas Bird Count, an annual ornithological census compiled by more than 50,000 bird enthusiasts. For more information or to participate in the count, see www.prbo.org or www.audubon.org. Some of the best places to observe the diverse variety of bird life are along the trails of Bear Valley, on the beaches and in the marshes of Limantour, in Bolinas Lagoon and the Audubon Canyon Ranch's Preserve, in the grasses and trees around Five Brooks Pond, in Abbotts Lagoon, along the Estero Trail and in the rocks and cliff areas near the lighthouse.

WHERE TO STAY

CAMPING

Within the boundaries of the National Seashore, there is only backcountry camping—that is, sites only accessible by hiking, biking, horseback, kayak or boat. There is no car or RV camping within the park. Backcountry camping requires a permit, which can be obtained at the Bear Valley Visitor Center. The sites are in high demand; reservations are recommended and can be made up to three months in advance

(415-663-8054; Monday-Friday 9 a.m.-2 p.m.).

Point Reyes Hostel
Point Reyes National Seashore, 415-663-8811, 888-464-4872 ext. 191; www.norcalhostels.org/reyes/index.html

Besides backcountry camping, this is the only option for those who want to stay overnight in Point Reyes. The Hostel provides dormitory-style shared basic accommodations in both gender-specific and co-ed rooms, sleeping up to ten people each. With a fully equipped, self-service kitchen, outdoor patio, picnic tables, barbecue grill, baggage and bicycle storage, secure lockers and complimentary linens, this is very convenient and adequate lodging for many visitors.

Dorm rooms, one private room.

HOTELS

Just outside Point Reyes National Seashore

★★★**Manka's Inverness Lodge**
30 Callendar Way, Inverness, 415-669-1034; www.mankas.com

Though a fire destroyed much of the main lodge and restaurant in 2006 (famously survived by actors Jake and Maggie Gyllenhaal, who were staying here for the holidays at the time), the lodge is reopened and as wonderfully quirky and rustic as ever. Surrounded by national park land, this old-time lodge sits in the hills above a small coastal village. 18 rooms. Restaurant. $$$

★★★ The Pelican Inn
10 Pacific Way, Muir Beach,
415-383-6000;
www.pelicaninn.com
Whitewashed walls and leaded windows frame this English-flavored inn, where an authentic pub thrills any guests who manage to tear themselves away from the views overlooking the nearby stables. Just 12 miles from Point Reyes, this lovely lodge treats guests to classic comfort with an elegant and personal touch.
7 rooms. Complimentary full breakfast. Restaurant, bar. $$$

— ALSO RECOMMENDED —

The Continental Inn
26985 Highway 1, Tomales,
707-878-2396;
www.thecontinentalinn.com
This newly built property is a replica of the original turn-of-the-century hotel that stood in the same spot. The rooms are decorated in an old-fashioned country style, while offering modern amenities such as DVD players, pillow-top mattresses, electric fireplaces and more.
9 rooms, 1 suite. Wireless Internet access. $

Olema Druids Hall
9870 Shoreline Highway 1,
Olema, 415-663-8727,
866-554-4255;
www.olemadruidshall.com
This exquisite inn offers lavish, first-class amenities and handsome accommodations with all of the intimacy of a bed and breakfast. Guests are treated to radiant-heated hardwood floors,

large Jacuzzi tubs, wood-burning fireplaces, luxurious bedding, plush bathrobes, Aveda toiletries and wireless Internet access—all in their own tastefully decorated rooms. Breakfast is local and organic.
4 rooms, 1 cabin. Lodge closed winter; cottage open year-round. Wireless Internet access. Complimentary continental breakfast. $$

Point Reyes Country Inn & Stables
12050 Highway 1, Point Reyes Station, 415-663-9696;
www.ptreyescountryinn.com
In addition to the intimacy and privacy offered by this classic bed and breakfast, the inn boasts horse stables and a remarkable proximity to the National Seashore, providing guests with more options for recreation. The elegant rooms all feature tasteful décor and a private balcony or garden. Private cottages and rooms over the stables have full kitchens.
8 rooms, 2 cottages. Complimentary full breakfast. $$

Southeast of Point Reyes National Seashore
These lodging options are just across the Golden Gate Bridge from San Francisco, offering equally convenient access to the city, the outdoors and wine country.

★★ Acqua Hotel
555 Redwood Highway, Mill Valley, 415-380-0400,
888-662-9555;

★
★
★
★

www.marinhotels.com
Modern design, lavish amenities, breathtaking views of Mount Tam and abundant access to the outdoors all meet in this boutique hotel, making it a first-class lodging choice for those who don't mind the 45-minute drive to the Seashore. Besides the deluxe bedding, large tubs, and private balconies, guests at the Acqua will enjoy evening wine and cheese service, a morning espresso bar, a stocked in-room refrigerator and daily newspaper service among other extras.

49 rooms. High-speed Internet access. Complimentary continental breakfast. Fitness center. $$

★★★Casa Madrona Hotel & Spa
801 Bridgeway, Sausalito, 415-332-0502, 800-288-0502; www.casamadrona.com

High above Sausalito, this inn elegantly blends 19th-century Victorian and New England style with purely modern amenities and uniquely California views. Its prime location on Sausalito's charming Bridgeway Street lends easy access to high-end clothing shops, galleries, souvenirs and more. A world-class spa and upscale Italian restaurant, offering countless ways to relax, await after a busy day of exploration.

63 rooms. Complimentary continental breakfast. Restaurant, bar. Spa. $$$

★★★The Inn Above Tide
30 El Portal, Sausalito, 415-332-9535, 800-893-8433;

www.innabovetide.com
Built over the water, all rooms have fabulous views of the bay and San Francisco. Soothing contemporary décor and generous attention to detail includes evening wine and cheese reception, luxury bedding, deep soaking tubs and fireplaces in some rooms, complimentary continental breakfast room service, daily newspaper delivery and more.

29 rooms. Wireless Internet access. Complimentary continental breakfast. $$$

★★★The Mountain Home Inn
810 Panoramic Highway, Mill Valley, 415-381-9000; www.mtnhomeinn.com

This romantic getaway on Mount Tam sits high above San Francisco, offering panoramic views of the splendid city below. Enjoy a complimentary breakfast, indulge in an elegant dinner prepared by chef Sander Stuip and lounge in the wine bar before retiring to one of the quaint rooms with a private balcony, fireplace or Jacuzzi.

10 rooms. Wireless Internet access. Complimentary continental breakfast. Restaurant, bar. $$

★★Waters Edge Hotel
25 Main St., Tiburon, 415-789-5999, 877-789-5999; www.marinhotels.com

Just like its sister hotels (the Acqua Hotel and Mill Valley Inn), the Waters Edge offers divine digs for travelers. With evening wine and cheese service, crisp luxurious featherbeds, hand-knit throws, fireplaces in guest rooms, conti-

★

★

★

★

★

nental breakfast delivered to your room each morning and access to a nearby health club, no amenity is spared. Some rooms also provide private decks and views of San Francisco and Angels Island. 23 rooms. Wireless Internet access. Complimentary continental breakfast. Fitness center. $$$

— **ALSO RECOMMENDED** —

Hotel Sausalito

16 El Portal, Sausalito,
415-332-0700, 888-442-0700;
www.hotelsausalito.com

This romantic boutique hotel is calling the francophile's name, as each bright, sunny gem of a room feels as if it's just been touched by the French Riviera. Lavishly inviting beds, daily newspaper delivery and complimentary coffee and pastries in the morning make this a reposeful retreat.

16 rooms. Complimentary continental breakfast. $$

Mill Valley Inn

165 Throckmorton Ave., Mill
Valley, 415-389-6608,
800-595-2100;
www.marinhotels.com

This European-style inn has a cozy mill town setting and California-style written all over it. Original North Bay crafts tastefully decorate the cozy rooms. With redwoods just out the door and the area's best outdoor recreation under an hour's drive away, this comfortable lodge is a good choice for any traveler looking for outstanding service at a fair price. The room rate includes evening wine service, continental break-

fast, morning espresso and daily newspaper.

25 rooms and cottages. Wireless Internet access. Complimentary continental breakfast. $$

WHERE TO EAT

In Point Reyes National Seashore

— **ALSO RECOMMENDED** —

Drakes Beach Café

1 Drakes Beach Road, Point
Reyes National Seashore,
415-669-1297

Once another throw-away concession stand that made the smashed PBJ in your backpack sound pretty good, this café has recently come of age. Even given its unbeatable location, at the tip of the Point with every window showing a view of the water, the cuisine is now stealing the spotlight: a fresh seafood chowder made from the bounty of the region's sea and farms, smoked salmon and caper quesadillas, locally raised grass-fed beef burgers and freshly cut and fried russet potatoes replace the dime-a-dozen fare of the old days; and dinner here is a new experience altogether with more locally grown, organic sustainable ingredients populating the always changing prix-fixe menu with dishes like pan-seared scallops on a bed of shaved fennel with a huckleberry vinaigrette and locally raised lamb with hearty lentils and red wine. Wine is BYOB.

California menu. Lunch, dinner (Friday and Saturday by reservation only.) $$

119

POINT REYES

★★★Manka's Inverness Lodge

**30 Callendar Way, Inverness,
415-669-1034; www.mankas.com**
This acclaimed restaurant is back
in business after a fire destroyed
the dining room in late 2006.
Strictly devoted to fresh, local
ingredients, the kitchen creates
mouthwatering, simple California
cuisine, with dishes that change
nightly but could include lamb
grilled in the fireplace, served with
duck confit hash.
California menu. Dinner. Closed
Tuesday-Wednesday; first six
weeks of the year. $$$

★★Olema Inn

**10000 Sir Francis Drake Blvd.,
Olema, 415-663-9559;
www.theolemainn.com**
Committed to doing fine dining
the California way—that is, using
only the freshest local, organic
and sustainable ingredients—the
winter menu here features such
extraordinary gourmet creations
as pan-roasted Sonoma pheasant
with a creamy fresh black truffle
risotto and winter squash.
French menu. Dinner, weekend
brunch. Closed Tuesday. Outdoor
seating. $$$

★Station House Café

**11180 Highway 1, Point Reyes
Station, 415-663-1515;
www.stationhousecafe.com**
One of the most popular spots to
grab a bite in West Marin, this
casual eatery cooks up traditional
American cuisine with a Califor-

nia twist. Think oyster omelets for
breakfast and a fresh halibut club
sandwich with chipotle aioli for
lunch.
American menu. Breakfast, lunch,
dinner. Closed Wednesday. Bar.
Children's menu. Outdoor seat-
ing. $$

— ALSO RECOMMENDED —

Hog Island Oyster Company

**20215 Highway 1, Marshall,
415-663-9218;
www.hogislandoysters.com**
The Hog Island Oyster Company
has farmed top-notch West Coast
oysters in the Tomales Bay since
1982. Thanks to the bay's plank-
ton-rich seawater, the beds pro-
duce more than 3 million oysters
annually. The farm is also a lead-
ing advocate of sustainable and
responsible aquaculture. Visitors
can buy fresh oysters to go or to
shuck and slurp onsite—the farm
provides waterfront picnic tables,
shucking knives and barbecue
grills.
Oyster bar. Open 9 a.m.-5 p.m.;
closed Monday. Outdoor seating.

Southeast of Point Reyes
National Seashore

★★Buckeye Roadhouse

**15 Shoreline Highway, Mill Valley,
415-331-2600;
www.buckeyeroadhouse.com**
The Roadhouse first opened in
1937 but has managed to keep the
feel of the place fresh. Traditional
American fare is served with a
touch of California, as exempli-
fied by the brick oven–roasted
chicken stuffed with pasilla chili
and avocado salsa.

American, Californian menu. Lunch, dinner, Sunday brunch. Bar. Children's menu. Business casual attire. Reservations recommended. Valet parking. Outdoor seating. $$

★★Frantoio Ristorante & Olive Oil Co.
152 Shoreline Highway, Mill Valley, 415-289-5777; www.frantoio.com

An olive oil company opening an Italian restaurant must be a recipe for success. And salads can't get any fresher treatment than the champagne vinegar and oil that dress the spinach, bacon and ricotta salad at Frantoio's. Those greens paired with a simple margherita pizza topped with extra virgin olive oil might be the best possible way to meet your daily good fat quota.

Italian menu. Dinner. Bar. Business casual attire. Reservations recommended. Outdoor seating. $$

★★Guaymas
5 Main St., Tiburon, 415-435-6300; www.guaymasrestaurant.com

This upscale Mexican restaurant overlooks the bay, offering plenty of tables outside. The extensive menu lets diners choose from both traditional fare, like pork tamales, and more creative dishes, like a Pacific snapper sautéed with mushrooms, jalapenos, onions, tomatoes and garlic—all made with fresh ingredients.

Mexican menu. Lunch, dinner. Bar. Children's menu. Outdoor seating. $$

★★Horizons
558 Bridgeway, Sausalito, 415-331-3232; www.horizonssausalito.com

With a deck over the Bay, this California-style seafood restaurant screams family vacation stop. Its menu should have something to please everyone in the clan, from Dungeness crab salads to fish and chips to surf and turf.

Californian, seafood menu. Breakfast, lunch, dinner, Saturday-Sunday brunch. Bar. Children's menu. Valet parking. Outdoor seating. $$

★★Mountain Home Inn
810 Panoramic Way, Mill Valley, 415-381-9000; www.mtnhomeinn.com

The ever-changing menu at this California café focuses on the fresh and local, resulting in nearby Niman Ranch pork in a barbecue sandwich with house-cut fries and pale ale–battered local cod served with house-cut chips and a jalapeño remoulade. They dress dinner up a bit more with a three-course, prix-fixe menu that may look something like a goat cheese tort with pecans and grapes; followed by a flash-grilled steak with rosemary fries, green beans and mustard; and ending with a molten chocolate cake with blueberry sauce.

American menu. Breakfast, lunch (Wednesday-Sunday), dinner

★

★

★

★

★

(Wednesday-Sunday). Bar. Outdoor seating. $$

★★Scoma's
588 Bridgeway, Sausalito, 415-332-9551; www.scomassausalito.com
Overlooking the bay with an alfresco dining deck for nice northern California days, this Sausalito ristorante serves seafood classics with an Italian flair, like a pistachio-encrusted wild king salmon in a balsamic butter sauce or the Lazy Man's Cioppiono, a seafood stew of crab, prawns, clams, fish and bay shrimp in a tomato garlic and white wine broth.
Italian, seafood menu. Lunch, dinner. Bar. Children's menu. Outdoor seating. $$

★★Servino Ristorante
9 Main St., Tiburon, 415-435-2676; www.servino.com
Nothing hits the spot after a long day of activity than sitting down and relaxing for a hearty meal with a lovely view. Try a waterfront table at Servino's and the cannelloni al forno, a homemade pasta with ground veal, fresh ricotta and a red sauce.
Californian, Italian menu. Lunch, dinner, Sunday brunch. Bar. Children's menu. Outdoor seating. $$

★Winship Restaurant
670 Bridgeway, Sausalito, 415-332-1454; www.winships.com
This family-friendly eatery is California's answer for diner devotees. Its long menu's fare ranges from a prawn Caesar salad to a vegetarian burrito to a crab-and-swiss melt on sourdough to a New York steak.
California menu. Breakfast, lunch. Bar. Children's menu. Casual attire. Outdoor seating. $

— ALSO RECOMMENDED —
Venice Gourmet
625 Bridgeway, Sausalito, 415-332-3544; www.venicegourmet.com
In addition to a wide selection of made-to-order sandwiches, like the San Francisco club made with roast beef and cheddar, this deli also sells a variety of unusual wines, cheeses, sauces, oils, vinegars, teas and kitchen accessories.
Deli. Open 9 a.m.-6 p.m. $

SHENANDOAH NATIONAL PARK

DESPITE SHENANDOAH NATIONAL PARK'S SMALLER SIZE IN RELATION to other parks—196,000 acres along an 80 mile sliver of land ranging from just two to 13 miles across—it's still one of America's most popular parks. More than 1.6 million people visit each year, with 400,000 of those coming to see the brilliant foliage that bursts forth each autumn. Most of the area is wooded in white, red and chestnut oak, as well as birch, maple, hemlock and nearly 100 other species of trees. The park remains open during winter months, and while the foliage is long gone by then, the clear forest view is often ideal for spotting park wildlife.

Another reason for the park's success is its location just 75 miles from the Washington, D.C., area. In fact, the park has had a long history with those who wanted to enjoy the area or exploit it. Native Americans hunted and gathered food in the region before hunters and trappers slowly took over the area in the 1700s. Homesteaders soon followed, and through the early 1900s, the land was stripped of its natural resources. In 1926, Congress authorized Virginia to purchase 280 overly exploited acres, and the idea for Shenandoah, one of the first nature reclamation projects in the United States, was born. A total of 1,088 additional privately owned acres were bought and 465 families relocated outside the newly authorized park boundaries before Franklin Roosevelt officially established Shenandoah National Park in 1935.

Luray, Virginia, 540-999-3500; www.nps.gov/shen

WHAT TO SEE

Skyline Drive, which runs north-south along the crest of the Blue Ridge Mountains for the entire length of the park, is one of the finest scenic trips in the East. Three major highways cut the park into three distinct sections: the very northern section of the park lies between Route 340 and Route 211, the central section between Route 211 and Route 33 and the southern section between Route 33 and I-64. To minimize vehicle-wildlife collisions, the speed limit is 35 mph, guaranteeing a relaxing pace that lets you take in the sights.

The drive is well marked with mile markers that will guide your trip through Shenandoah; the northern Front Royal entrance is Mile 0.0, and the southern Rockfish Gap entrance is Mile 105. From the north, enter the park through the **Front Royal North Entrance Station** (from I-66 and

★
★
★
★

Highways 340, 522 and 55) before making a stop at the **Dickey Ridge Visitor Center** (Mile 4.7, 540-635-3566; open late March-late April and November, Thursday-Monday 8:30 a.m.-5 p.m.; late April-October, daily 8:30 a.m.-5 p.m.). In the central section, Park Headquarters and **Thornton Gap Entrance Station** are on Route 211, while Big Meadows, also known as the **Byrd Visitor Center**, is on Mile 51 of Skyline Drive (open late March-November, daily 8:30 a.m.-5 p.m.). **Swift Run Gap Entrance** (from Highway 33), **Loft Mountain Information Center** at Mile 79.5 (late May-early November, weekends and holidays 8:30 a.m.-5 p.m.) and the **Rockfish Gap Entrance Station** (from I-64 and Hwy 250 and the Blue Ridge Parkway) serve the park's southern section.

Once you've entered the park through one of the four entry points (a vehicle fee good for seven days is $15 March-November, $10 December-February), the best way to see the park is by driving through the three sections along the 105-mile **Skyland Drive**—Shenandoah's only public road. A whopping 75 overlooks along the way offer incredible scenic views of the Blue Ridge Mountains, Shenandoah Valley, the eastern Piedmont and the Alleghenies. Also take note of the unmowed area abutting Skyline Drive—this land is left uncut to enable growth of the myriad wildflowers native to the park.

In the beginning of the northern section, the **Shenandoah**

Valley Overlook (Mile 2.8) looks onto the Valley and the start to the Massanutten Mountains, which run southward through the valley for 55 miles. Further down the road, the **Hogback Overlook** (Mile 20.7), formed from remnant granite, is at 3,400 feet, the highest peak in the north portion of the park. The **Crescent Rock Overlook** (Mile 44) is the ideal spot to see the cliffs and slopes of Hawksbill Mountain, the highest point in the park at 4,051 feet. Named for Union officer General William B. Franklin, the **Franklin Cliffs Overlook** (Mile 49) gives visitors a good history lesson with a description of General Thomas Jackson's Confederate troop maneuvers during the Civil War. Near the end of the south section, drivers enjoy views of **Paine Run Hollow** and the Trayfoot and Rocks Mountains from the **Horsehead Mountain Overlook** (Mile 88.5).

Besides scenic overlooks, six picnic areas within the park offer grills and picnic tables for a meal alongside breathtaking views. Make time for a stop at **Dickey Ridge** (mile 4.7), **Elkwallow** (mile 24.1; open year-round), **Pinnacles** (mile 36.7; open year-round), **Lewis Mountain** (mile 57.5) or **South River** (mile 62.8; open year-round), all off Skyline Drive.

Besides panoramic vistas from elevated vantage points throughout the park, there are also a couple of specific sites to look for on your journey. Cascading 93 feet in two drops, **Overall Run Falls** (access parking at mile 22.2) is the

124

SHENANDOAH

highest waterfall in Shenandoah National Park, among a series of smaller falls you'll notice from Skyline Drive or from many of the hiking trails. Finally, to see one of a very small number of man-made sights in Shenandoah, **Corbin Cabin** in the park's central section, is a must-see. For a glimpse into early 20th-century life in the mountains, up the steep, 1.5-mile Corbin Cabin Cutoff Trail (mile 37) is a rustic log cabin built in 1909 by George Corbin. It was condemned in 1936 but saved after the park service took over the property. Today it is one of six cabins in Shenandoah and is available for short stays (contact the Potomac Appalachian Trail Club, 118 Park St. SE, Vienna, 703-242-0315; www.potomacappalachian.org).

WHAT TO DO

HIKING

Appalachian Trail

Perhaps one of the most well-known hiking trails in the United States, the Appalachian Trail slithers for 2,176 miles from Maine to Georgia. Shenandoah contains more than 101 miles of the fairly smooth trail that is accessible off of Skyline Drive. The park has 400 miles of other trails, from easy to difficult, spread along its length. Following is a sampling of what's available.

Fox Hollow (north)

1.2-mile loop

Trailhead: Across Skyline Drive from Dickey Ridge Visitor Center, Mile 4.6

In the north section, Fox Hollow Trail is an easy trail with a self-guiding tour including old homesites, farm fences and a cemetery.

Limberlost Trail (central)

1.3-mile loop

Trailhead: Parking area near Mile 43

Appropriate for all hiking levels, the Limberlost Trail follows a gentle grade as it passes through a hemlock forest, orchards and stands of mountain laurel.

Stony Man Nature Trail (central)

1.6-mile loop

Trailhead: Parking area at Mile 41.7

An upward amble along Stony Man Nature Trail ends at the cliffs of Stony Man's Summit. From 4,011 feet, the second-highest point in the park, the views of the Shenandoah Valley from atop the rocky cliffs are unparalleled.

── MODERATE ──

Big Devils Stairs (north)

5.4 miles round-trip

Trailhead: Gravel Springs Gap parking area at Mile 17.6; take Appalachian Trail to Gravel Springs Hut, head east on Bluff Trail; after crossing Big Devils Stairs Gorge take Big Devils Stairs Trail south.

125

SHENANDOAH

For a slightly more difficult trek, the Big Devils Stairs Trail covers 5.4 miles of great canyon, stream and cascade views.

Hightop Summit (south)
3.6 miles round-trip
Trailhead: Park at Smith Roach Gap, Mile 69.9; start on the fire road for 30 feet, then follow the white blazes of the Appalachian Trail.

In late spring, wildflower fans flock to the Hightop Summit Trail (Mile 66.7) to see blooming flowers as well as great views of the tallest peaks in the park's south section.

——— STRENUOUS ———
Rocky Mount-Gap Run (south)
9.6 miles round-trip
Trailhead: Mile 76.2; park just south of trailhead at Two Mile Run Overlook.

For a real workout, the Rocky Mount Trail is a 6.9-mile round-trip climb to 2,739 feet (total elevation change of 1,600 feet), ending on the summit with vistas that span from Two Mile Ridge to Rocky Mountain and the Blue Ridge.

Whiteoak Canyon Trail (central)
4.6 miles round-trip
Trailhead: Parking area at Mile 42.6

The Whiteoak Canyon Trail, ascending 1,040 feet, is a challenging climb but rewards hikers with views of a gorge stream and an 86-foot waterfall (the second highest in the park).

RANGER PROGRAMS

Go straight to the experts to learn about and experience everything the park has to offer. The Live Birds of Prey program gives guests a chance to meet owls and raptors up close while learning about their habitats. Ranger's Choice Talks are a series of informative lectures that can include anything from the park's bears to wildflowers. For a more active experience, take a ranger-led walk or sign up the little ones to become Junior Rangers—a 1.5-hour program in the spring, summer and fall with hands-on activities for kids ages 7–12. (Check out www.nps.gov/shen/planyourvisit/rangerprograms.htm for more times, schedules and information.)

HORSEBACK RIDING

Exploring the park on horseback is a great way to experience Shenandoah, and there are more than 180 miles of trails open to horse owners. Alternatively, the Skyland Stables (Skyland Drive, Mile 42.5, 540-999-2212 advance, 540-999-2210 same-day; late March-November) can arrange guided rides along forest trails. Pony rides are available for children under 4'10". (For more information, check out www.nps.gov/shen/planyourvisit/horseback_riding.htm or www.visitshenandoah.com.)

CAVERNS

Going underground is a great way to explore Shenandoah—the

★
★
★
★
★

region is dotted with large caves worth seeing. At **Luray Caverns** (970 W. Highway 211/340, Luray, 540-743-6551; www.luraycaverns.org), natural corridors connect huge cathedral-like rooms (one is 300 feet wide and 500 feet long with a soaring 140-foot ceiling) that occupy 64 underground acres. Colorful rock formations, some as delicate as lace, drip like melting wax from the ceilings and walls. **Skyline Caverns** (10344 Stonewall Jackson Highway, Front Royal, 540-635-4545, 800-296-4545; www.skylinecaverns.com) boasts rare white-spiked calcite orchids that cling to the cave, and colorful lighting emphasizes the rocky caverns. The **Grand Caverns Regional Park** (Dogwood Ave., Grottoes, 540-249-5705, 888-430-2283; www.uvrpa.org) has Civil War–era graffiti from Confederate and Union soldiers scrawled on the walls.

WILDLIFE

Hosting a wide array of animals, Shenandoah is a sanctuary that makes for great wildlife viewing.
Mammals: More than 50 species of mammals live in Shenandoah National Park, including some that are abundant and easy to spot from the park trails and overlooks. Keep an eye out for **white-tailed deer**, **gray squirrels** and **striped skunks.** Other, seldom seen animals include the **shrew** and **bobcat**. Bears are one of the park's mammal success stories: Nearly eliminated in the early 1900s, today there are hundreds

thanks to better management and ecological conditions.
Fish: Besides the **bluehead chub** and **fantail darter**, **brook trout** are one of the 30-plus species of fish that thrive here. In fact, these trout live in more than 50 of the nearly 100 streams running through the park due to the cool, clear waters that they prefer.

BIRDS

Ranging from **barred owls** and **red-tailed hawks** to **warblers** and **Carolina chickadees**, birds are by far the largest group of animals with more than 200 transient and resident species represented in the park. The most common woodpecker, the small and usually friendly **downy**, is a year-round park resident and one of the few birds seen in the area during the winter. Much rarer, the brightly colored **scarlet tanager** is a bird-watcher's prize sighting.

WHERE TO STAY

CAMPING

There are four campgrounds within the park. Closest to the north entrance, the **Mathews Arm Campground** (Mile 22.1; $15 per night; open late May-October) is just miles from Overall Run Falls and Elkwallow Wayside. For a more secluded site, **Big Meadows** (Mile 51.2; $20 per night during reservation season, $17 per night in late spring and early fall; open late March-November) is located further into the park near three waterfalls and the Meadow. **Lewis Mountain** (Mile 57.5; $15 per night; open mid-April to October) is first-come, first-served. It's the smallest of the campgrounds but offers a great opportunity to feel somewhat alone without having to head deep into the backcountry. Atop Big Flat Mountain, **Loft Mountain** (Mile 79.5; $15 per night; open mid-May to October) is the biggest campsite. It has great views, two nearby waterfalls and trails into the Big Run Wilderness. Reservations can be made for all sites, except Lewis Mountain, by calling 877-444-6777 or online at www.recreation.gov. Campers are also free to explore the park's 196,000 acres of backcountry. Free permits to set up a site away from the four campgrounds are available during business hours at a visitor contact station. For more information, check out www.nps.gov/shen/planyourvisit/camping.htm.

HOTELS

Luray

★★Big Meadows Lodge
Skyline Drive, Mile 51.2, Luray,
540-999-2221, 888-896-3833;
www.visitshenandoah.com
Located right in the park, guests will enjoy the panoramic views of Shenandoah Valley, and the numerous accessible hiking trails nearby. Plan on a good night's sleep—beds are comfortable, and rooms have no phones or Internet to keep you awake (a few rooms have TVs).

97 rooms, suites and cabins. Closed early November-late April. Restaurant, bar. **$**

★Luray Caverns Motel West
1001 W. Highway 211, Luray,
540-743-6551, 888-941-4531;
www.luraycaverns.com
Near the west entrance to the Luray Caverns and Shenandoah, this colonial-style motel has awesome views of the Blue Ridge Mountains and the park. Rooms are large and inexpensive.
20 rooms. Complimentary continental breakfast. Pool. **$**

★★Skyland Resort
Skyline Drive, Mile 41.7, Luray,
540-999-2211, 888-896-3833;
www.visitshenandoah.com
Next to Whiteoak Canyon Falls, Skyland's rustic cabins, lodge rooms and suites are 3,700 feet above the Shenandoah Valley and have incredible valley views. First opened as a dude ranch in the late 1800s, Skyland still offers guests a range of activities, from horseback riding to nature hikes. At night, grab a glass of legal Moonshine in the bar before heading back to your quarters. Rooms have no phones.
177 rooms, suites and cabins. Closed December-late March. Restaurant, bar. Pets accepted. **$**

— ALSO RECOMMENDED —
Cabins at Brookside
2978 E. Highway 211, Luray,
540-743-5698, 800-299-2655;
www.brooksidecabins.com
The privacy and seclusion of your own log cabin is the draw to this

vacation development located 4.5 miles from the entrance to Skyline Drive. The cabins have plush country décor and front porches, and are set into the quiet woods; they have no TVs or phones to disturb your rural retreat. A cozy restaurant on the property serves home-style food.

9 cabins. Restaurant. $

Mayneview Bed and Breakfast

439 Mechanic St., Luray,
540-743-7921;
www.mayneview.com

This historic Victorian inn is nestled in the heart of the Shenandoah Valley and has a wonderful wraparound porch. Built in 1865 for use as a hunting lodge, it also served as a station for the underground railroad during the Civil War. Rooms are cozy and furnished with antiques. Visitors can take day trips to the famous Luray Caverns, the New Market Battlefield and nearby shops.

5 rooms. Give advance notice of children under 6. Complimentary full breakfast. Pets accepted. $

Harrisonburg

★Hampton Inn

85 University Blvd., Harrisonburg,
540-432-1111, 800-426-7866;
www.hamptoninn.com

This traditional hotel (offering free breakfast and drinks) is located just off I-81 and is close to several college campuses and historic battlefields. Skyline Drive and Blue Ridge Parkway are also nearby.

163 rooms. Wireless Internet access. Complimentary continental breakfast. Fitness center. Pool. Business center. $

★★The Village Inn

4979 S. Valley Pike, Harrisonburg,
540-434-7355, 800-736-7355;
www.thevillageinn.info

This well-maintained motel is located in a rural setting and has a children's play area, an outdoor pool and whirlpool, shuffleboard, a walking trail and a creek at the back of the property. A country buffet breakfast is served Monday through Saturday.

37 rooms and suites. High-speed Internet access. Restaurant. Pool, whirlpool. Pets accepted. $

Luray

★Brookside

2978 E. Highway 211, Luray,
540-743-5698, 800-299-2655;
www.brooksidecabins.com

The home-style cooking and freshly baked bread and desserts make the Brookside a local favorite. Service is quick and friendly, and the menu selection is extensive. After a meal of everything from homemade soup to peanut butter pie, diners are sure to go away satisfied. Lunch and dinner buffets are offered daily with breakfast buffets as well on the weekends.

American menu. Breakfast, lunch, dinner. Closed four weeks in December. Children's menu. Casual attire. $

SHENANDOAH

★
★
★
★
★

★Parkhurst

2547 W. Highway 211, Luray,
540-743-6009

Situated near the Luray Caverns, this restaurant is known for its exceptional service and great food (everything from steak to homemade pies). There's also an adjacent wine shop, so you can stock up for later. The restaurant wine list includes some local selections. American menu. Lunch, dinner. Bar. Casual attire. Outdoor seating. $

— ALSO RECOMMENDED —

Artisan Grill

2 E. Main St., Luray,
540-743-7030;
www.artisansgrill.com

At this casual restaurant located next door to an art gallery, dishes are named after famous artists: the Rembrandt is a hot corned beef with Swiss cheese sandwich, while a Gaugin is mozzarella, tomato, basil and vinaigrette on whole-grain bread. It also serves burgers, soups and salads.

American menu. Lunch, dinner. Casual attire. $

Southern Station Diner

915 E. Main St., Luray,
540-743-6001

This simple down-home diner is a local favorite. Breakfast is served any time of day, and the big homemade meals like cheese steak, pancakes or eggs are always popular choices.

American menu. Breakfast, lunch, dinner. Casual attire. $

Harrisonburg

★★Village Inn Restaurant

4979 South Valley Pike,
Harrisonburg, 540-434-7355,
800-736-7355;
www.thevillageinn.travel

Attached to the Village Inn and located on a semirural road off I-81, this comfortable, family-friendly restaurant specializes in home-style country cooking. Known for its country breakfast buffets, which include country sausage and the less commonly seen scrapple, the third-generation-owned Village Inn is a great escape from the typical interstate restaurants. Lunch is served buffet-style as well.

American menu. Breakfast, lunch, dinner. Closed Sunday. Casual attire. $$

— ALSO RECOMMENDED —

Cally's Restaurant & Brewing Co.

41-A Court Square, Harrisonburg,
540-434-8777;
www.callysbrewing.com

This downtown microbrewery is a great place to come for beers and pub grub like burgers and sandwiches after a day in the park. It's open seven days a week and has a great brunch on Sundays (10 a.m.–2 p.m.).

American menu. Lunch, dinner, Sunday brunch. Bar. Casual attire. $

Joshua Wilton House

412 S. Main St., Harrisonburg,
540-434-4464, 888-294-5866;
www.joshuawilton.com

A great upscale restaurant set in a historic Victorian home in the old town, the Joshua Wilton House has an indoor dining room with a cozy fireplace and an outdoor eating area. Local farmers supply the restaurant with the freshest ingredients for dishes, including corn husk–wrapped salmon, crispy quail and chicken parmesan. Wash it down with wine from the extensive list boasting more than 100 vintages.

American menu. Dinner. Closed Sunday-Monday. Bar. Business casual attire. Outdoor seating. $$

SHENANDOAH

★
★
★
★
★

THEODORE ROOSEVELT NATIONAL PARK

★

★

★

★

★

THIS NATIONAL PARK WAS ESTABLISHED IN 1947 AS A MONUMENT TO the 26th U.S. president, Theodore Roosevelt, who first came to the badlands of North Dakota in September 1883 to hunt buffalo and other large game. He eventually became interested in the open-range cattle industry and purchased an interest in the Maltese Cross Ranch near Medora, then returned a year later and established another ranch, the Elkhorn, about 35 miles north of the small cattle town. The demands of his political career and failures at raising cattle eventually forced him to abandon his ranching ventures, but he often cited his experiences in the rugged North Dakota region as the main reason he was able to become president. While in the Badlands, Roosevelt witnessed firsthand how overgrazing was destroying the grassland and hunting was wiping out several species of animals, including the bison that he originally came to catch. As president, he took the knowledge he'd gleaned during his time in the west to develop conservation programs and champion the preservation of America's natural resources through the creation of five national parks.

This park preserves his efforts as well as the magnificent badlands landscape as Roosevelt knew it. Wind and water have carved curiously sculptured formations, tablelands, buttes, canyons and rugged hills from a thick series of flat-lying multihued sedimentary rocks, which were first deposited here by waters flowing from the freshly risen Rocky Mountains between 55 and 60 million years ago. Thick, dark layers of lignite coal, which are sometimes fired by lightning and burn slowly for many years, are exposed in eroded hillsides. The blazes often bake adjacent clay layers into a red, bricklike substance called scoria, or "clinker," adding to the badland's amazing palette of color.

The park is unique in that its sections are not connected; substantial distance lies between the two main units. The North Unit is located 70 miles above the South Unit. Between the two sections lies the small Elkhorn Ranch Unit, which connects to the South Unit via gravel roads. The Little Missouri River must be forded to reach Elkhorn Ranch, so check with a visitor center for directions and current river depth information before you head out.

Medora, North Dakota, 701 623-4466 (South Unit); Highway 85, 16 miles south of Watford City, North Dakota, 701-842-2333 (North Unit); www.nps.gov/thro

WHAT TO SEE

Due to the park's divided geography, it's best to choose either the South Unit, characterized by its paved roads, scenic drives and series of overlooks, or the North Unit, the less developed and more rugged of the two, to explore in a single day. Be on the lookout for landmarks, as there is rich history in the park and the surrounding towns.

South Unit

To explore the more developed South Unit, start at the **Medora Visitor Center** (I-94, exits 24 and 27 at Medora, 701-623-4466; open year-round, 8:00 a.m.-4:30 p.m., with extended summer hours). Picture President Roosevelt living in his **Maltese Cross Cabin**, the three-room ranch he had built in about 1883 (open for self-guided tours September-May). Originally constructed near the Missouri River, the cabin has since been relocated here, and contains some of the original household items Roosevelt used, as well as additional artifacts from the same period. Past the cabin, follow the park road to the **Medora Overlook** for a view of its namesake town, which was established in 1883 as a cattle hub just months before Roosevelt arrived in the

Badlands. Next, make time for a stop at the **prairie dog town** (one of three dog towns in the South Unit) to the east of the park road, where these squirrel cousin critters bark out warnings to each other while popping in and out of their underground network of burrows. Heading further north, the **Skyline Vista** demonstrates how the badlands formed, with views of the flat prairie that drops off into the eroded badlands below, followed by the **River Woodland Overlook** with views of the erosion-causing Little Missouri River. Veering toward the right, the 36-mile **Scenic Loop Drive** begins its route around the park, with its first overlook at **Scoria Point,** where the ancient volcanic ejecta, scoria (otherwise known in the park as "clinker"), tinted the earth. Further along the loop, the **North Dakota Badlands Overlook** has another spectacular scenic view before the road begins a long backstretch, which passes several popular hiking trails as well as prairie dog towns. At the northernmost tip of the Scenic Loop, you can access the Third Unit of the park, **Elkhorn Ranch**, via a 20-mile dirt road (inquire at the visitors center or call for specific directions and road conditions). Continuing on the loop toward Cottonwood and back to the Medora Visitor Center, you'll pass **Peaceful Valley**, an 1880s ranch near the beginning of the Loop Drive and the park entrance.

133

THEODORE ROOSEVELT

Exit the park and head 7 miles east of Medora on I-94 to the **Painted Canyon Visitor Center** (I-94, exit 32, 701-575-4020; April to mid-November, daily 8:30 a.m.-4:30 p.m. with extended summer hours). At the most visited site in the park, an overlook treats visitors to unparalleled panoramic vistas of the Badlands that stretch as far as the eye can see, exhibiting the spectacular range of colors for which the area is named. For an especially beautiful, kaleidoscope-colored view, go near sunrise or sunset. Keep your eyes out for wild horses, elk and bison as they frequently roam the grounds of the Painted Canyon.

North Unit

From Painted Canyon, head north on U.S. 85 for about 70 miles to the **North Unit Visitor Center** (701 842-2333; year-round, 9 a.m.-5:30 pm). Because of its isolated location, unspoiled wilderness expanses and limited road, it's arguably the most beautiful unit of the park—and one which avid hikers prefer for its rugged trails and, in winter, snowshoeing sites. From the visitor center, be on the lookout for longhorn steers as you begin the scenic drive that runs 14 miles from east to west. After around three and a half miles on the drive, the **Slump Block Pull-out** is the first notable stop. In the distance, giant blocks of bluff have slowly slid, or "slumped," from the steep canyon walls to the valley below. This geographic process took place as sediment underneath the top-heavy pieces

gradually eroded away. Other fascinating and unique results of this erosion can be seen at the next two stops, the **Cannonball Concretions Pullout**'s sandstone spheres and the **Caprock Coulee Pullout**'s pedestal rocks. Aptly named, the formations at these sites look as though a sculptor might have carved them carefully, when in fact the erosion process is solely responsible for their beauty. Past these famous formations, the road meanders toward a switch-back to the **River Bend Overlook,** where the Little Missouri Valley can be seen flanked by the Badlands. The road eventually gives way to grassy plateaus before ending at the **Oxbow Overlook** for yet another unforgettable Badlands vista.

WHAT TO DO

HIKING

Theodore Roosevelt National Park contains more than 100 miles of hiking trails for everyone from novice to experienced hikers. Take plenty of water with you, and give bison a wide berth.

South Unit

──────── **EASY** ────────

Coal Vein Trail
0.8-mile loop
Trailhead: Off Scenic Loop Drive just north of Paddock Creek.
The 0.8-mile Coal Vein Trail at Mile 15.6 runs along a seam of coal that was ignited decades ago and blazed from 1951 to 1977. It

gives a perfect up-close demonstration of how the kiln-like process created the area's red-tinted scoria.

Wind Canyon Trail

0.5 miles round-trip

Trailhead: Northwestern corner of Scenic Loop Drive.

Hikers reaching the bluff tops of the steep Wind Canyon Trail will appreciate the Little Missouri River view. The northwest-facing canyon shows how the trail got its name—over time, winds whipping up Badland debris have sandblasted the canyon rock into its current smooth formation.

——————— MODERATE ———————

Buck Hill

0.5 miles round-trip

Trailhead: Scenic Loop Drive between North Dakota Badlands and Boicourt Overlooks.

Just north of the Painted Canyon, the trek up the steep paved path to Buck Hill yields 360-degree views from this 2,855-foot incline.

Jones Creek Trail

3.7 miles, 7.4 miles round-trip

Trailheads: Scenic Loop Drive, parking areas just north of Boicourt Overlook and just south of Beef Corral Bottom.

For a more challenging trail, try the Jones Creek Trail. It snakes through a usually dry creek bed that runs through eroded buttes in the heart of the badlands.

Painted Canyon Trail

0.9-mile loop

Trailhead: Painted Canyon picnic area

See the Painted Canyon's colorful buttes up close on this trail that descends the canyon wall.

North Unit

——————— EASY ———————

Little Mo Nature Trail

1.1-mile loop

Trailhead: Juniper Campground

This self-guided nature trail travels through badlands and river woodlands where hikers may see deer and beaver. The trail guide is available at the trailhead or on the park Web site.

——————— MODERATE ———————

Buckhorn Trail Loop

11-mile loop

Trailhead: Caprock Coulee Nature Trailhead

Accessed from the Caprock Coulee Nature Trailhead, the 11-mile Buckhorn Trail Loop passes by a prairie dog town about a mile into the loop. Set aside a half or full day for this hike.

Upper Caprock Coulee Trail

3.3-mile loop, 4.1-mile loop with Caprock Coulee Nature Trail

Trailhead: 1.5 miles west of Juniper Campground.

A challenging trek, the Caprock Coulee Trail winds through coulees, or dry water gulches, that cut into the grassy plains. The nature trail section is self-guided.

135

THEODORE ROOSEVELT

★
★
★
★
★

GUIDED TOURS

Listen to a 20-minute ranger talk on topics that change daily from mid-June to Labor Day (Medora Visitor Center), gather around for an evening campfire lecture at Cottonwood or Juniper Campground (mid-June to September) or head to Roosevelt's one-story pine home, Maltese Cross Cabin just behind the Medora Visitor Center (September-May) for a tour. A few of the president's personal possessions are still inside the cabin, including a rocking chair and writing hutch. For a longer excursion, half-day hikes with rangers throughout the badlands include visits to more remote areas like the Elkhorn Ranch site.

THEODORE ROOSEVELT

RIDING

Horseback riding enthusiasts can bring their own horses into the park or schedule a ride with the Peaceful Valley Ranch/Shadow Country Outfitters from May to September (701-623-4568; www.home.ctctel.com/peacefulvalley). The ranch can accommodate riders of all skill levels (some restrictions apply). A basic tour lasts about an hour and a half and includes informative talks on the park's history and wildlife. For more experienced riders, a daybreak ride begins at 7:30 a.m. and lasts anywhere from two and a half to five hours—a great way to see the park without having to hike it.

WILDLIFE

Theodore Roosevelt National Park is full of interesting wildlife. What you see depends on where you're at in the park, the season—and luck.

Prairie dogs: Prairie dogs are a perennial favorite of visitors to the Theodore Roosevelt National Park. There are five species of this member of the squirrel family, but only the black-tailed prairie dog lives in the park. A family of these social animals makes its home in about an acre of interconnected underground burrows called a coterie. Prairie dogs are able to identify members of their own family by "kissing" or sniffing each other. They warn others of potential threats, like humans, through high-pitched squeaks, or barks. Three large prairie dog towns are spread around the South Unit, while in the North Unit, the animals can be found by taking a one-mile hike that starts at the Caprock Coulee parking lot.

Wild horses: Escaped horses brought by Spanish settlers in the 16th century eventually formed herds that could number well into the thousands. These mustangs are known as feral horses, which means they're related to domesticated stock. Used by Plains Indians to hunt buffalo, the horses ran wild through the region until the middle of the 1800s, when ranchers and cattlemen settling the area considered them a nuisance and largely exterminated the herds. Preservation efforts began in the 1950s, and today the park maintains between 70 and 110 feral horses. They stick mainly to the South Unit's eastern section at Painted Canyon. **Bison:** With their massive heads and humped backs, bison are the park's most exciting animals to see. Lumbering throughout the park, this member of the cow family is the largest mammal in North America and can weigh as much as 2,000 pounds when fully grown. Once estimated to number in the tens of millions on America's plains and prairies, westward expansion proved deadly for these giant animals, as explorers and hunters killed them for sport, food and their hides. By the early 1900s, as few as 300 remained in the wild. The government recognized the threat of extinction and passed laws in 1894 that led to the protection of the species. Today, more than 125,000 of the herbivores roam the United States, including 200–400 in Theodore Roosevelt National Park's South Unit and 100–300 in the North Unit.

Prairie rattlesnakes: "Rattlesnakes are only too plentiful everywhere; along the river bottoms, in the broken, hilly ground, and on the prairies and the great desert wastes alike," wrote Theodore Roosevelt during his time in the Badlands. Today they still slither throughout the region and often make their homes in deserted prairie dog holes. The park's only poisonous reptile, prairie rattlesnakes only attack if provoked.

BIRDS

Of the 186 species of birds detected in Theodore Roosevelt National Park, you're likely to see some of the more common ones, such as the chickenlike **sharp-tailed grouse** and **ring pheasant**, as well as the spectacular **great blue heron** with its six-foot wing span. Some of the rarer species can be spotted, depending on the season. While the **golden eagle** is fairly common throughout the year, the **prairie falcon** is only occasionally seen during winter, and the famed **bald eagle** is most likely to be seen—if at all—during its spring and fall migrations.

WHERE TO STAY

CAMPING

The **Juniper Campground** is the only camping area serving the North Unit. The 50 campsites and the pull-through RV sites are filled on a first-come, first-served basis. Water and restrooms (but no showers) are available throughout the campground May-September. Fees are $10 May-September, $5 October-April. Additionally, one large site for seven to 60 people is available by reservation (701-842-2333).

The South Unit has two sites open year-round. The **Cottonwood Campground** is first-come, first-served and has 76 sites, including many RV pull-through sites. Water and restrooms (but no showers) are available May-

THEODORE ROOSEVELT

★

★

★

★

September. Fees are $10 May-September, $5 October-April. There is also a group site for seven to 20 people (701-623-4730 ext. 3417) at one end of the campground.

The **Roundup Horse Campground,** a single site available for just one group (20 people with 20 horses or 30 people without horses, minimum of six people), is open May-October. Usage is limited to five nights per year. Reservations must be made by fax or mail (for details, see www.nps.gov/thro/planyourvisit/roundup-group-horse-campground.htm).

Backcountry camping is allowed with a free permit obtained at one of the park's visitor centers. For the South Unit and Elkhorn Ranch, permits can be picked up at the Medora Visitor Center; for North Unit camping, they're available at the North Unit Visitor Center.

HOTELS

North Unit

★**Comfort Inn**
493 Elk Drive, Dickinson, 701-264-7300, 877-424-6423;
www.comfortinn.com
Families with kids will appreciate the large indoor water park that includes a two-story spiral slide and hot tub, as well as the suite-style accommodations. Rooms are well priced, and the hotel's side street location—less than an hour from the heart of the park's South Unit—makes for a good night's sleep.

115 units. High-speed Internet access. Complimentary continental breakfast. Fitness center. Pool. Pets accepted. $

South Unit

★**AmericInn Medora**
75 E. River Road S., Medora,
701-623-4800, 800-396-5007;
www.americinn.com
Conveniently located just a mile from the park in the restored cattle town of Medora, this affordable chain hotel offers spacious rooms, some with microwaves and refrigerators.
52 rooms, 2 suites. Wireless Internet access. Complimentary continental breakfast. Pool. $

—— **ALSO RECOMMENDED** ——
Days Inn-Grand Dakota Lodge
532 W. 15th St. Dickinson,
701-483-5600, 800-329-7466;
www.daysinn.com
With its welcoming lobby fireplace and onsite Red Pheasant Restaurant, the hotel promises a true "lodge" experience with spacious rooms that were renovated in 2005. The Grand Dakota Lodge is convenient for nighttime dining after a day exploring the park's South Unit just 35 miles to the west.
149 units. High-speed Internet access. Complimentary continental breakfast. Restaurant. Fitness center. Pool. Business center. Pets accepted. $

★

★

★

★

★

Roosevelt Inn

600 Second Ave. SW (Highway 85 West), Watford City, 701-842-3686, 800-887-9170; www.rooseveltinn.com

Just 15 minutes from the park, the Roosevelt Inn has a number of affordable room options, including a suite suitable for families featuring three double beds and two bathrooms. For more deluxe accommodations, request one of the two new suites with Jacuzzi, fireplace and large-screen TV. The inn was renovated to include an indoor pool.

46 rooms, 4 suites. High-speed Internet access. Pool. $

Rough Riders Hotel

301 Third Ave., Medora, 701-623-4444, 800-633-6721

Antique furnishings outfit the small rooms at this hotel near the park, but there's more to its history than just tables and chairs. Originally built in 1884, the structure now housing the hotel was frequented by Theodore Roosevelt and served as a stop on his 1900 campaign trail. Since then, the building has served as a restaurant, café and bar before being refurbished in 1962 into its current Rough Riders Hotel state. 9 rooms. Open mid-April to early September. $

WHERE TO EAT

North Unit

— ALSO RECOMMENDED —

TJ's Pizza and Suds

605 Main St. S., Watford City, 701-842-2771

Go to TJ's for variety in the menu and reliable staples: This family restaurant serves up hearty dinners like goulash and baby back ribs (with soup or salad, potato, vegetable and dessert). If you visit during lunch, try the pizza or one of the hot subs, including cheese steak, meatball and hot sausage. American menu. Breakfast, lunch, dinner. Casual attire. $

South Unit

— ALSO RECOMMENDED —

The Cowboy Café

215 Fourth St., Medora, 701-623-4343

A line of American flags wave outside the two-story rustic wooden building that houses the Cowboy Café. On the inside, cowboy pictures and old-fashioned tin cups, plates and utensils line the walls. The service is friendly, and the pies—including ground cherry, sour cream raisin and peach—are always a treat for dessert. American menu. Meals. Casual attire. $

Little Missouri Saloon & Dining

440 Third St., Medora, 701-623-4404

Enjoy the friendly service and great bar food at this local favorite. When you're through with

139

THEODORE ROOSEVELT

your meal, head downstairs and sidle up to the bar to enjoy the live music during weekends in the summer.

American menu. Meals. Bar. Casual attire. **$**

Pitchfork Steak Fondue
Tjaden Terrace, Medora

At this popular restaurant steaks are cooked on pitchfork skewers and served with fondue dipping sauces such as horseradish, curry and mustard crème, and are served with homemade potato chips and fresh salads. Lemon bars are the perfect dessert afterward.

Steak menu. Dinner. Closed early September-May. Children's menu. Casual attire. **$**

Rough Riders Dining Room
301 Third Ave., Medora,
701-623-4444

In the historic restored Rough Riders Hotel built circa 1880, dining in this restaurant, with its antique furnishings and western-style food, is like stepping back to the turn of the century. The restaurant also has an impressive past: Theodore Roosevelt used to dine here on his frequent trips through Medora. It's also one of the only fine-dining establishments in town.

American menu. Meals. Closed Labor Day-Memorial Day. **$$**

140

YELLOWSTONE AND GRAND TETON NATIONAL PARKS

THE WORLD'S FIRST NATIONAL PARK, 3,000 SQUARE MILES OF RAMBLING wilderness open to exploration since 1872, welcomes visitors from all over the globe through its five entrances in three states (Wyoming, Montana and Idaho) onto 370 miles of scenic public roads. You'll travel past impressive granite peaks and through lodgepole pine forests that open onto meadows dotted with wildflowers and elk. Beyond the beautiful panorama, Yellowstone boasts a marvelous list of sights and attractions: a big freshwater lake that ranks as the largest in North America at high elevation (7,733 feet); a waterfall almost twice as high as Niagara; a dramatic, 1,200-foot-deep river canyon; and the world's most famous geyser, Old Faithful.

Long before its beauty was world renowned, as many as 11,000 years ago, Native Americans began to explore the area. In fact, there's evidence that they created the park's first trail system, now known as the Bannock Trail, to give them better access to the plant, animal and mineral resources of the area. Portions of it are still visible. John Colter of the Missouri Fur Trading Company, who had been a member of the Lewis and Clark party, is believed to be the first non-Native American to explore the area, including Yellowstone Lake, as he sought trade partnerships with several area tribes. Another trapper, Jim Bridger, who was famous for telling a good tall tale, told stories of Yellowstone's "rivers that ran so fast they got hot on the bottom" and places where he can see "Hell bubbling up." His tales were dismissed as lies.

Today more than 3 million visitors and some 4,300 employees a year could attest that some rivers in Yellowstone do run warm and mud does spontaneously bubble up from the ground. In spite of the swarming summer crowds that traipse over its 1,100 miles of trails each year, most of Yellowstone has been left in its natural state, with 97 percent of the park's 2.2 million acres undeveloped, preserving the area's beauty and delicate ecological balance. Yellowstone is one of the world's most suc-

YELLOWSTONE/GRAND TETON

cessful wildlife sanctuaries, drawing many tourists solely for the animal-viewing opportunities the park offers. More wild animals live in Yellowstone than almost any other place in the country. Within its boundaries are a wide variety of species, including grizzly and black bears, elk, deer, pronghorn antelope and bison.

Besides intimate encounters with wildlife, Yellowstone also gives geology buffs close-up looks at the Continental Divide, Yellowstone Volcano, and much more. It's a playground for nature lovers of all kinds.

N.E. Entrance Road and Grand Loop Road, Cody, Wyoming, 307-344-7381; www.nps.gov/yell

WHAT TO SEE

The **Grand Loop Road**, a main access way within the park, winds approximately 140 miles past many major points of interest.

From the North Entrance, it begins in the Mammoth Area. Take it five miles south along the Gardiner River to reach the **Mammoth Hot Springs**. There, the park headquarters and museum (open year-round) are stationed in buildings built by the U.S. Cavalry to house the Army troops who protected the park before the creation of the National Park Service in 1916. **The Albright Visitor Center** provides a general overview of the natural and human history of the park. Naturalist-guided walks through the springs are conducted on boardwalks over the terraces (summer).

Where the Grand Loop crosses the Gardiner River, there is a sign marking the **45th parallel** of latitude, the midway point between the equator and the North Pole. A parking lot on the east side of the road is designated for visitors who'd like to take a dip in the **Boiling River**, a large hot spring. Bathing is allowed only in the des-ignated spot, which is about a half mile along the trail from the parking area, where the spring enters the Gardiner River and creates clouds of steam. The hot spring is closed in spring when water levels are dangerously high.

The **Norris Geyser Basin**, 21 miles south of Mammoth Hot Springs, is the hottest thermal basin in the world, sitting on the intersection of three major faults. It provides a multitude of displays; springs, geysers, mud pots and steam vents hiss, bubble and erupt in a showcase of thermal forces at work. Here are **Steamboat Geyser**, the tallest geyser in the world, and rare acid geysers, such as **Echinus Geyser** (pH 3.5 approximately). The **Norris Geyser Basin Museum** has self-explanatory exhibits and dioramas (June-Labor Day, daily). A self-guided trail (2.5 miles) offers views of the **Porcelain and Back basins** from boardwalks (mid-June to Labor Day). The **Museum of the National Park Ranger** is also nearby, with exhibits portraying the history of the profession of the park ranger and the National Park Service.

★
★
★
★
★

At **Madison**, 14 miles southwest of Norris, the **West Entrance Road** (Highway 20-91 outside the park) joins the **Grand Loop Road**. Heading south of Madison, it is a 16-mile trip to **Old Faithful**. Along the route are four thermal spring areas; numerous geysers, mud pots and pools provide an appropriate prologue to the spectacle ahead. Old Faithful has not missed a performance in the more than 100 years since eruptions were first recorded. Eruptions occur on average every 70 to 90 minutes. This area, the Upper Geyser Basin, contains more hydrothermal features than any other part of the park, at least 150 within one square mile. A nearby visitor center provides information, exhibits, and a film and slide program (May-October and mid-December to mid-March, daily).

From Old Faithful, it is 17 miles east to **West Thumb Geyser Basin** and nearby **Yellowstone Lake**, the largest natural freshwater lake at high elevation (about 7,000 feet) in the United States. Early explorers thought that the shape of the lake resembled a hand, with the westernmost bay forming its thumb. A variety of rare species of waterfowl make their home along its 110 miles of shoreline. The 22-mile road from the South Entrance on the **John D. Rockefeller, Jr. Memorial Parkway** (Highway 29-287 outside the park) meets the Grand Loop Road here.

Northeast of West Thumb, about 19 miles up the western shore of Yellowstone Lake, the road leads to **Lake Village** and then to **Fishing Bridge**. At Fishing Bridge, the road splits: 27 miles east is the East entrance from Highway 14/16/20, and 16 miles north is **Canyon Village**. On the way to Canyon Village, the road passes **Hayden Valley**, a prime wildlife-viewing area. Canyon Village is near **Upper Falls** (a 109-foot drop) and the spectacular **Lower Falls** (a 308-foot drop). The colorful and awesome **Grand Canyon** of the Yellowstone River can be viewed from several points; there are self-guided trails along the rim and naturalist-led walks (summer). Groomed cross-country ski trails are open in winter. The **Canyon Visitor Education Center** teaches how the Yellowstone Volcano, geysers, hot springs and geologic history shaped the park and its life (mid-May to late September, daily).

Nineteen miles north of Canyon Village is **Tower**. Just south of Tower Junction is the 132-foot Tower Fall, which can best be observed from a platform at the end of the path leading from the parking lot. The Northeast Entrance on Highway 212 is 29 miles east of Tower; **Mammoth Hot Springs** is 18 miles west.

The rest of the park is wilderness with more than 1,100 miles of marked foot trails. Inquire at one of the visitor centers in the area before hiking in the backcountry. The official park season is May 1 through October 31. However, Highway 212 from Red Lodge,

★

★

★

★

Montana, to Cooke City, Montana (outside the northeast entrance), is not open to automobiles until about May 30 and closes around October 1. In winter, roads from Gardiner to Mammoth Hot Springs and to Cooke City are kept open, but the road from Red Lodge is closed; travelers must return to Gardiner to leave the park. The west, east and south entrances are closed to automobiles from November 1 to about May 1 but are open to oversnow vehicles from mid-December to mid-March. Dates are subject to change due to weather conditions and conservation measures. For current road conditions and other information, contact Park Headquarters at 307-344-7381. The entrance permit, $25 per vehicle per visit, is good for seven days in Yellowstone and Grand Teton.

WHAT TO DO

BACKPACKING

Permits are required for backcountry camping and should be picked up in person 48 hours before the trip from one of the following locations between 7 a.m. and 4:30 p.m.: Bechler Ranger Station, Canyon Ranger Station/Visitor Center, Grant Village Backcountry Office, Bridge Bay Ranger Station, Mammoth Ranger Station/Visitor Center, Old Faithful Ranger Station, South Entrance Ranger Station, Tower Ranger Station or West Entrance Ranger Station. Reservations for some permits can be

made 48 hours in advance by calling 307-344-2160; nonrefundable $20 fee.

Guided backcountry camping trips are also available through a number of independent guiding companies. For more information, visit www.nps.gov/yell/planyourvisit/hikebusn.htm.

BIKING

Bicycles are available for rental at Old Faithful and allowed on public roadways and other designated routes but not backcountry trails. Cyclists must exercise extreme caution when riding on Yellowstone's heavily trafficked, narrow, winding roads. Safety equipment, including a helmet, is recommended. Stop at a visitor center for more information on specific trails where bicycling is permitted.

BOATING, CANOEING AND KAYAKING

All private boats, motorized and non-motorized, require a permit (motorized: $20 annual, $10 seven-day; nonmotorized: $10 annual, $5 seven-day). Boaters can obtain permits at the South Entrance, Lewis Lake Campground, Grant Village Backcountry Office and Bridge Bay Ranger Station. Jet skis and similar watercraft are prohibited in the park. Xanterra Parks & Resorts offers canoe rentals at Bridge Bay Marina on Yellowstone Lake. Guided canoeing, kayaking and fishing trips are also available through independent companies that have been granted permission by Yellowstone to do business in the park. Find more information at www.nps.gov/yell/planyourvisit/boatbusn.htm.

CROSS-COUNTRY SKIING AND SNOWSHOEING

Skiing and snowshoeing are permitted on all unplowed roads and trails. Backcountry permits are required for overnight trips. Contact a park ranger before setting out on a day trip for an update on the current conditions. Besides taking all of the precautions necessary for any trip in the wilderness, winter trips require special planning for limited daylight, extreme temperatures and snow conditions.

FISHING

The fishing season in Yellowstone runs from Saturday of Memorial Day weekend through the first Sunday in November. Though no state license is required, fishing in Yellowstone National Park requires a permit; anglers 16 years and older must have a $15 three-day permit, a $20 seven-day permit or a $35 season permit. Rowboats, powerboats and tackle may be rented at Bridge Bay Marina. Permits are also required for all vessels (see "Boating"). Information centers near Yellowstone

Lake are located at Fishing Bridge and Grant Village (both open daily Memorial Day-Labor Day). Only barbless hooks are permitted. The **Firehole River,** which starts south of Old Faithful and flows northward into the Madison River, is world-famous for its abundance of healthy brown, brook and rainbow trout. The **Madison River** offers blue-ribbon fly fishing for its healthy stocks of mountain whitefish and brown and rainbow trout.

HIKING

With 1,100 miles of trails, hiking is one of the best ways to see and explore Yellowstone's wilderness. Here are some trail suggestions at various levels of difficulty. Before starting one of these or for other ideas, stop at a ranger station or visitor center for information.

———————— **EASY** ————————

Cascade Lake Trail
4.5 miles round-trip
Trailhead: Cascade Lake Picnic Area, 1.5 miles north of Canyon Junction on the Tower-Canyon Road.
Though the trail can be wet and muddy as late as July, this short hike winds through meadows for optimal wildlife- and wildflower-viewing in season.

Storm Point Trail
2-mile loop
Trailhead: Pullout at Indian Pond, 3 miles east of Fishing Bridge Visitor Center.

With views of Yellowstone Lake and Indian Pond, the trail starts out weaving through meadows. It takes a turn through the forest before leading out to rocky Storm Point, where a large colony of yellow-bellied marmots live. From there, the trail travels through a lodgepole pine forest and back to Indian Pond.

Ice Lake Trail
0.6 miles round-trip
Trailhead: 3.5 miles east of Norris on the Norris-Canyon Road.
A short walk will get you to this small, pretty lake in a lodgepole pine forest.

─────── **MODERATE** ───────
Observation Point Loop Trail
1.1-mile loop
Trailhead: Firehole River footbridge behind Old Faithful Geyser.
The view of the Upper Geyser Basin from the overlook makes the 200-foot climb worth your while.

Purple Mountain
6 miles round-trip
Trailhead: 0.25 mile north of Madison Junction on the Madison-Norris Road.
A steady climb (1,500-foot elevation gain) through a burned lodgepole pine forest leads to a good viewpoint of the Firehole Valley and Gibbon Valley.

Mallard Lake Trail
6.8 miles round-trip
Trailhead: Old Faithful Lodge cabin area
Travel through lodgepole pine forests, meadows and rocky slopes before reaching Mallard Lake.

Bunsen Peak Trail
10 miles round-trip
Trailhead: Entrance to Old Bunsen Peak Road, five miles south of Mammoth toward Norris.
This trail climbs gradually (1,300 feet) to the summit of Bunsen Peak and gives hikers views of the Blacktail Plateau, Swan Lake Flats, Gallatin Mountain Range and Yellowstone River Valley. You can return the same way you came, or head to the Osprey Falls trailhead (about 2 miles) and return via the Old Bunsen Peak Road Trail. If you've allowed enough time, you can hike an additional 2.8 miles to Osprey Falls.

─────── **STRENUOUS** ───────
Avalanche Peak Trail
5 miles round-trip
Trailhead: West end of Eleanor Lake, across the road to the east of the small creek.
Without switchbacks, this steep trail climbs up stiffly (1,800 feet), passing through a forest of whitebark pines and an old avalanche slide area before opening onto a meadow at the base of the bowl of Avalanche Peak, boasting some of the best panoramic views in the park. The trail climbs on through scree (broken rock) along the Avalanche Peak ridgeline.

★
★
★
☆
☆

HORSEBACK RIDING/ LLAMA PACKING

Guided one- and two-hour tours of the wilderness can be made on horseback with Xanterra Parks and Resorts from Mammoth Hot Springs, Tower-Roosevelt and Canyon Village. Horseback and wagon rides that end with a steak dinner by a campfire are also available. Reservations are recommended (307-344-7311). Guided llama tours are also available from park-approved vendors; see www.nps.gov/yell/planyourvisit/stockbusn.htm. Private horses are not allowed in the park before July 1 due to wet trail conditions.

WILDERNESS EDUCATION

The Yellowstone Association, a non-profit partner of the Park Service, offers many educational programs and seminars for adults looking for more in-depth information than the average tour might provide. **Field Seminars** delve into individual aspects of the Yellowstone ecosystem. **Ed-Ventures** are naturalist-led excursions, which may include a walk or hike as part of an educational program (for example, "Geysers, Mud Pots and Hot Springs"). For reservations call 307-344-2293; www.yellowstoneassociation.org.

For kids, the park service offers a **Junior Ranger Program** to teach children about natural wonders and how they can help to protect them. To receive a Junior Ranger patch, children are required to attend a ranger-led program, hike on a park trail, and complete several age-appropriate activities on park resources, issues and concepts, such as geothermal geology. For more information and a Junior Ranger assignment, stop at any visitor center in the park.

TOURS

Various informational bus tours run through the park in the summer. Contact tour operators for details and reservations: Adventure Yellowstone (406-585-9041; www.national-park-tours.com), All Yellowstone Sports (800-548-9551; www.allyellowstone.com), Flagg Ranch Resort (307-543-2861, 800-443-2311; www.flaggranch.com), Grand Teton Lodge Company (307-543-2811; www.gtlc.com) and Xanterra Parks and Resorts (307-344-7311, 866-439-7375; www.travelyellowstone.com).

GRAND TETON NATIONAL PARK
These rugged, block-faulted mountains began to rise about 9 million years ago, making them some of the youngest on the continent. The strikingly jagged appearance of the Tetons is dramatically enhanced by the absence of foothills, leaving impressively vertical granite peaks fully exposed from the spacious Jackson Hole Valley at their base up to the sky. Geologic and glacial

★
★
★
★

forces combined to buckle and sculpt the landscape into a stunning setting of canyons, cirques and craggy peaks, which cast their reflections across countless clear alpine lakes. The marvelous scenery of this park draws nearly 4 million visitors a year. The Snake River winds gracefully through a high-altitude valley—or a "hole" in old fur trappers' speak—where mountain streams converge, making an ideal habitat for beaver and other furry animals. John Colter passed through the area between 1807 and 1808, but it was in 1822 that Dave E. Jackson of St. Louis responded to a newspaper ad for hunters in the Rocky Mountains. In 1826, he and a couple of his friends bought the fur company, and by 1829, they were doing so well that the trapping area came to be known as "Jackson's Hole."

The fight for the conservation of this region was a long one, spanning decades of frustration, compromise and admirable dedication to the ideal of preservation. In 1897, the superintendent of Yellowstone first suggested expanding the southern boundary of Yellowstone into Jackson Hole to protect the area's migrating elk. By 1912, the National Elk Refuge was established, and today is a popular Jackson Hole tourist attraction. A bill introduced by a Wyoming congressman to, again, expand Yellowstone's southern boundary passed the House in 1919 but failed in the Senate. A few years later, the superintendent of Yellowstone took John D. Rocke-

feller, Jr., and his family to see the Tetons. The spiky peaks and the quickly intruding construction must have made an impression on Rockefeller because the next year, he dedicated himself to the preservation of the area and established the Snake River Land Company as a cover. He promptly began purchasing land on both sides of the Snake River from the area's cattle ranchers with the intention of one day donating it all to the federal government.

In 1929, Congress and President Calvin Coolidge finally signed legislation to preserve the Teton Range and the glacial lakes directly at their feet but left out the Jackson Hole Valley. Then in 1943, President Franklin Delano Roosevelt accepted Rockefeller's donation of 35,000 acres, for which he'd paid $1.5 million, and created the Jackson Hole National Monument. This secured the protection of the lovely low-lying lands—but enraged cattle ranchers, who felt they'd been duped. Finally in 1950, the legislature and President Harry Truman agreed on expanded protection for the area and consolidated the Jackson Hole and Teton areas to create Grand Teton National Park. **Highways 26-89-191, Moose, Wyoming, 307-739-3300; www.nps.gov/grte**

WHAT TO SEE

Grand Teton National Park is set in **Jackson Hole**, an 80-mile-long and 15-mile-wide valley that includes National Forest and the **National Elk Refuge** (307-733-9212). The refuge is 25,000 acres of land dedicated to elk, and more than 1,000 of these graceful animals spend their winters here. Throughout the year, more than 47 mammals and 147 bird species make the park their home. Grand Teton is bordered to the north by the **John D. Rockefeller, Jr. Memorial Parkway**, 24,000 acres of land dedicated by congress to the generous philanthropist in 1972. The Rockefeller Parkway, administered by Grand Teton, acts as a natural bridge between the two parks.

Entering Grand Teton from the north by way of the Rockefeller Parkway, Highway 89-191-287 skirts the eastern shore of Jackson Lake for 16 miles to Jackson Lake Junction. About three-quarters of the way there, find Colter Bay Village with the **Colter Bay Visitor Center and Indian Arts Museum** (309-739-3594; mid-May to mid-October) on Jackson Lake. The museum has a wide variety of Native American artifacts, donated by the Rockefellers, on exhibit.

At Jackson Lake Junction, the road turns eastward five miles to **Moran Junction** (at Highway 26) and continues another two miles to the east entrance. The Teton Park Road begins at Jackson Lake Junction and borders the mountains for 12 miles to **Jenny Lake** and the **Jenny Lake Visitor Center**, open May 13-September 28. The center offers information on park geology, guided walks and other ranger-led programs. From the South Jenny Lake Junction, the Teton Park Road continues toward the park headquarters at Moose Junction, passing **Menor's Ferry Historic Area**, a historic homestead and country store that belonged to William D. Menor. The early resident of Jackson built a ferryboat on the Snake River that became vital to many of the settlers of Jackson Hole. At Moose Junction, 12 miles north of Jackson, is the **Craig Thomas Discovery and Visitor Center** (307-739-3399; year-round). It offers natural history exhibits, an extensive bookstore, guided tours and other ranger-led programs and is open year-round. Highway 89-191-26 parallels Teton Park Road from Moran Junction to the south entrance on the east side of the Snake River. The **Chapel of the Transfiguration**, located in Moose, is a log chapel with a large picture window over the altar framing the mountains (daily; services held late May-September).

All highways have a continuous view of the Teton Range, which runs north-south. Highway 26-89-191 is open year-round from Jackson to Flagg Ranch on the Roosevelt Parkway, as is Highway 26-287 to Dubois. Secondary roads and Teton Park Road are open May-October. The park is open year-round (limited in winter), with food and lodging available in the park from mid-May through September and in Jackson. A 24-hour recorded message

★
★
★
★

gives information about weather: 307-739-3611.

Outside the park on Highway 26-89-191 to Jackson is the **National Museum of Wildlife Art** (2820 Rungius Road, Jackson, 307-733-5771, 800-313-9553; www.wildlifeart.org; daily 9 a.m.-5 p.m.). Nearly blending into the hillside across from the National Elk Refuge, this organic-looking structure (made of red sandstone from Arizona) houses the largest arts facility dedicated to the theme of wildlife, including works by John James Audubon and others. A restaurant and gift shop are onsite. In winter, sleigh tours of the National Elk Refuge originate here, and combination museum admission-sleigh tour packages are available.

If you're starting from Jackson, literally surrounding the town is the **Bridger-Teton National Forest** (307-739-5500; www.fs.fed.us/btnf/), more than 3.3 million acres offering much to explore. The forest was the site of one of the largest earth slides in U.S. history, the Gros Ventre Slide (1925), which dammed the Gros Ventre River (to a height of 225 feet and a width of nearly 1/2 mile). The slide formed **Slide Lake**, which is approximately three miles long. There are scenic drives along the Hoback River Canyon and the Snake River Canyon and in Star Valley. Unspoiled backcountry includes parts of Gros Ventre, Teton and Wind River ranges along the Continental Divide and the Wyoming Range. **Teton Wilderness** (557,311 acres) and **Gros Wilderness** (247,000 acres) are accessible on foot or horseback. You'll find swimming, fishing, rafting, hiking, mountain biking, winter sports areas and camping here. Also in the forest is **Bridger Wilderness**, where there's fishing, boating and big-game hunting.

The Jackson area also has some fun events in the summer and fall. From early July to late August, the **Grand Teton Music Festival** (307-733-3050; www.gtmf.org) in Wilson (7 miles west of Jackson) features a virtuoso orchestra of top professional musicians from around the world performing many different programs of chamber music and orchestral works. And from mid-September to early October, Jackson hosts the **Jackson Hole Fall Arts Festival** (www.jacksonholechamber.com/fall_arts_festival), a three-week celebration of the arts featuring special exhibits in more than 30 galleries, as well as demonstrations and special activities. Also included are dance, theater, mountain films, Native American arts and culinary demonstrations.

WHAT TO DO

BACKPACKING

Backcountry camping requires a permit, which can be obtained at Colter Bay and Craig Thomas Visitor Centers or Jenny Lake Ranger Station. Permit reservations ($25 fee), accepted January 1 through May 15, are recommended, as some areas fill up early. For reservations, go to www.nps.gov/grte/planyourvisit/back.htm.

Guided backpacking trips for 15- to 17-year-olds are offered by Teton Valley Ranch Camp (307-773-6122, 307-733-2958; www.tvrcamp.com). During the two-week trip, teens will learn wilderness safety, ecology, first aid, fire safety and minimum impact camping principles, among other things. Jackson-based Wilderness Ventures (307-733-2122, 800-533-2281; www.wildernessventures.com) also offers a variety of guided adventure travel trips in the area for junior high and high school students. Activities include backpacking, hiking, whitewater rafting, sea kayaking, rock climbing and more.

BOATING AND RAFTING

Boaters and anglers can enjoy placid lakes or wild streams; the Colter Bay, Signal Mountain and Leek's marinas have ramps, guides, facilities and boat rentals. Many river and lake trips are offered, and you can choose an adventure to suit your individual tastes. Five-, 10- and 20-mile trips on rubber rafts navigate the Snake River. A self-guided trail tells the story of Menor's Ferry (1894) and the Maude Noble Cabin; Jenny Lake has boat trips and boat rentals; and Jackson Lake cruises are available, some reaching island hideaways for breakfast cookouts.

Boat rentals also are available at Jackson Lake. The Grand Teton Lodge Company (307-543-2811; www.gtlc.com) offers a full-day guided bus and boat trip covering major points of interest in the park from June to mid-September. A park permit is required for private boats, and a Wyoming fishing license is required and may be obtained at several locations in the park.

MOUNTAINEERING

Climbers can tackle summits via routes of varying difficulty; the more ambitious may take advantage of classes from Exum Mountain Guides (307-733-2297; www.exumguides.com) and Jackson Hole Mountain Guides (307-733-4979, 800-239-7642; www.jhmg.com), which range from a beginner's course to an attempt at conquering the 13,770-foot Grand Teton, considered one of the major North American peaks. Detailed information on routes, backcountry and conditions is available at www.tetonclimbing.blogspot.com. Trips involving any technical climbing or mountaineering require permits, which can be picked up at the Jenny Lake Ranger Station.

HIKING

There are more than 200 miles of trails in this relatively small park. Here are a few day hike suggestions. Stop at a ranger station before heading out to check on

YELLOWSTONE/GRAND TETON

conditions or for additional trail suggestions.

Lakeshore Trail
2 miles round-trip
Trailhead: Colter Bay
This flat trail hugs the eastern then northern shore of Colter Bay before it emerges onto a Jackson Lake peninsula that offers views of the northern Tetons.

Flagg Canyon Trail, Rockefeller Parkway
5 miles round-trip
Trailhead: Flagg Ranch Village on the Rockefeller Parkway; access from the east side of the Polecat Creek Loop Trail.
This easy hike with little elevation change offers fantastic views of the Snake River.

Hermitage Point
8.8 miles round-trip
Trailhead: Colter Bay
This gentle hike with a 100-foot elevation change offers an intimate look at the park's wildlife habitats from forests to meadows to ponds.

———— MODERATE ————

Hidden Falls
5 miles round-trip
Trailhead: Jenny Lake
This hike hugs Jenny Lake's south shore before climbing 150 feet to a viewpoint of the 200-foot waterfall.

Two Ocean & Emma Matilda Lake
12.9 miles round-trip
Trailhead: Two Ocean Lake
This trail first travels along the lovely north shore of Two Ocean Lake, then climbs to the panoramic Grand View Point. The hike continues along the south shore of Emma Matilda Lake before making its way back around to Two Ocean Lake. The elevation change is 710 feet.

Forks of Cascade Canyon
13 miles round-trip
Trailhead: Jenny Lake
This trail travels into Cascade Canyon and offers views of Grand Teton, Mount Owen and Teewinot. Be prepared for a 1,057-foot elevation gain.

———— STRENUOUS ————

Amphitheater and Surprise Lakes
9.6 miles round-trip
This stiff climb (2,958 feet) is rewarded with views of serene glacial lakes and subalpine meadows.

HORSEBACK RIDING

Corrals at Jackson Lake Lodge and Colter Bay have horses accustomed to rocky trails; and pack trips can be easily arranged. Several independent stables offer commercial trips at various lengths and levels: Flagg Ranch Resort (800-443-3211; www.flaggranch.com), Grand Teton Lodge Company (307-543-2811; www.

gtlc.com), Gros Ventre River Ranch (307-733-4138; www.grosventreriverranch.com), Triangle X Ranch (307-733-2183; www.trianglex.com), and Signal Mountain Lodge (307-543-2831; www.signalmtnlodge.com).

MOUNTAIN BIKING

Teton Mountain Bike Tours (Jackson, 307-733-0712, 800-733-0788; www.tetonmtbike.com) offers guided mountain bike tours for all ability levels. Mountain bikes, helmets, transportation and local guides are provided; day, multi-day and customized group tours are available.

RANGER PROGRAMS

Slide-illustrated talks on the park and its features are held each night (mid-June to Labor Day) at the amphitheaters at Colter Bay, Signal Mountain and Gros Ventre. Ranger-led hikes, children's activities, snowshoe hikes (December-March) and wildlife viewing are also available.

SKIING

Snow King Ski Resort (400 E. Snow King Ave., Jackson, 307-733-5200, 800-522-5464; www.snowking.com), six blocks south of Town Square in Jackson, has a triple and two double chairlifts and a surface tow, ski school, rental-repair shop, snack bar and resort facilities. Its longest run is nearly one mile with a vertical

drop of 1,571 feet. Open November-March, daily.

Jackson Hole Resort (7652 Granite Ridge Loop Road, Teton Village, 307-733-2292, 888-333-7766; www.jacksonhole.com), 30 minutes from downtown Jackson, offers 2,500 acres of terrain, a 4,139-foot vertical rise and a 459-inch average annual snowfall. This ski resort offers some of the most notoriously tough terrain in the U.S., and delivers challenging runs at every level of ability. Its lifts include one eight-person lift, six quads, two triples, two doubles and one surface tow. Ski school, child care, snowshoeing, cross-country skiing, dog sledding and more are available. Open December-April, daily.

TRAM

The Aerial Tramway (307-733-2291; www.jacksonhole.com/info/pr.tram.asp), which has run just outside the park's southern boundary from Teton Village for 40 years has been taken out of service to be replaced with a new tram in December 2008. The tram has a vertical lift of 4,600 feet, over a 2.5-mile ride from the valley floor to the top of **Rendezvous Peak** for spectacular views. There are trailheads at the top for those who prefer to hike down or continue farther.

WILDLIFE

The greater Yellowstone area is a paradise for animals and the people who love them, with a greater concentration of large and small mammals than anywhere else in the lower 48 states. You may encounter elk, bison, black bears, grizzly bears, bighorn sheep and coyotes among others. However, the parks' big cats—bobcats, lynx and mountain lions—are very rarely seen; any sighting of one or its tracks should be reported to the park service. Early morning and evening, when most animals tend to feed, are typically the best times to spot wildlife. Although it is not unusual to encounter animals along park roads, they are more commonly seen on backcountry trails and in more remote areas.

Bighorn Sheep: These surefooted animals habitually climb very steep terrain high in the cliffs to escape predators such as coyotes, eagles and mountain lions. They range in color from light brown to chocolate and have horns. They can be observed in Yellowstone in the Gardiner River Canyon crossing from the cliffs to the river and grazing on grasses in fall and winter.

Bison: The big guys on campus, bison bulls can weigh more than 1,800 pounds. There are more than 4,000 wild bison in Yellowstone. They can be found in large herds in Yellowstone's Hayden Valley in spring, early summer and during their fall rut—mating season—which begins in late July or early August. In Grand Teton,

look for them eating grasses in the sagebrush flats above the Snake River and along Teton Park Road between Signal Mountain and North Jenny Lake Junction.

Black Bears: Don't be deceived by their name; in the Rocky Mountains, only about 50 percent of the black bears are black with a light brown muzzle. The others range from brown to cinnamon to blonde. These animals are common in the park and are generally not aggressive. They rely on their climbing skills to escape predators and danger. Black bears are more active during the day than grizzlies. Watch for them in forests and in small clearings near forested areas. They are most commonly seen in Yellowstone along the road from Mammoth Hot Springs east through Tower-Roosevelt to the northeast entrance of the park, as well as frequently near Old Faithful, Madison and Canyon Village. In Grand Teton, they are often spotted in Cascade and Death Canyons and near Two Ocean and Emma Matilda Lakes.

Coyotes: These small members of the dog family have coats ranging from gray to tan and have pointed ears and noses. They are on average about one quarter the size of wolves, but they are fierce predators nonetheless. The cartoon character wasn't named Wile E. at random; these clever and skillful hunters manage to prey on everything from mice and ground squirrels to elk, bison and moose. Coyotes can almost always be seen in Yellowstone's Hayden Valley.

★
★
★
★
★

Elk: Having the largest population of any large mammals in the park, these beautiful animals are easy to find. The park service reports that more than 30,000 elk spend their summers in Yellowstone and approximately 15,000 to 22,000 arrive for the winters. Their coats are reddish-brown with dark manes. The bulls grow antlers from their first year on. The maturity of a bull can be determined by how many points, or tines, are on each side of his rack. Antlers with six to eight tines can weigh more than 30 pounds. In Grand Teton, look for them from Highway 89-191 in the lush meadows along the northeastern edge of Jackson Lake, in Willow Flats from the Willow Flats Overlook a quarter mile south of Jackson Lake Lodge, in grassy meadows along the Snake River, at Hermitage Point and along Beaver Creek.

Grizzly Bears: Weighing as much as 700 pounds, these bears are about twice as big as black bears of the same sex and age. They are more active at night and best spotted through binoculars or a telephoto lens just after sunrise and just before sunset in open meadows. The best places in Yellowstone to look for them are along the road from Tower-Roosevelt south through Canyon Village, Yellowstone Lake area and Fishing Bridge toward the east entrance of the park. They are also often spotted southeast of Yellowstone Lake and in the Gallatin Mountains in the northwest area of the park. In Grand Teton, they are seen near Two Ocean and Emma Matilda Lakes.

Moose: The largest member of the deer family, Moose bulls can weigh up to 1,300 pounds. These giants are frequently seen near water. In Yellowstone, look for them near the Bechler and Falls Rivers, Yellowstone Lake, Soda Butte Creek, Pelican Creek, Lewis River, Gallatin River and in the Willow Park area between Mammoth and Norris. In Grand Teton, look along the trails in the Colter Bay area, in the Willow Flats area from the back deck of Jackson Lake Lodge, at the Oxbow Bend of the Snake River, in the Blacktail Ponds area a half mile north of Moose on Highway 26-89-191 and along creeks in Cascade and Death Canyons.

Wolves: Native to the park when it was established in 1872, the wolf populations diminished throughout the 20th century until there was no evidence of them in Yellowstone in the 1970s. In 1995 and 1996, the park service reintroduced the species to the park with great success, and there are now more than 300 wolves living in the area in and around Yellowstone.

BIRDS

While the greater Yellowstone area is indeed a wildlife wonderland, it is not a birding hotspot compared with other places in North America. A few of its interesting native species include the **Trumpeter Swan**; the largest species of North American wildfowl, with its neck and legs extended, it can measure nearly six feet long. As one might

★
★
★
★

suspect, this bird has a unique trumpetlike call. Yellowstone is home to one year-round flock and one migrating winter flock of the swans. The long-legged **Sandhill Crane** is another one of the area's interesting birds. This gray bird is usually seen in pairs until migration time, when it joins up with flocks of as many as 200. Their unique loud, rattling, guttural call makes them more easily heard than seen. Look for them in the south end of Yellowstone's Hayden Valley. Hayden Valley in general is one of the better places to watch for birds in the park: keep an eye out for ducks, geese, American white pelicans and bald eagles. Try the Gardiner River Canyon to see osprey and more eagles. And for a good chance at spotting a variety of Yellowstone's avian life, hike the Pelican Creek Trail, which begins at the Pelican Creek Bridge one mile east of the Fishing Bridge Visitor Center. In Grand Teton, look for pelicans, geese and waterfowl on the northeastern shores of Jackson Lake and in the Willow Flats area between Jackson Lake Dam and Colter Bay.

WHERE TO STAY

CAMPING

Yellowstone

During peak season in July and August, campsite demand often exceeds supply; many sites are occupied by mid-morning, and those that take reservations are booked long in advance. Planning ahead is a must. The following campgrounds take reservations: Bridge Bay, Canyon, Madison, Grant Village and Fishing Bridge RV Park. For same-day reservations, call 307-344-7901. For future reservations, call 307-344-7311 or 866-439-7375. More RV sites are available at Flagg Ranch south of Yellowstone's boundary in the Rockefeller Parkway area, in West Yellowstone and north of the park in Gardiner. Overnight vehicle camping or stopping outside designated campgrounds is not permitted. Seven additional National Park Service campgrounds at Yellowstone are operated on a first-come, first-served basis: Indian Creek, Lewis Lake, Mammoth, Norris, Pebble Creek, Slough Creek and Tower Fall. Arrive early in the day to secure a site. Campfires are prohibited except in designated areas or by special permit obtained at ranger stations. Backcountry camping is available by permit only, given out no more than 48 hours in advance in person at ranger stations. Backcountry sites can be reserved for a $20 fee.

Grand Teton

Five National Park Service campgrounds are maintained within the park: Colter Bay, Signal Mountain, Lizard Creek, Gros Ventre and Jenny Lake (the most popular). They do not accept reservations. Jenny Lake typically fills by mid-morning during peak season, but the others don't fill until late in the day, if at all. Flagg Ranch in the Rockefeller Parkway area also offers tent sites and RV sites, but reservations are recommended: Colter Bay, Gros Ventre and Jenny Lake Campgrounds (800-628-9988), Flagg Ranch Campground (800-443-2311), Lizard Creek Campground (800-672-6012), Signal Mountain Campground (800-672-6012).

HOTELS

YELLOWSTONE NATIONAL PARK

★★Lake Yellowstone Hotel
Yellowstone National Park,
307-344-7311, 866-439-7375;
www.travelyellowstone.com
This lodge dating back to 1891 on the shore of Yellowstone Lake is listed on the National Register of Historic Places and is the oldest hotel in the park. Refurbished to recapture the grand ambiance of the roaring '20s, this elegant hotel offers a wide range of accommodations from deluxe suites to simple cabins. No TVs.
158 rooms. Closed mid-October to late May. Restaurant, bar. $$

★★Old Faithful Inn
307-344-7311, 866-439-7375;
www.travelyellowstone.com
This national historic landmark was designed by architect Robert C. Reamer, who said its asymmetry was intended to reflect the chaos of nature. Built in 1904, the log and wooden shingle exterior conveys an apropos rustic ambiance. With its convenient location near Old Faithful, guests here have countless activities at their fingertips. No TVs.
327 rooms. Closed mid-October to early May. Restaurants, bar. $$

★★Old Faithful Snow Lodge
307-344-7311, 866-439-7375;
www.travelyellowstone.com
This lodge is the newest of Yellowstone's hotels, completed in 1999, but was designed to fit harmoniously into its mountain environment and among the historic buildings it joined. A wildlife theme is carried throughout the décor in the inn's comfortable rooms and furnishings. No TVs.
95 rooms. Closed mid-October to mid-December and mid-March to early May. Two restaurants, bar. $$

NORTH OF YELLOWSTONE NATIONAL PARK
Gardiner, MT

★★Best Western Mammoth Hot Springs
W. Highway 89, Gardiner,
406-848-7311, 800-780-7234;
www.bestwestern.com
No surprises here: This recently renovated Best Western offers comfortable accommodations with satellite TV and high-speed Internet just outside Yellowstone's north entrance.
85 rooms. High-speed Internet access. Restaurant, bar. Casino. Pool. Pets accepted. $

★Yellowstone Village Inn
Highway 89, Gardiner,

406-848-7417, 800-228-8158; www.yellowstoneinn.com

A departure from the dime-a-dozen chain motels surrounding it, this local joint offers a bit more personality but similarly basic accommodations with TV and Wi-Fi. Rooms with kitchenettes are also available.

43 rooms. Wireless Internet access. Complimentary continental breakfast. Pool. $

EAST OF YELLOWSTONE NATIONAL PARK
Cody, WY

★★Holiday Inn
1701 Sheridan Ave., Cody, 307-587-5555, 800-315-2621; www.blairhotels.com, www.holidayinn.com

Just over 50 miles from Yellowstone's east entrance, this Holiday Inn in downtown Cody offers comfortable accommodations and family-friendly amenities, including a heated outdoor pool, gym and tickets to local events and attractions.

189 rooms. Wireless Internet access. Restaurant, bar. Airport transportation available. Fitness center. Pool. $

★

★

★

★

★

— ALSO RECOMMENDED —
Absaroka Mountain Lodge
1231 Northfork Highway, Cody, 307-587-3963; www.absarokamtlodge.com

Dating back to 1910, this historic family-friendly lodge is just 12 miles east of Yellowstone's entrance. The Absaroka warmly welcomes guests with espresso, cocktails, board games, nightly movies and home-cooked meals next to crackling fires before they retire to cozy rustic cabins on Gunbarrel Creek. Fishing, a variety of horseback riding options and other family activities are available. All-inclusive packages are available.

18 cabins. Restaurant, bar. $

WEST OF YELLOWSTONE NATIONAL PARK

★★Holiday Inn Sunspree Resort West Yellowstone
315 Yellowstone Ave., West Yellowstone, 406-646-7365, 800-646-7365; www.doyellowstone.com

Meeting the standards expected from a Holiday Inn, this hotel also offers close proximity to Yellowstone. Its restaurant features a restored railcar from the "Yellowstone Special" train, which brought visitors to Yellowstone at the turn of the century. The menu features cuisine with a western flair such as buffalo and elk. Kids 12 and under eat for free.

123 rooms. High-speed Internet access. Restaurant, bar. Fitness center. Pool. Airport transportation available. $$

★★Stage Coach Inn
209 Madison Ave., West Yellowstone, 406-646-7381, 800-842-2882, 800-561-0815; www.yellowstoneinn.com

This unique western lodge with rustic décor featuring a bison antler motif throughout treats guests to comfortable, spacious rooms with cable TV and plenty of places to kick back after a long day in the park. Try a cocktail next to the fireplace in the lounge, which offers poker tables, video poker, keno, live entertainment during peak season and a big-screen TV. 83 rooms. Complimentary continental breakfast. Restaurant, bar. $

IN GRAND TETON NATIONAL PARK

★★★Jackson Lake Lodge
North Highway 89 and 1191, Moran, 307-543-3100, 800-628-9988; www.gtlc.com
This full-service lodge in Grand Teton National Park offers spectacular views of Mount Moran and the Tetons across Jackson Lake. Its grand lobby has two fireplaces and 60-foot picture windows framing the view, as well as a collection of Native American artifacts and western art.

37 rooms, 348 cottages. Closed early October to mid-May. Two restaurants, bar. Pool. Airport transportation available. $$

★★Togwotee Mountain Lodge
Highway 26/287, Moran, 307-543-2847, 800-543-2847; www.togwoteelodge.com
On the eastern rim of the Jackson Hole valley, one hour's drive from the town of Jackson, this comfortable lodge provides guests a year-round destination for mountain adventures, including snowmobiling and dog sledding in the winter and fishing, horseback riding, whitewater rafting, mountain biking and more in the summer.
35 rooms, 54 cabins. Restaurant, bar. $

— **ALSO RECOMMENDED** —

Jenny Lake Lodge
Jenny Lake, Grand Teton National park, WY
800-628-9988, 307-733-4647; www.gtlc.com/
At the base of the beautiful Tetons, within short walking distance of trailheads and three lakes, this historic lodge made up of cabins dating back to the 1920s presents travelers with the finest service in a unique atmosphere. The charming cabins provide reposeful retreats, equipped with down comforters and handmade quilts. The nightly rate includes breakfast, a five-course prix fixe dinner, horseback riding and bicycling.
37 historic cabins. Restaurant. Complimentary full breakfast, 5-course dinner, horseback riding, and bicycling. $$$

SOUTH OF GRAND TETON NATIONAL PARK
Jackson, WY

★Wyoming Inn
930 W. Broadway, Jackson, 307-734-0035, 800-844-0035; www.wyoming-inn.com
The stone fireplace in this lodge's warm lobby establishes a welcoming ambiance that is carried through with tasteful western-themed décor and thoughtful touches. Snacks, juices, and fresh-baked chocolate chip cookies are available compliments of the hotel throughout the day.
73 rooms. Wireless Internet access. Complimentary full breakfast. Airport transportation available. $$

★★★Rusty Parrot Lodge & Spa

175 N. Jackson St., Jackson, 307-733-2000, 888-739-1749; www.rustyparrot.com

Just minutes from Grand Teton and Yellowstone National Parks and Jackson Hole, the lodge is also only three blocks from Town Square. Rustic rooms are filled with mountain-style touches: antler chandeliers, handmade furniture and goose-down comforters. A hearty breakfast is included in the rates. To rejuvenate the body and the spirit after a day on the trails, try one of the many treatments available at Body Sage, the on-site day spa.

31 rooms. Complimentary full breakfast. Restaurant, bar. Whirlpool. Spa. $$$

★★★Spring Creek Ranch

1800 Spirit Dance Road, Jackson, 307-733-8833, 800-443-6139; www.springcreekranch.com

Hovering 1,000 feet over the town of Jackson, this resort offers a stunning view of the Teton Mountain Range. The accommodations run the gamut from lovely inn rooms to large mountain homes. In the inn, guests will enjoy evening turndown service, wood-burning and gas fireplaces and massage services.

122 rooms. Wireless Internet access. Restaurant, bar. Airport transportation available. Fitness center. Tennis. Pool. Spa. $$$

★★★The Wort Hotel

50 N. Glenwood St., Jackson, 307-733-2190, 800-322-2727; www.worthotel.com

Reflecting the history and culture of Jackson Hole, this popular country inn is decorated with fabrics and furnishings of the Old West. The rooms are equipped with every possible comfort: goose down comforters, plush bathrobes, Starbucks coffee, Aveda beauty products, a humidifier and a welcoming teddy bear.

55 rooms, 4 suites. High-speed Internet access. Two restaurants, bar. Airport transportation available. Fitness center. $$$

★★★★Amangani

1535 N. East Butte Road, Jackson, 307-734-7333, 877-734-7333; www.amanresorts.com

Perched on the edge of a butte outside one of the country's most popular ski resorts, this American outpost of the acclaimed Aman resort group is a welcoming blend of Eastern minimalism and Western style—and a perfect (if expensive) retreat after a visit to one of the parks. With only 40 rooms, the atmosphere is one of relaxation and renewal. Rooms are streamlined and contemporary with fireplaces and deep soaking tubs, while the resort's public spaces take advantage of the impressive mountain views. The culinary staff at the Grill keep the focus on fresh organic ingredients, and the staff at the onsite health center accommodate every whim, from private yoga sessions to soothing spa treatments.

40 rooms. Wireless Internet access. Restaurant, bar. Airport transportation available. Fitness center. Pool. Spa. **$$$$**

Teton Village, WY

★★Alpenhof Lodge

3255 W. Village Drive, Teton Village, 307-733-3242, 800-732-3244; www.alpenhoflodge.com

For a little piece of Europe in the heart of the Rockies, guests head to the Alpenhof and find that no thought to their comfort is spared in deluxe rooms with handcrafted Bavarian furniture, fireplaces, balconies, lavish robes and down comforters. Some even provide Jacuzzi tubs and heated tile floors. In winter, fondue parties are held, compliments of the house. The lodge has ski-in/ski-out access.

42 rooms. Closed November. Wireless Internet access. Complimentary continental breakfast. Two restaurants, bar. Pool. **$$**

★★★★★Four Seasons Resort Jackson Hole

7680 Granite Loop Road, Teton Village, 307-732-5000; www.fourseasons.com/jacksonhole

If you're looking to stay somewhere in style, this is the place to do it. Laidback western flair is paired with big-city attention to detail at this full-service resort set amid the natural beauty of the Teton Mountains. Rooms are warm and welcoming with gas fireplaces and décor that hints at the area's Native American

heritage. Besides ski-in/ski-out access to the area's famous trails, the resort boasts a ski concierge, who handles lift tickets, advises skiers on trails and assists with equipment selections. Guests can reward themselves after a day of skiing, fly-fishing or hiking with a meal at the cozy Westbank Grill, where local specialties such as mustard- and tarragon-crusted Colorado lamb fill the menu. Top off the evening with a soak in one of the outdoor hot pools while you feast on s'mores.

124 rooms. Wireless Internet access. Three restaurants, two bars. Airport transportation available. Fitness center. Pool. Spa. Pets accepted. **$$$$**

★★The Inn at Jackson Hole

3345 W. Village Drive, Teton Village, 307-733-2311, 800-842-7666; www.innatjh.com

This rustic lodge with modern amenities and a variety of comfortable rooms is in the Teton Village part of the Jackson Hole ski area. It is only 12 miles from Jackson and near Grand Teton National Park, Jackson Hole and Yellowstone National Park and has ski-in/ski-out access.

83 rooms. Two restaurants, bar. Pool. **$$**

★★★Teton Mountain Lodge

3385 W. Village Drive, Teton Village, 307-734-7111, 800-631-6271; www.tetonlodge.com

A luxury retreat, this lodge provides not only fine furnishings but attentive service and extras like

spa treatments, concierge service, nightly turndown and overnight laundry. Ski-in/ski-out access.

129 rooms. High-speed Internet access. Restaurant, bar. Fitness center. Pool. $$$

WHERE TO EAT

IN YELLOWSTONE NATIONAL PARK

★★Lake Yellowstone Hotel Dining Room

Highway 89, Yellowstone National Park, 307-344-7311, 866-439-7375; www.travelyellowstone.com

The park's finest dining is presented in its oldest, most elegant hotel. Highlights on its upscale menu are such specialties as farm-raised bison, wild Alaskan Salmon and Montana tenderloin, all to be enjoyed with views of lovely Yellowstone Lake.

American, seafood menu. Breakfast, lunch, dinner. Closed October-May. Bar. Children's menu. Reservations recommended for dinner. $$

— ALSO RECOMMENDED —

Canyon Lodge Dining Room

Grand Canyon of the Yellowstone, Yellowstone National Park

For casual dining at affordable prices, the Canyon Lodge eateries fit the bill. A cafeteria and deli provide visitors with quick meals when they're on the go. The full-service dining room offers both full and continental breakfast menus, a number of burgers and salads for lunch and a dinner menu ranging from a wild Alaska Sockeye salmon burger to chicken-fried steak.

American menu. Breakfast, lunch, dinner. Closed mid-September through May. Children's menu. $$

Grant Village Dining Room

Grant Village, southwestern shore of Yellowstone Lake, Yellowstone National Park, 866-439-7375; www.travelyellowstone.com

Overlooking the lake, guests in this restaurant can enjoy a breakfast buffet, sandwiches and salads in the afternoon and a full dinner menu presenting such western specialties as a farm-raised bison meatloaf with rosemary gravy, mashed red potatoes and sautéed spinach.

American menu. Breakfast, lunch, dinner. Closed October-late May. Children's menu. Reservations required for dinner.$$

Obsidian Dining Room

Old Faithful Snow Lodge, Old Faithful, Yellowstone National Park, 866-439-7375; www.travelyellowstone.com

This homey dining room offers a full breakfast menu with such specialties as a vegan breakfast burrito and eggs Benedict with wild Alaska salmon. The lunch menu is varied with soups, salads and tasty sandwiches, like a honey mustard chicken sandwich served on a pretzel roll. Evening house specialties include Rocky Mountain farm-raised trout and a unique eggplant "mignon" served with fresh mozzarella, wild mushroom orzo and tomato fondue.

American menu. Breakfast, lunch, dinner. Closed mid-October to mid-December and March-May. $$

NORTH OF YELLOWSTONE NATIONAL PARK
Gardiner, MT

★★Yellowstone Mine
Highway 89, Gardiner, 406-848-7336

Relax by the fire in this full-service restaurant and bar while enjoying a hand-cut steak, prime rib or maybe a pasta with a cocktail. Steak menu. Breakfast, dinner, Sunday brunch. Bar. Children's menu. Casual attire. $$

— ALSO RECOMMENDED —
Sawtooth Deli and Café
220 Park St., Gardiner, 406-848-7600

Diners here can start the day with a hearty western huevos rancheros or a breakfast burrito. At lunch, the menu ranges from deli sandwiches to barbecue to brick-oven pizzas. And for dinner, the Sawtooth offers a variety of pastas, seafood and steaks. Beer and wine are served. An outdoor seating area is available.
American menu. Breakfast, lunch, dinner. Outdoor seating. $

Tumbleweed Bookstore & Café
501 Scott Street, Gardiner, 406-848-2225

Browse the new and used books and then sit down to a cup of freshly brewed coffee or a bitter espresso drink and a sandwich.

American menu. Breakfast, lunch. $

EAST OF YELLOWSTONE
Cody, WY

★★Maxwell's
937 Sheridan Ave., Cody, 307-527-7749

For carefully prepared casual meals served with a smile, locals and tourists alike head to Maxwell's. Go for lunch and order a buffalo burger or a fresh spinach salad.
American menu. Lunch, dinner. Closed Sunday. Children's menu. Casual attire. Outdoor seating. $$

— ALSO RECOMMENDED —
Wyoming's Rib and Chop House
1367 Sheridan Ave, Cody, 307-527-7731; www.ribandchophouse.com

Many claim this joint serves up the best baby-back ribs—anywhere. The filet mignon is also highly recommended. The menu isn't limited to satiating carnivore cravings, though. There are also many salads and seafood dishes to choose from, as well as an ample wine list.
American menu. Dinner. $$

WEST OF YELLOWSTONE NATIONAL PARK

★★Three Bear Restaurant
205 Yellowstone Ave., West Yellowstone, 406-646-7353; www.threebearlodge.com

Hearty breakfasts abound here for guests prepping for a big day in the park. And when they return, there's something on the dinner menu for everyone, from big buffalo burgers to the catch of the day.

American menu. Breakfast, dinner. Closed late March-early May, late October to mid-December. Bar. Children's menu. Casual attire. $$

— ALSO RECOMMENDED —

Beartooth Barbecue

111 N. Canyon St., West Yellowstone, 406-646-0227

For a mountain appetite, try Beartooth's ribs with their tasty sauce and local brews on tap. The pulled pork is also popular.

Barbecue menu. Lunch, dinner. $

Running Bear Pancake House

Corner of Madison and Hayden, West Yellowstone, 406-646-7703

Travelers looking for a hearty breakfast that will stick to their ribs till it's time for lunch at the top of the trail leave the Running Bear satisfied. The pancake sandwich is a particular hit, making a real meal of the Bear's specialty pancakes by adding ham or bacon between them and an egg on top. Or opt for a traditional stack with a creative addition like coconut. Lunch offerings include burgers, salads and sandwiches.

American menu. Breakfast, lunch. $

IN GRAND TETON NATIONAL PARK

— ALSO RECOMMENDED —

Jenny Lake Lodge

Jenny Lake, Grand Teton National Park, 307-733-4647; www.gtlc.com

The always-delicious, five-course prix-fixe dinner here is dining at its finest. An extensive, award-winning wine list and impeccable service make this a first-class restaurant. Breakfast is also a prix-fixe affair, featuring such gourmet treats as Belgian waffles with pecans and crab cake eggs Benedict. Lunch is á la carte. Foodies shouldn't miss this exquisite restaurant in such an unlikely yet stunning location.

Continental menu. Breakfast, lunch, dinner. Reservations required for breakfast and dinner. Jacket suggested at dinner. $$$

John Colter Café Court

Colter Bay Village, Grand Teton National Park

Visitors looking for a quicker meal or snack can get it here. With everything from Mexican food to pizza, the options should make everyone in the family happy. Box lunches packed for picnics on the trail are also available.

International menu. Lunch, dinner. Closed mid-September through May. $

SOUTH OF GRAND TETON NATIONAL PARK

Jackson, WY

★★Calico Restaurant

2650 Teton Village Road, Jackson, 307-733-2460; www.calicorestaurant.com

This family-friendly eatery produces not only primo pizzas, which is how it got its start, but also an array of traditional Italian dishes, including, chicken parmesan, ravioli and risotto.

Italian menu. Dinner. Bar. Children's menu. Casual attire. Outdoor seating. $$

★★★Blue Lion

160 N. Millward St., Jackson, 307-733-3912; www.bluelionrestaurant.com

Housed in a charming old home, this restaurant offers creative preparations of a wide variety of dishes from a southwestern duck cakes appetizer to a rack of lamb rubbed with Dijon mustard and served with both a peppercorn-rosemary sauce and jalapeno-mint sauce. The restaurant also offers a good wine list.

American menu. Dinner. Bar. Children's menu. Casual attire. Reservations recommended. Outdoor seating. $$$

★★★Snake River Grill

84 E. Broadway, Jackson, 307-733-0557; www.snakerivergrill.com

Hardwood floors and a cozy stone fireplace are set in the center of this tastefully appointed rustic restaurant. Diners will appreciate its charming northwest ambiance as much as its creations from the kitchen. Dishes such as a steak tartare pizza appetizer and a roasted elk chop served with a pumpkin tart, green beans and coffee-bourbon steak sauce provide a unique gourmet dining experience.

American menu. Dinner. Closed April and November. Bar. Casual attire. Reservations recommended. Outdoor seating. $$$

★★★Sweetwater

85 S. King St., Jackson, 307-733-3553; www.restauranteur.com/sweetwater

Housed in an 1890's log cabin about two blocks from the Jackson town square, this restaurant provides a creative take on a traditional American menu, from the chile-lime crab cakes appetizer to the 14-ounce prime rib served with strawberry au jus and feta cheese.

American menu. Lunch, dinner. Closed first two weeks in April. Children's menu. Casual attire. Reservations recommended. Outdoor seating. $$$

Teton Village, WY

★★★The Alpenrose in the Alpenhof Lodge

3255 W. Village Drive, Teton Village, 307-733-3242, 800-732-3244; www.alpenhoflodge.com

At the base of the Jackson Hole ski area, the restaurant at this Bavarian-style lodge is the most well-regarded dining room in the area. Here the emphasis is on hearty dishes of western-influenced con-

★
★
★
★

tinental cuisine. Variations on classic themes include the tableside preparation of caribou steak Diane or a great bananas Foster. The property's upstairs bistro offers more casual fare.

American menu. Dinner. Closed Sunday-Monday; also November. Bar. Casual attire. $$$

★★★The Westbank Grill at the Four Seasons Resort

7680 Granite Loop Road, Teton Village, 307-732-5000; www.fourseasons.com/ jacksonhole

The Westbank Grill is the finest example of western flavors merged with sophistication. It also offers diners awe-inspiring views of the Teton Mountains. The restaurant is divided into an indoor dining room and outdoor terrace. The dining room boasts a large stone fireplace; tile floors; dark, exposed wood beams; vaulted ceilings; and, of course, plenty of windows. The outdoor terrace is heated and provides an outdoor fireplace. The menu focuses on Jackson Hole's abundance of wild game, fish and beef. Choices range from buffalo jerky–wrapped Hudson Valley foie gras to pan-seared wild king salmon to smoked, salt-roasted pheasant to mesquite-smoked and pepper-crusted buffalo tenderloin. Be sure to try the signature entrée: espresso-rubbed antelope loin. The Westbank Grill is a great place to recuperate from an active day.

American menu. Breakfast, lunch, dinner. Bar. Children's menu. Business casual attire. Reservations recommended. Outdoor seating. $$$

★

★

★

★

★

YOSEMITE NATIONAL PARK

YOSEMITE IS ONE OF THE MOST POPULAR AND BEST-KNOWN NATIONAL parks in the world, and as the primary guinea pig in the experiment of national land protection, it deserves that status. Not only was Yosemite one of the first U.S. national parks, but Yosemite Valley was the very first bit of scenic land set aside for protection by any federal government. By the mid-19th century, tourists had heard tales of "the Incomparable Valley" from descriptions written by their astounded contemporaries, such as Horace Greeley and Ralph Waldo Emerson. Word of Yosemite's majesty spread throughout the United States and the world. Early opportunists and entrepreneurs saw money-making potential in this influx of sightseers and soon began constructing hotels and residences in the wilderness. The area was developed further and further with livestock set to pasture in Yosemite's meadows and orchards planted in its valley. As a result, the fragile ecosystem suffered, and conservationists appealed their novel idea of governmental land protection to President Lincoln. In 1864, Abraham Lincoln granted the land to the state of California as an "inalienable public trust."

In 1890, naturalist John Muir, the "father of our parks system," successfully lobbied for Yosemite to receive protective status equal to Yellowstone's under the newly established park system. Muir's devotion to the area came after abandoning everything else to live in the park, exploring and reveling in what he called "the most songful streams in the world . . . the noblest forests, the loftiest granite domes, the deepest ice-sculptured canyons." The park's storied waterfalls are an awe-inspiring sight from the valley in spring and early summer when the snowmelt is most plentiful. But look beyond the falls. Within its nearly 2,000 square miles—95 percent of which is designated as official wilderness—Yosemite offers stunning granite peaks, vast high country, elevations soaring from 1,800 to over 13,000 feet, exquisite alpine and subalpine meadows, glorious wildflowers, thousands-year-old giant sequoias, pristine lakes, unspoiled snowfields, remarkable glaciers, 800 miles of trails, meandering streams and sandy river beaches.

Then there's Yosemite Valley itself, the seemingly miraculous result of years of interaction between glaciers and rocks. What could have ended up looking like just another valley, nature endowed with countless gifts of random, immeasurable beauty, including the famously grand curve of Half Dome, the staggeringly sheer granite wall of El Capitan, and the magnificent annual roar of Yosemite and Bridalveil Falls. The sport of rock climbing was born here, inspired by the dramatic granite walls and their surrounding beauty. It's to see those same stones and streams that day-trippers and globetrotters have been traveling to this little remote valley for a century and a half. All in all, the number of visitors surpasses 3 million a year now. Fortunately, the views are powerful enough that they tend to distract from the crowds.

Yosemite, California, 209-372-0200 (general park information); www.nps.gov/yose; www.yosemite.org

WHAT TO SEE

From hot spots teeming with tourists to downright solitude in distant wilderness, Yosemite is a big place to explore. Coming into the park ($20 per vehicle, valid for seven days) on Highway 41 at the **South Entrance** on Wawona Road, visitors are almost immediately faced with one of the park's great attractions, **Mariposa Grove**. This is the largest and most visited of Yosemite's three groves of giant sequoia trees. The two-mile road to the grove is closed to cars from November to April, depending on conditions, but can be walked, skied, or snowshoed anytime. Merced and Tuolumne groves are near Crane Flat, northwest of Yosemite Valley. The **Grizzly Giant** in Mariposa Grove, 209 feet high and 34.7 feet in diameter at its base, is estimated to be 2,700 years old.

Continuing on Wawona Road, you'll come to the **Wawona Information Station** where, during the summer months, you'll find rangers who can answer questions and help plan your trip. At Wawona, you may choose to stop at the **Pioneer Yosemite History Center**. A tribute to the park's beginnings, the center teaches about Yosemite's role in inspiring the creation of national parks worldwide and features a collection of the park's historic buildings and artifacts. From Wawona, the drive to Yosemite Valley is a little less than an hour. If you're driving straight into the valley via Wawona Road, you would be remiss to not stop at the **Tunnel View Point** at the east end of the Wawona Tunnel. From here, you'll get your first views of Bridalveil Fall and El Capitan climbing up out of the valley.

Before reaching the turn toward the valley, though, you'll come to the **Glacier Point Road** turnoff, which makes one of the best starting points if this is your first trip to the park. This scenic drive leads to one of the most spectacular viewpoints in the park. The exquisite panorama at **Glacier Point** from the rim 3,214 feet above Yosemite Valley captures views of the high Sierra and the valley below and faces Half Dome head-on in all its glory. But that's not all. Across the valley from here are Yosemite Falls, the Royal Arches, North Dome, Basket Dome, Mount Watkins and Washington Column. Up the Merced Canyon are Vernal and Nevada falls. Griz-

★
★
★
★

zly Peak, Liberty Cap, and the towering peaks along the Sierras' crest and the Clark Range mark the skyline. The road is closed to vehicles in winter but open to skiers and snowshoers.

It takes a little less than an hour from Glacier Point to drive down into **Yosemite Valley** from here. Obviously a must-see, and the main reason most people come to this park, the valley lies at the foot of such wonders as the 5,000-foot **Half Dome**, the 3,000-foot sheer granite wall of **El Capitan** and roaring **Yosemite** and **Bridalveil Falls**. Driving east into the canyon, there are several sights. Follow signs for **Yosemite Village** to reach the **Yosemite Valley Visitor Center** (209-372-0200), the largest information station in the park, where you'll find details on all there is to see and do during your stay. Next to the visitor center is the **Yosemite Museum** with displays that explore the cultural history of the indigenous Miwok and Paiute peoples and an art gallery. Just behind the museum is the **Indian Village of Ahwahnee**, a reconstructed Miwok-Paiute village with a self-guided trail, which is always open. Across the street from the museum, you will find the historic **Yosemite Cemetery**. The village is also home to the **Ansel Adams Gallery**, formerly known as Best's Studio, featuring the photography that made the park's landmarks recognizable to people across the country. Prints of Adams' work are available here along with contemporary photog-raphy and other fine art, handicrafts, books and souvenirs.

Traveling a bit farther east into the valley leads to the **Ahwahnee Hotel**, a National Historic Landmark. This hotel's rustic architecture is as strikingly grand and majestic as the natural granite walls surrounding it. It's worth a stop even for a tour or a bite to eat. Continuing to the end of the valley on Southside Drive, you'll find **LeConte Memorial Lodge** (late May-September), a National Historic Landmark and now a Sierra Club–operated visitor center. The Lodge offers a library and educational programs. Beyond that, you'll reach the **Nature Center at Happy Isles** (May-September), where you can learn about the area's wildlife and different environments from family-oriented natural history exhibits.

There are many ways to explore all there is to see in Yosemite Valley (see "What to Do"), and a whole vacation at the park could be spent in just this area. But other parts of the park are equally unforgettable. For a little solitude or to experience the more remote wilderness, take Northside Drive back west and out of Yosemite Valley to El Portal Road to **Big Oak Flat Road** toward Highway 120. About 30 minutes, or 16 miles, out of Yosemite Valley, just past the junction with Highway 120, is **Crane Flat**, an area of forest and meadow that gives access to the **Tuolumne** and **Merced Groves** of giant sequoias. There are no roads to the groves; the big trees are a two- to three-mile

★
★
★
★

hike from Crane Flat. Beyond Crane Flat to the north is the **Big Oak Flat Information Station** at the Big Oak Flat entrance to the park. Exiting the park there and taking Evergreen Road north to the **Hetch Hetchy entrance** will get you to **Hetch Hetchy Road** (closed overnight) and eventually the **Hetch Hetchy Reservoir**, about an hour and a half from Yosemite Valley without stops. This reservoir provides much of San Francisco's drinking water, and the area has many less popular wilderness trails.

Heading east from the junction of Big Oak Flat Road and Highway 120, the highway becomes **Tioga Road**. Closed in winter, this road climbs steadily and serves as the threshold of the vast wilderness—mountain peaks, passes and lakes—of the high country, accessible only via horseback or on foot. The road also passes **Tenaya Lake,** the park's most accessible mountain lake, and about an hour and a half from Yosemite Valley reaches **Tuolumne Meadows**, an unbeatable destination for hikers, and the **Tuolumne Meadows Visitor Center**. Also in the area is the **Parsons Memorial Lodge** (late June-early September), where visitors can learn about the history of Tuolumne Meadows and hike 30 minutes to the spot where John Muir and a friend came up with the idea of establishing Yosemite as a national park.

WHAT TO DO

BACKPACKING

Yosemite Mountaineering School & Guide Service (209-372-8344; www.yosemitepark.com) offers both group and customized overnight backcountry camping trips, as well as overnight Learn-to-Backpack Trips. Experienced guides will share not only their knowledge of gear, wilderness and navigation skills but also information on Yosemite's geology, history, plants and wildlife. Reservations are required.

Experienced backcountry campers have countless options in Yosemite's vast wilderness. Free permits are required year-round for overnight trips, and Yosemite uses a trailhead quota system to reduce impact on the most popular areas and limit the number of people starting off on a particular trail on a given day (see www.nps.gov/yose/planyour-visit/wildpermits.htm). Permit reservations can be made up to 24 weeks in advance for $5 per person at www.yosemitesecure.org/wildpermit. They must be picked up in person the day of or the day before the hike.

BIKING

Yosemite Valley offers bike rentals and more than 12 miles of paved bike paths. Cyclists are also permitted to ride on regular roads as long as they follow traffic laws. Unfortunately, mountain biking and off-trail riding aren't allowed in the park.

BUS TOURS

Below are a few of the guided bus tours available. For more information or to make reservations for any of these tours, call 209-372-4386.

Big Trees Tram Tour: This 75-minute tour through Mariposa Grove details the history of the ancient trees and is available in multiple languages. Adult $16, child $11. May-October.

Toulomne Meadows Tour: An eight-hour tour, this route takes visitors out of the valley on scenic Tioga Road, making stops at Olmstead Point, Tenaya Lake and Toulomne Meadows, where you have time to take a short hike or relax and enjoy the scenery. Adult $23, child $11.50. July-Labor Day.

Valley Floor Tour: This two-hour bus tour, guided by park rangers, acquaints visitors with the most famous sites in the Yosemite Valley, as well as its history, geology and ecology. The tour departs several times daily from Yosemite Lodge at the Falls. Adult $22, child $11.50. Year-round.

FISHING

With 58 streams and a combined length of 770 miles, the wild and scenic Merced River and countless mountain lakes, you're bound to find a good spot. All lakes and reservoirs are open year-round. The stream and river season begins on the last Saturday in April and ends November 15. Valid California sport fishing licenses are required. Bait fishing is prohibited. Inquire in the park about special regulations.

GOLFING

The first regulation course in the Sierra Nevada, Wawona Golf Course, established in 1918, features a 9-hole par-35 course in a spectacular setting. It's one of the few organic golf courses in the United States and is a certified Audubon Cooperative Sanctuary. For more information and tee times, call 209-375-6572.

HIKING

With 800 miles of trails, just think how much you'd be missing if you didn't go for a hike. Below is just a sampling of the wide variety of hikes available. For guided hikes, call 209-372-4386.

──────── **EASY** ────────

Bridalveil Fall
0.5 miles
Trailhead: Bridalveil Fall parking area

An easy paved trail takes you directly from the parking lot to the bottom of this famous fall.

Lower Yosemite Falls
1-mile loop; half of loop is wheelchair accessible
Trailhead: Lower Yosemite Falls

A quick, easy walk will get you to great views of both Upper and Lower Yosemite Falls in spring

★
★
★
★

and early summer. The waterfall is usually dry by late July or August.

Mirror Lake

2 miles round-trip/5 miles round-trip with full loop around lake; trail to lake is wheelchair accessible.

Trailhead: Mirror Lake Trailhead

A gentle walk on a paved trail leads directly from the trailhead to the serene Mirror Lake. Turn right off of the main trail at the stone bridge for the 5-mile loop.

———— MODERATE ————

Valley Floor Loop

6.5 miles round-trip for half loop, 13 miles round-trip for full loop

Trailhead: Camp 4

This long but easy hike hits the valley's highlights. Walk on some of the oldest trails in the park to catch views of Sentinal Rock, Cathedral Rocks, El Capitan, Three Brothers, Bridalveil Fall and Yosemite Fall. The half loop crosses the Merced River. To complete the full loop, continue to Bridalveil Fall.

Gaylor Lakes

2 miles round-trip; 500-foot elevation gain

Trailhead: Tioga Pass Entrance Station

This worthy hike will earn you views of Mount Dana and Dana Meadows and surrounding peaks from the ridge top. Then descend 200 feet to Lower Gaylor Lake.

Upper Cathedral Lake

7 miles round-trip; 1,000-foot elevation gain

Trailhead: Cathedral Lakes, 0.5 mile west of Tuolumne Meadows Visitor Center.

The steady climb to Upper Cathedral Lake offers impressive views of Cathedral Peak's stunning granite spires, beautiful mountain meadows and, of course, the tranquility of the alpine lakes at the top. A spur trail near the top of the main trail leads down to Lower Cathedral Lake.

Glen Aulin

11 miles round-trip

Trailhead: Soda Springs

A classic Yosemite hike, this one takes you by the meadows, granite domes and waterfalls that characterize the park. Four miles from the trailhead, you will reach Tuolumne Fall and White Cascade. If 11 beautiful miles aren't enough for you, continue on to California Fall, upping the round-trip to 15 miles, or Waterwheel Fall, 17 miles.

—— MODERATE TO STRENUOUS ——

Vernal Fall

1.6 miles round-trip to bridge; 400-foot elevation gain,

3 miles round-trip to Vernal Fall; 1,000-foot elevation gain

Trailhead: Happy Isles

The Vernal Fall bridge is just 0.75 miles from the trailhead and offers a spectacular view of the falls. If you continue past the bridge, take the Mist Trail at the fork for another 0.5 mile up 600 slippery and steep granite steps. Beware of your footing—waterfall spray adds an additional challenge to the hike.

★

★

★

★

Upper Yosemite Fall

7.2 miles; 2,700-foot elevation gain

Trailhead: Yosemite Falls Trailhead Camp 4

A stiff hike up one of Yosemite's oldest trails will reward you with fantastic views of the valley from 2,425 feet above and an intimate look at the impressive Yosemite Fall when it's roaring in spring and early summer.

MULE AND HORSEBACK RIDING

There are three stables in the park: Tuolumne Stable, Yosemite Valley Stable and Wawona Stable. They offer two- and four-hour, and all-day rides through stunning scenery on sure-footed animals. You may also ride your own mule or horse on most trails. Check with a wilderness permit station for regulations.

RAFTING AND KAYAKING

Both are permitted on the Merced River between Stoneman Bridge and Sentinal Beach and on the South Fork of the Merced in the Wawona area. Each occupant must have a flotation device. Rafts are typically for rent in the park in June and July. Kayaking is also permitted in Tenaya Lake.

ROCK CLIMBING

A mecca for rockaholics, Yosemite might be the perfect place to pick up a new hobby. Yosemite Mountaineering School (209-372-1000; www.yosemitepark.com) offers beginner Go-Climb-a-Rock classes, Crack Climbing classes and more.

SKIING

If you visit the park in winter, cross-country skiing, ice skating in Yosemite Valley and snowshoeing in the Badger Pass area are a blast. Badger Pass (801-559-4884; www.badgerpass.com) makes a good family ski destination with 85 percent of the mountain devoted to beginner and intermediate trails. The area is equipped with one triple, three double and one cable tow lift, ski patrol, and rentals. Open mid-December to late March, daily 9 a.m.-4 p.m., depending on conditions.

WILDLIFE

From the low, dry foothills to the highest peaks, Yosemite's animal habitats are so greatly varied that they allow more than 250 species of fish, amphibians, reptiles, birds and mammals to make the park their home. Lower elevations have relatively high diversity, thanks to the milder climate. Fewer species live at higher elevations. Here is a brief guide to some of Yosemite's most interesting types of wildlife and how you might be able to identify them.

Black Bears: The last of the Yosemite grizzlies was shot in the early 1920s, leaving only their

173

YOSEMITE

★

★

★

★

cousins, the black bears to call this park home. In Yosemite, the black bears are rarely black; they are usually more brown, blonde, cinnamon, and even white. It is extremely important not to feed bears (or any wildlife for that matter) or leave food out. Though bears instinctively eat a variety of natural foods, these intelligent mammals will readily adapt and eat human food if it becomes available. This poses a problem, as bears exposed to human foods then change their habits and begin to seek those foods in campgrounds, parking lots and from backpackers. These typically nonthreatening animals can then become very aggressive toward humans, and park management must take action by killing the bear. Campgrounds provide bear-safe boxes for overnight food storage. Backpackers must carry a bear canister (a portable container for storing food) with them. And day hikers should take care to close all car windows and doors completely when leaving a vehicle unattended for the day and not to store food (including canned drinks) in the car at night.

California Ground Squirrel: Frequently spotted in the summer, these burrowing critters have patchy gray and white fur. They become less active or hibernate in the winter.

Coyotes: These speedy canines are more likely to be heard than seen. Their nightly yipping echoes off the granite walls of the park.

Marmots: These cuddly looking large, golden-brown rodents are often spotted from Olmstead Point to Tuolumne Meadows and as far up as the highest peaks in the park. They love to burrow in broken rock slide.

Mountain Lions: Primarily nocturnal, the mountain lion typically avoids developed areas and is rarely seen by humans. These animals are also referred to as panthers, pumas, or cougars.

Mule Deer: Also called "black-tailed deer" for their distinguishing characteristic, they are one of the most commonly seen animals throughout the park. Watch for them in meadows and oak groves—and, of course, in front of your car. More people are attacked each year in Yosemite by mule deer than by any other animal—they may seem tame, but don't approach them!

Rainbow Trout: The rainbow trout with multicolored scales and a large pink band across its body is found in the lower Merced River in Yosemite Valley and Tuolumne River.

Rattlesnake: Easy to distinguish by the rattle at the end of its tail, this is the only poisonous snake of the 13 species found in the park. Its role in Yosemite's ecosystem is to keep the rodent population under control. They are not often encountered, but watch for them in dry, rocky places. If you see one, walk around it.

Western Gray Squirrel: These bushy-tailed squirrels are one of the most commonly seen animals in the park and are often spotted even in winter.

BIRDS

Dark-Eyed Junco: This small slate-gray bird has two white tail feathers, which "flash" when it takes flight, and black on its head.

Golden Eagle: Named for its crown of feathers, this formerly endangered species is doing well in Yosemite.

Great Gray Owl: Yosemite is the southernmost habitat worldwide for these large speckled birds. They can be found in Yosemite Valley, often in trees at the edge of meadows.

Peregrine Falcon: The peregrine is the fastest bird of prey in the world, swooping to speeds of up to 200 miles per hour. This formerly endangered species has made a strong comeback. Several pairs nest on the cliffs of Half Dome, El Capitan and the Hetch Hetchy area from March through July.

Raven: Typically seen in pairs, these large black birds are very intelligent, and are known for their acrobatic flying.

Red-Tail Hawk: This red-tailed bird of prey is very common in Yosemite from the Valley to Tuolumne Meadows.

Stellar's Jay: This blue-feathered bird with a black crest and a loud voice is characterized by its mischievousness. It's often seen snatching unwatched food in picnic areas.

CAMPING

According to his good friend Teddy Roosevelt, John Muir said that camping is "the only way in which to see at their best the majesty and charm of the Sierras," and if you're down with dirt, we second that. Yosemite has 13 campgrounds, including accommodations for traditional tent camping, RVs and canvas tents, and of course, an extensive backcountry for the more adventurous. Camping is limited to 30 days in a calendar year; May to mid-September, camping is limited to seven days in Yosemite Valley, in the rest of the park to 14 days. Campsites in the valley campgrounds, Hodgdon Meadow, Crane Flat, Wawona and half of Tuolumne Meadows campgrounds may be reserved in advance (877-444-6777; www.recreation.gov). Reservations are highly recommended, as these sites are routinely booked solid in the summer. Other park campgrounds are on a first-come, first-serve basis and typically fill very early in the day. Winter camping is permitted in the Valley, Hodgdon Meadow and Wawona only.

HOTELS

In the Park

★★★The Ahwahnee Hotel

Yosemite Valley, Yosemite National Park, 209-372-1407, 801-559-4884; www.yosemitepark.com

Opened in 1927, this storied

175

YOSEMITE

★

★

★

★

hotel is a celebration of Native American and colonial American design. Its wooded, natural setting is perfectly complemented by the Native American décor, including artifacts and artwork created by the Yosemite Miwok. The rooms and suites may appear rustic, but their amenities are world-class. The public spaces are especially glorious, with impressive stained glass windows, intricate stonework and mosaics in the lobby, as well as a lounge, solarium and dining room.

93 rooms, 6 suites, 24 cottages. Restaurant, bar. Tennis. Pool. $$$$

★★Wawona Hotel

Yosemite National Park, Wawona, 209-375-6556, 801-559-4884; www.yosemitepark.com

Since 1856, Yosemite visitors have been stopping here for hearty meals and a comfortable place to lay their heads. A National Historic Landmark, the aged white wooden buildings with charming Victorian interiors and large verandas overlooking the lawns make a comfortable place to relax after enjoying all of the golf, swimming, tennis, fishing, hiking, mule and horseback rides and tours that the area has to offer. Rooms with and without private bathrooms can be combined to create suites.

104 rooms. Restaurant, bar. Pool. $

★★Yosemite Lodge at the Falls

Highway 41/140, Yosemite National Park, 559-252-4848,
801-559-4884; www.yosemitepark.com

This family-friendly lodge offers the convenience of prime location in the middle of beautiful Yosemite Valley and all the modern amenities and comforts of a hotel. Wi-fi, an ATM, a full-service post office, a heated pool and an amphitheater for nightly ranger programs are all available onsite. The hotel staff will also arrange tours, lessons and horseback rides or rent bikes for guests. And after a long day in the outdoors, guests can sit down to dinner with a spectacular view of Yosemite Falls from the hotel restaurant.

249 rooms. Wireless Internet access. Two restaurants, bar. Pool. $$

— ALSO RECOMMENDED —

The Redwoods in Yosemite

8038 Chilnualna Falls Road, Wawona (Inside Yosemite's south entrance), 209-375-6666; www.redwoodsinyosemite.com

These privately owned vacation homes and cabins in the forests of Yosemite offer accommodations from one to six bedrooms to suit every guest's needs. From rustic to modern, the selection varies widely, but in each rental, guests can expect a fully equipped kitchen, fireplace or wood-burning stove with firewood, and a barbecue grill. There are two markets, a post office and gift shop within walking distance.

130 homes. Wireless Internet access in some homes. Pets accepted. $$

Big Oak Flat Entrance (West of Highway 120)

★★The Groveland Hotel

18767 Main St., Groveland, 209-962-4000, 800-273-3314; www.groveland.com

A great place to relax after spending time in the mountains and just a half hour from the park entrance, this Victorian style bed-and-breakfast, built in 1849, features old-world charm updated with modern amenities. Throughout the inn, you'll find European antiques, romantic floral décor, featherbeds and free Wi-Fi—not to mention decadent wine and cheese or champagne and chocolate room service options and a full menu of spa treatments.

17 rooms. Wireless Internet access. Complimentary continental breakfast. Restaurant, bar. $

— ALSO RECOMMENDED —

Evergreen Lodge

33160 Evergreen Road, Groveland (8 miles from Highway 120 west entrance), 209-379-2606, 800-935-6343; www.evergreenlodge.com

These charming forest cabins accommodating up to six people make the perfect lodging for a family vacation, offering privacy, modern amenities such as satellite radio and activities for the whole family. The onsite tavern, popular with locals, offers ten beers on tap, an extensive list of California wines and frequent live music; the restaurant serves three meals a day, and a general store sells quick to-go meals and other necessities.

In the recreation building, guests can relax by the fireplace with board games, puzzles, books, or a massage. Knowledgeable staff can help you plan and book tours, hikes and more.

68 cabins. Wireless Internet access. Restaurant, bar. $$

Arch Rock Entrance (West of Highway 140)

★★Yosemite View Lodge

11136 Highway 140, El Portal, 209-379-2681, 888-742-4371; www.yosemite-motels.com

Offering basic accommodations just outside the park, this motel features three pools, family suites with kitchenettes, two restaurants and a bar. The best part is it's only a stone's throw from the park, which makes hitting the trails early a lot easier.

278 rooms. Two restaurants, bar. Pool. $

— ALSO RECOMMENDED —

Little Valley Inn

3483 Brooks Road, Mariposa (35 miles from Yosemite's Highway 140 entrance), 209-742-6204, 800-889-5444; www.littlevalley.com

A quiet cabin in the woods, this bed and breakfast features rooms with private entrances and decks plus refrigerators, a family-sized room with a full kitchen and a tranquil setting about a 40 minute drive from the entrance to Yosemite. A breakfast buffet is served each morning. Guests can pan for gold in the seasonal creek.

6 rooms. Complimentary continental breakfast. $$

Wawona Road/South Entrance (South of Highway 41)

★★Best Western Yosemite Gateway Inn

40530 Highway 41, Oakhurst, 559-683-2378, 800-780-7234; www.bestwestern.com

There's something to be said for knowing what to expect, and this classic American chain dependably offers comfortable accommodations at an affordable price. Only 15 miles from the south entrance of the park, the hotel offers sightseeing tours departing from the lobby, guided hiking trips and fly fishing. Bass Lake is also nearby for easy access to water sports.

105 rooms, 17 suites. High-speed Internet. Restaurant, bar. Fitness center. Pool. Pets accepted. $

★★★★Chateau du Sureau

48688 Victoria Lane, Oakhurst, 559-683-6860; www.chateausureau.com

Tucked away in the heart of the Sierra Nevada forest near Yosemite is a lovely hideaway known as Chateau du Sureau. Foodies have been coming to the Elderberry House restaurant since 1984 for its haute cuisine, and the restaurant did so well that owner Erna Kubin-Clanin opened an inn to accommodate her guests. This charming Provençal-style castle features quaint balconies and a dramatic round fieldstone tower. The grounds are planted with manicured topiaries, and the stucco walls are dotted with elderberry bushes that also cover the castle's rolling grounds. Inside, chambermaids in black with white linen aprons deliver baskets of goodies and tea. There is no front desk, no check-in formalities. The unique bedrooms, nearly all of which have fireplaces, include canopy and sleigh beds, cathedral ceilings and views of the Sierra Nevada Mountains. After a long day on the trails, nothing soothes like a visit to the Spa du Sureau, featuring a decadent double treatment room with a black marble fireplace, two massage tables separated by translucent drapes, lounge chairs and a Jacuzzi. The spa also features a Hydrostorm shower system—one of only a handful in the country that uses aroma and color therapy aquatics.

10 rooms. Closed two weeks in January. Complimentary full breakfast. Restaurant, bar. Spa. $$$$

★★The Pines Resort

54432 Road 432, Bass Lake, 559-642-3121, 800-350-7463; www.basslake.com

Less than 30 minutes from the park entrance, this family-friendly lakefront resort offers something to keep everyone busy from boat rentals, tennis and karaoke to spa services. Accommodations range from resort-style suites to two-story rustic chalets with private decks and picnic tables, barbecue grills and fully equipped kitchens for the convenience of large groups.

84 chalets, 20 suites. High-speed

★

★

★

★

★

Internet access. Complimentary continental breakfast. Restaurant, bar. Tennis. Pool. Whirlpool. $$

★★★Tenaya Lodge at Yosemite
1122 Highway 41, Fish Camp, 559-683-6555, 888-514-2167; www.tenayalodge.com

Situated on 35 acres adjacent to the Sierra National Forest and just two miles from Yosemite, this elegant mountain retreat is just the place to see the sights without forsaking the comforts of home. The newly renovated guest rooms and suites share an upscale yet rustic appeal. Guests are supplied with all-natural, eco-friendly bath amenities. Activities are plentiful, both on the property and off, including a terrific children's program. Enjoy fine dining at Sierra, while Jackalopes Bar & Grill is ideal for the entire family.

244 rooms. Wireless Internet access. Three restaurants, bar. Fitness center. Pool. Spa. $$

— ALSO RECOMMENDED —

The Homestead
41110 Road 600, Ahwahnee, 559-683-0495, 800-483-0495; www.homesteadcottages.com

At this tranquil family-run lodge just 30 minutes south of the park, guests get as much or as little individual attention as they want. Six separate charming cottages offer comfort, privacy and convenience for optimal relaxation. They all have fully equipped kitchens stocked daily with coffees, teas, hot chocolate, milk, juice, muffins, fruit, granola and other essentials. A gas barbeque and patio is available to guests. On top of all this, there are also high-quality horse accommodations for those who want to bring along their equine friends.

6 cottages. Complimentary continental breakfast. $

The Hounds Tooth Inn
42071 Highway 41, Oakhurst, 559-642-6600, 888-642-6610; www.houndstoothinn.com

On 3.5 acres, 12 miles from Yosemite, this Victorian-style bed-and-breakfast offers itself as a relaxation refuge for those looking to explore the park or simply the peace and quiet. Each room is unique, some offering spas, fireplaces and views. Each afternoon, complimentary wine, coffee and teas are served. The breakfast includes various breads, cereals, fruit, sweet cake, juice, coffees, teas and a hot dish, providing plenty of hiking fuel.

12 rooms, 1 cottage. Complimentary full breakfast. $$

Tioga Road/East Entrance (East of Highway 120)

★The Yosemite Gateway Motel
51340 Highway 395, Lee Vining, 760-647-6467; www.yosemitegatewaymotel.com

For Yosemite visitors heading to the park from the east and seeking a basic room on a budget, the Gateway Motel fits the bill. The motel is just 14 miles east of the park and offers a pleasant view of Lake Mono.

18 rooms. Whirlpool. $

★
★
★
★

In the Park

── **ALSO RECOMMENDED** ──

The Ahwahnee Dining Room

The Ahwahnee Hotel, Yosemite National Park, Yosemite Valley, 209-372-1489, 801-559-4884; www.yosemitepark.com

The architecture alone is enough to make a meal here worthwhile with a grand 34-foot-high beamed ceiling and floor-to-ceiling windows exposing the beauty beyond the glass. But the gourmet California cuisine, including organic, sustainable and locally grown ingredients, could easily stand alone. Try a specialty such as the roast prime rib of California grass-fed beef au jus or the spinach and chickpea crêpes.

California menu. Breakfast, lunch, dinner, Sunday brunch. Bar. Reservations recommended. Business casual attire for dinner. Outdoor seating. $$$

Mountain Room Restaurant

Yosemite Lodge at the Falls, Yosemite National Park, Yosemite Valley, 209-372-1274

The Mountain Room offers views of the spectacular Yosemite Falls and a central location, not to mention fresh California cuisine with chef's specialties such as smoked trout cakes and mahi-mahi Monterey.

California menu. Dinner. Bar. Children's menu. Reservations for parties of 9+ only. $$

Pizza Deck

Curry Village, Yosemite National Park, Yosemite Valley

For casual outdoor dining after a long day in the park, you can gaze at views of Glacier Point and Royal Arches with a cold one while waiting for your pizza to bake.

Pizza. Lunch, dinner. Open weekends/holidays only December to mid-March. Casual attire. Outdoor seating. $

Wawona Dining Room

Wawona Hotel, Yosemite National Park, Wawona, 209-275-1425, 801-559-4884; www.yosemitepark.com

This Victorian fine dining room serves traditional cuisine influenced by fresh, seasonal ingredients and contemporary culinary trends, resulting in such entrées as a grilled pork tenderloin served with mashed sweet potatoes, braised greens and bourbon apple compote. At lunch, don't miss the restaurant's award-winning white turkey chili, which has been featured in multiple cookbooks.

American menu. Breakfast, lunch, dinner, Sunday brunch. Bar. Reservations recommended. Outdoor seating. $$

Big Oak Flat Entrance (West of Highway 120)

★★The Victorian Room

18767 Main St., Groveland, 209-962-4000, 800-273-3314; www.groveland.com

This restaurant in The Groveland Hotel features the same charming Victorian décor as the rest of the

180

YOSEMITE

★
★
★
★
★

establishment and offers a California menu, including entrées such as pan-seared Pacific salmon with an organic three-grain rice pilaf, smoked wild char roe and a white wine butter sauce.

California menu. Dinner. Closed Monday. Bar. Children's menu. Reservations recommended. Outdoor seating. $$

Arch Rock Entrance (West of Highway 140)

— ALSO RECOMMENDED —

Mariposa Pizza Factory
5005 Fifth St. at Highway 140, Mariposa, 209-966-3112; www.mariposapf.com

The slogan "We toss 'em, they're awesome" pretty much says it all. Hungry hikers will be satisfied by the selection of pastas, calzones, sandwiches and soups, and a salad bar.

Pizza, fast food. Lunch, dinner. $

Wawona Road/South Entrance (South of Highway 41)

★★★★Erna's Elderberry House
48688 Victoria Lane, Oakhurst, 559-683-6800; www.chateausureau.com

This restaurant offers an exquisite seasonal menu of California cuisine served in a setting decorated with antique French Provençal furnishings, brocade tapestries and original oil paintings. Since 1984, Erna Kubin-Clanin has guided the kitchen toward farm-raised meats and local produce. Prix fixe menus change daily and consist of six courses paired with three or four California or international wines. The 725-bottle wine list is overseen by Erna's daughter, Renée, and includes several rare, cult California wines, as well as many Austrian selections in honor of Erna's birthplace.

California, French menu. Dinner, Sunday brunch. Closed first two weeks in January. Bar. Business casual attire. Reservations recommended. Valet parking. Outdoor seating. $$$$

Tioga Road/East Entrance (East of Highway 120)

★★Whoa Nellie Deli
22 Vista Point Road (Highway 120 west off 395), Lee Vining, 760-647-1088; www.thesierraweb.com/tiogagasmart

From pizza to sandwiches to cappuccinos, this gas station deli offers a surprisingly gourmet array of choices. The varied international menu features such specialties as the lobster taquitos on a bed of Brazilian black beans with tomatillo pineapple salsa and greens. There's sure to be something here to quell every hiker's hunger.

Deli. Breakfast, lunch, dinner. Box lunches available. Bar. Outdoor seating. $

181

YOSEMITE

★

★

★

★

INDEX

INDEX

INDEX

INDEX

INDEX

INDEX

INDEX

INDEX

INDEX

INDEX

YOSEMITE NATIONAL PARKS, 167

INDEX

ARCTIC OCEAN

CHUKCHI
SEA

BEAUFORT SEA

Barrow

Wainwright

Prudhoe
Bay

Point
Hope

Mackenzie
Bay

IVVAVIK
NATL. PARK

Inuvik

Arctic Circle

Noatak

Uvulok

Colville

ALASKA

YUKON
TERR.

VUNTUT
NATL. PARK

Ft. McPhe

RUSSIA

KOBUK VALLEY
NATL. PARK

Kotzebue

Kobuk

GATES OF
THE ARCTIC
N.P. & PRES.

Porcupine

CANADA

U.S.

Arctic Ci

Bering Strait

Selawik

Koyukuk

U.S.

Fort Yukon

Allakaket

Circle

Yukon

11

5

Peel

Teller

Nome

Norton Sound

St. Lawrence I.

Unalakleet

St. Michael

Ruby

Manley Hot
Springs

Nenana

Eagle

Fairbanks

Dawson

Delta
Jct.

CONTINENTAL DIVIDE

Stewart

11

Mayo

2

95

Yukon

Grayling

Ophir

Poorman

3

108

Tok

138

75

2

Beaver
Creek

Pelly

Fa

4

Carmac

St.
Mary's

Kuskokwim

DENALI
NATL. PARK
AND PRES.

175

147

8

123

5

Whit

KLUANE
N.P. &
RES.

1

Talkeetna

Glennallen

McCarthy

3

Bethel

Anchorage

LAKE CLARK
NATL. PARK
AND PRES.

Kenai

35

Palmer

1

4

Valdez

WRANGELL-
ST. ELIAS
N.P. AND
PRESERVE

Haines
Jct.

3

Tes

Nunivak
Island

Kuskokwim
Bay

Iliamna
L.

229

9

Cordova

7

Ska

Haines

BERING
SEA

Dillingham

Naknek

Homer

Seldovia

Seward

KENAI FJORDS
NATL. PARK

Yakutat

GLACIER BAY NATL.
PARK & PRES.

Bristol
Bay

KATMAI
NATL. PARK
AND PRES.

GULF OF
ALASKA

Chichagof I.

S

Unimak
Island

Sand
Point

Kodiak

Kodiak Island

Baranof I.

W.

K

Unga
Island

Chignik

Trinity
Islands

PACIFIC OCEAN

King
Cove

Chirikof
Island

Unalaska

Unalaska
Island

0   100   200   300 MI

0   100 200 300 400 KM

Queen C.

© GeoNova

ALASKA

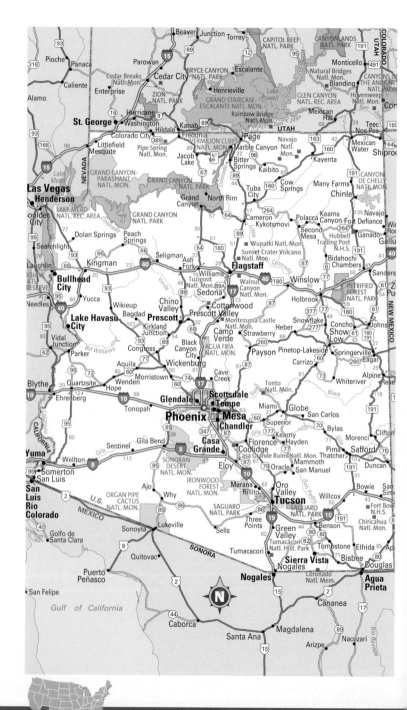

ARIZONA

FLORIDA

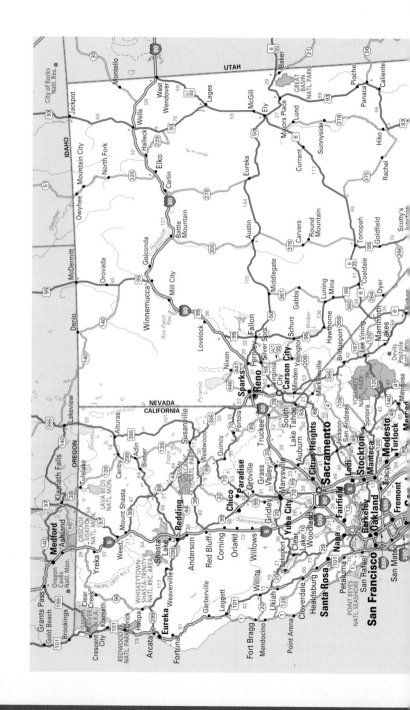

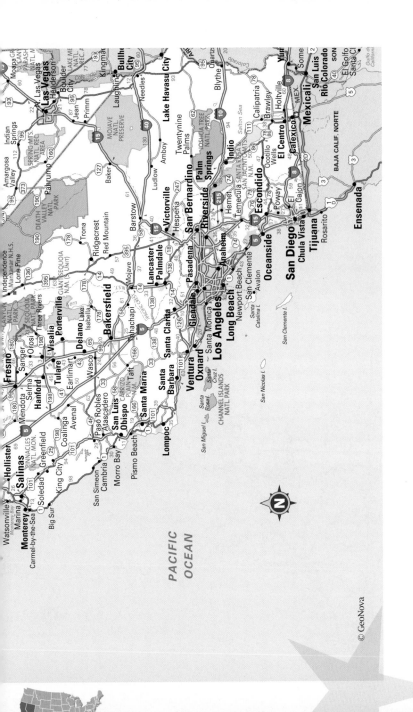

CALIFORNIA

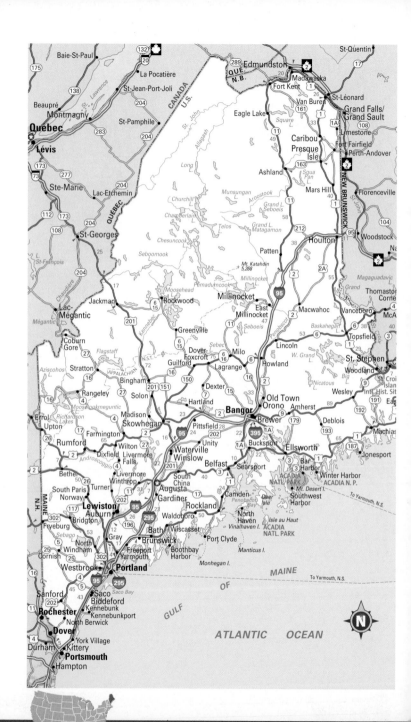

MAINE

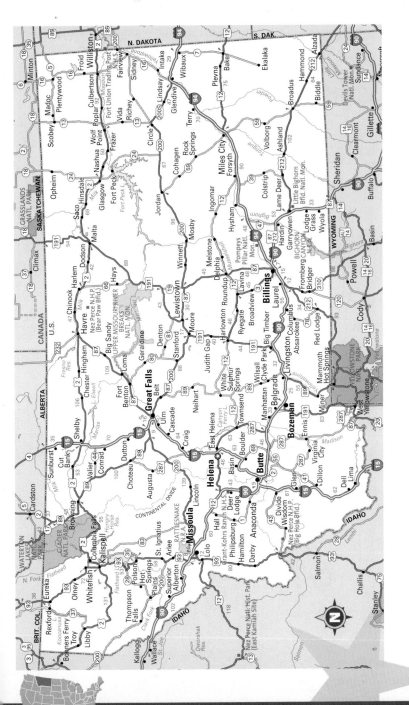

MONTANA

0 20 40 60 80 MI
0 20 40 60 80 100 120 KM

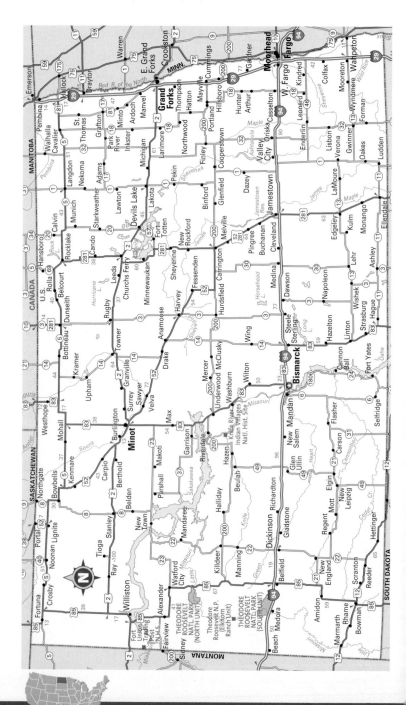

NORTH DAKOTA

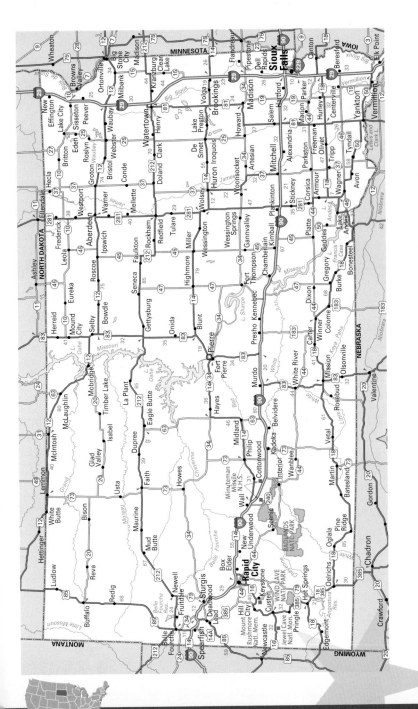

SOUTH DAKOTA

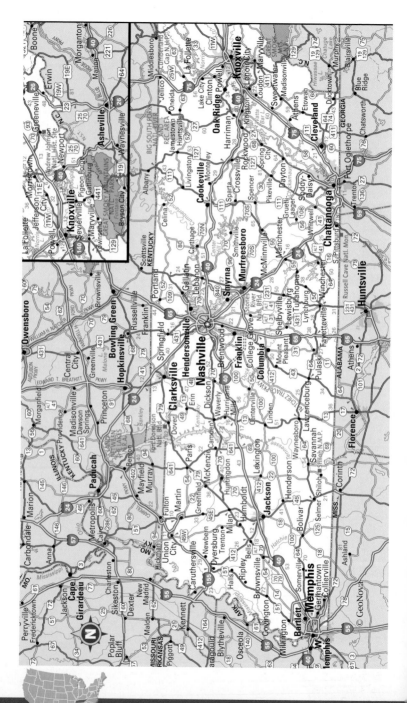

TENNESSEE

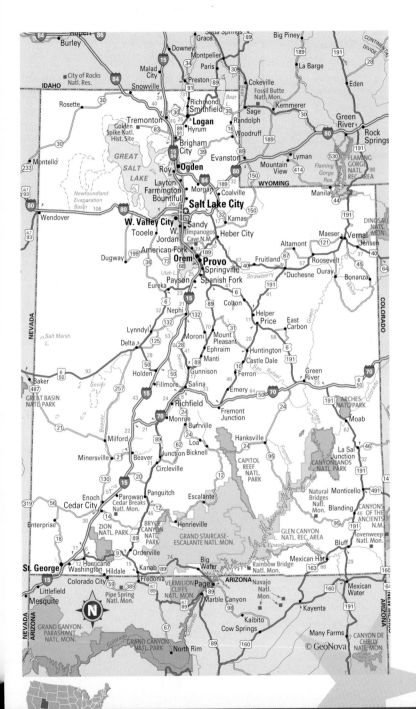

UTAH

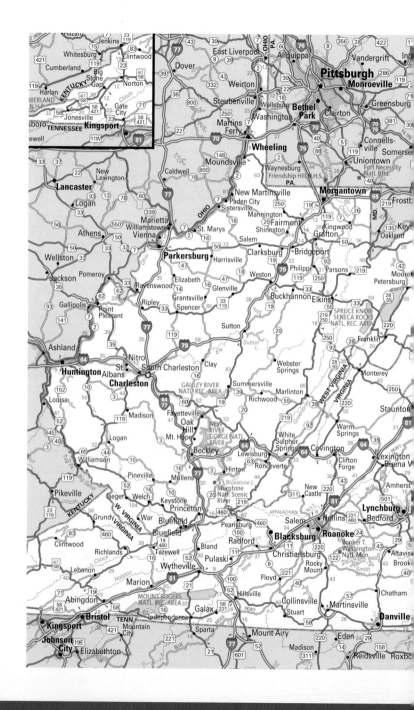

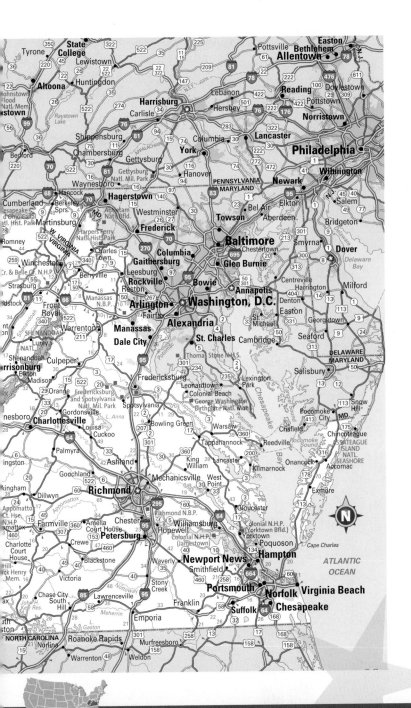

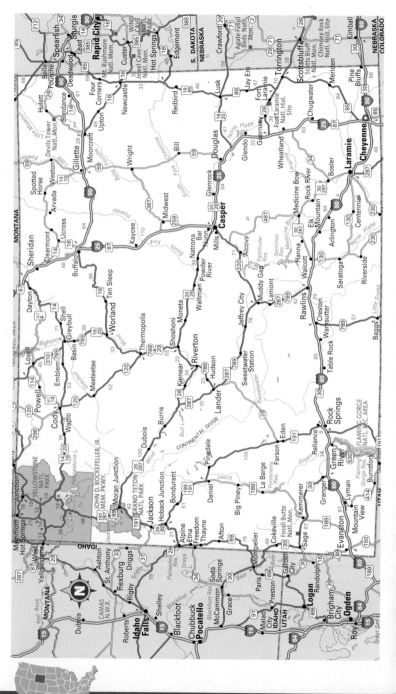

WYOMING

DAWN ARRIVES IN ACADIA NATIONAL PARK

YOSEMITE VALLEY

AN ALPINE MEADOW IN OLYMPIC

A STREAM IN GLACIER

© Istock/ Aimin Tang

THORS HAMMER AT SUNRISE IN BRYCE CANYON

GREAT SMOKY MOUNTAINS

A VIEW OF THE COLORADO RIVER IN GRAND CANYON.

© National Park Service/ Ray Mathis

NOV   2009